Foundations of Education

Foundations of Education

Srinibas Bhattacharya

ATLANTIC
PUBLISHERS & DISTRIBUTORS (P) LTD

Published by
ATLANTIC
PUBLISHERS & DISTRIBUTORS (P) LTD
7/22, Ansari Road, Darya Ganj, New Delhi-110002
Phones : +91-11-40775252, 40775214, 23273880, 23275880
Fax: +91-11-23285873
Web: www.atlanticbooks.com
E-mail: orders@atlanticbooks.com

Printed & bound in India by Atlantic Print Services

A FEW WORDS

Education is a growing science and its foundations are to be explored with reference to its various dimensions. It is an interdisciplinary approach demanding a critical study of the different perspectives and interaction between them.

The first couple of sections are an attempt to discuss the twin basis of education, viz. philosophical and sociological as they emerge as the cornerstones of the foundation of education as a faculty. In fact, philosophy is a must for the development of any art or science as it provides values and direction in addition to be total outlook behind creative work. It is, therefore, imperative to deal at length with the interaction between philosophy of education and the problem of values in education. In addition, topics like "Man in Education" and "Aims of Education" have found proper place in this Volume. Lastly, current trends of education including peace education have been included in this section.

The other foundation of education which has been discussed in detail is the sociological foundation of education. Obviously education is incomplete unless it is set in social perspectives. It goes without saying that education rests upon social forces, needs and demands. The expectations and aspirations of a changing society are projected through educational system of a nation or country. The sociological perspective is thus very significant and it demands special attention today. The present Volume, therefore, has emphasized the role of culture and community in our changing society with their bearing on education. It is challenging to cope with the problems of social stratification and disintegration demanding solution through education. Needless to mention that our society today is more complex than ever before as we as human beings are living in the midst of confusion and conflict. In fact we are in the grip of transition when man is almost lost in utter bewilderment.

The second section of the Volume, viz. the *Sociological Foundation of Education* thus attempts to deal with this vital issue at length and studies some of the sensitive frontiers like education for national integration and education for national understanding. The last section has been designed keeping in view the needs of the students and educators of Psychology of Education as it is written in Indian perspective in a non-traditional way. I hope this modest attempt will be rewarded with positive reactions from every corner.

SRINIBAS BHATTACHARYA

CONTENTS

PART III

PSYCHOLOGICAL FOUNDATION OF EDUCATION

PART I

PHILOSOPHICAL FOUNDATION OF EDUCATION

1

INTRODUCTION

PHILOSOPHY AND EDUCATION

Significance of education cannot be fully appreciated unless it is looked at in proper perspectives.

Education has more than one perspective, viz., philosophical, sociological and psychological. A comprehensive view of education leads to a sound philosophy of education.

In the field of social science there is a considerable overlap between one aspect and the other. Yet, they have something in common. All these disciplines are related to men. Thus education as a subject for study draws its materials from different areas including Psychology Philosophy, Sociology, etc.

The philosophical perspectives provide the basis of education in terms of values, aims and objectives. Education as a subject should have a value-orientation for its impact on philosophy society and other factors of education.

The interaction between these areas has made the interdisciplinary approach feasible today.

The philosophical basis of education seeks to support the need for a direction which education should follow. It provides directives and offers values to which education should be oriented from time to time. It is assumed that the knowledge of metaphysics and ethical thinking helps an educationist to put education in the proper perspective.

The philosophical basis makes education more purposive towards ends which are fundamentally good. Thus education without philosophical basis remains rather shaky.

In the words of Reid, "If education is a purposive activity of the utmost importance for the welfare and growth of young human beings, the most careful critical and constructive thought about ultimate purpose of education is surely necessary''

Values are different and the bases of education, society and social perspectives are hard to ignore. The social environment determines, no doubt, the needs and problems to be met by means of education.

The principles of sociology when applied to education create the required perspective for its effective operation in the context of social interaction in a community. School is considered as a community where students, teachers and administrators are like community members. Teachers function like parents and heads are like leaders in the community. The students socialize while learning and playing with their peer groups.

Social control is exercised within the school when socialization takes place.

The various forms of interaction within and outside groups determine the quality of learning experience.

Education is life itself. It is dynamic. It involves the process of interaction. It is also viewed as an experience which is gathered in our life time.

As education is life, so life also is education. We learn by living and live by learning. Living and learning go together. Education has more than one dimension. In a formal sense education comes through learning but in general it involves experience, stimulation and growth. Formal education is only one way of promoting the growth, enriching experience and developing attitude. Thus various domains of human life are touched by means of education. In other words, thinking, feeling and acting are enriched by means of educational experience.

It is obvious to have a philosophical foundation of Education. Without a philosophical basis education tends to lose its direction. Philosophy provides the values, goals and wisdom. In fact, if we are to educate, we must do it with a sense of direction. Priority of values should also be determined for being instilled in the mind of the learners. As philosophy is the key to love and wisdom, it is a necessity in life and education. Our life demands not only knowledge but also wisdom. Without it education is of no avail. From the dawn of civilisation man has been marching in search of wisdom and he is still doing so. In fact, this eternal search goes on. Various experiments are projected through education, so that humanity, happiness and harmony be wedded together.

As mentioned before, education has more than one perspective. It appears that philosophy is the starting point of human progress. It is like a beacon star in the darkness of ignorance. Man finds his way with the help of philosophy which shows the path of life shrouded in mystery. Without the philosophical foundation, therefore, education will be like a boat without a rudder. No doubt, metaphysics is the origin of philosophy. It is not everything in education. Philosophy of education is however limited in its approach as there are other perspectives of education. Exploration and experimentation are the twin methods of unveiling the mystery of life. It is imperative that there should be a direction and destination for whatever we want to do. Thus philosophy of education in general is important as it is the application of philosophy in the field of education. On the whole we attempt to educate for helping individuals to reach perfection. To attempt to educate is to do something intentional and purposive towards what is believed and to be good.

EDUCATION AND PHILOSOPHY

Aims of education come under the purview of philosophical foundation of education because one should know the ends and not the means alone. Education comes from the Latin word "Educare" that is to bring up to foster, to lead. It is, therefore, necessary to set some objectives to be reached through education. Whitehead says, "The only object of education is the development of complete life". Thus it involves a continuous process of socialisation for adjustment to reality. In other words, education consists in the manipulation of experiences and the potential of an individual towards better adjustment to life. In fact, education and life are inseparable.

A persisting controversy over the priority of values has disturbed the desired balance in educational planning. The various schools of education are emerging in a complex world-society today. Education was bipolar, but today it has become multipolar. This has added to the complexity of the problem confronting the planners in education. There are so many considerations like mind, matter, individual, society, community, group, nation and universe. It is not an easy task to come up with a perfect framework of education which meets all the challenges presented by the different frontiers of life.

FUNCTION OF PHILOSOPHY

The speculative function of educational philosophy is, therefore, closely related to its function of determining the values which education ought to pursue. Taken together, these aspects of educational philosophy would seem to indicate that it has a prospective reference and that it anticipates and directs practice. While there are many who agree that philosophy should provide certain ideas at which teachers should aim, there are others who take a less ambitious view of educational philosophy. Philosophy is retrospective rather than prospective in character. It is more of conservation than progression. The place of Dewey's concept of democracy in education and pragmatism in education deserves special mention. Most readers would admit of its profound limitations when applied to education. We run into problems when philosophy has to decide what is feasible. It is not proper for philosophy to decide what to do in any particular case as it deals with knowledge and not with opinions.

Two types of educational philosophy seem to be emerging. One stresses a dynamic nature, rich with novelty and varied individualities. It does not overlook the need for stability but it also refers to the social culture which is constantly subject to revision in the light of future events. The other approach to educational philosophy gives full recognition to dynamic world. It also points out the stable factors of culture and the primordial traits of reality. It would be proper to keep both these perspectives in view.

The function of education is not only to help the individual to adjust to his environment but also to contribute to the social and cultural environment. In other words, education helps one's adjustment to environment either by passive acquiscence or by active interaction with it. If we go back to the fundamental issue as to whether education should have a philosophy or not, we find a difference of opinion. As mentioned earlier, there are many who hold the view that education is a dynamic process and should have no definite and permanent goal. In that case philosophy of education will have limited significance. Of course, education should have some fundamental and basic aims. Otherwise it will be completely at the mercy of time agent. According to Bertrand Russell, education should have an autonomous existence. It should be effective when it evolves some process for meeting the fundamental needs of society.

As suggested by some educationist like Dewey education should be one of the most dynamic forces. He objects to any static and fixed goal being set as he believes in pragmatism and progress. We should be aware of means to the end and the end as well. Dewey's philosophy of education strongly believes in creative functions of school. Perfection for him is not easy to reach as it involves a continuous pursuit.

Another aim of education is to pass on the social heritage which is the result of the stored experience. While transmitting the heritage the school can either be conservative or be progressive. It is also the function of education to provide knowledge of the various perspectives. In short, philosophy helps to develop a comprehensive outlook. It is through philosophy alone that one's approach to life proves effective. The modern philosophy in education involves a rational outlook which takes into consideration the entire spectrum of life before conclusion. In other words, education without philosophy is incomplete as they are mutually interdependent.

PHILOSOPHY AND EDUCATIONAL ASSUMPTIONS

As mentioned earlier, education is a purposive activity towards the following ends which are deemed to be good:

(a) Acquisition of skills.

(b) Passing on of the cultures and traditions of society.

(c) The development of critical minds.

(d) The development of character and personality along the right line.

Philosophy applied to education helps the educationist to put his thought and work into proper perspective. The philosophical assumptions with implications about four different things are around:

(a) Belief about Values.

(b) Belief about Religions.

(c) Non-religious Metaphysical Belief.

(d) Belief about Knowing.

(a) *Belief about Values.* The four kinds of assumptions affect education. They overlap with one another. Beliefs about values are important in educational thought and practice.

All the factors of education are influenced by the values. The aims and objectives, the content of the curriculum, the teachers' outlook, the methods of teaching and evaluation are all influenced by belief about values. There are certain educational values which appear to be more desirable than the others. Love for the children and love for knowledge are the most desirable attributes of a good teacher. Similarly a deeper understanding of human nature and education enriches the professional growth of a teacher.

(b) *Belief about Religions.* Belief about religion leads to belief about values. Humanism which is characterised by concern for human beings is a matter of prime concern almost in every religion. There is difference between kinds of humanism leading to differences about religion, but the importance of human being is acknowledged by every one.

A humanist believes in the well-being and the happiness of human beings. Nevertheless there are differences between kinds of humanism leading to difference around religion. It is easy to misunderstand the distinction between the types of humanism. The beliefs about religion are the determining factors which form the basis of classification of humanism. This belief helps the teacher to develop his own philosophy as a guiding force in his personal and professional life.

(c) *Non-religious Metaphysical Belief.* There are many forms of metaphysics in which religion is not directly involved. This has a bearing on educational assumptions. In psychological studies we usually make our objective approach without any reference to religious or metaphysical belief.

(d) *Belief about Knowing.* It is not belief but facts which guide our assumptions. Particularly behaviourism depends more on facts and objective data. Moreover, it assumed that education is conditioning. From this point of view a child is to be moulded and shaped according to the expectation of the society.

2

PHILOSOPHICAL FOUNDATION OF EDUCATION

NATURE, SCOPE AND FUNCTION OF PHILOSOPHY

The traditional concept of philosophy has been developed for ages with reference to metaphysics. It deals with the knowledge of the universe, the ultimate reality and its source or origin. Thus philosophy directs its enquiry into life in its totality. It also deals with the aim and purpose as well as some other relevant issues and problems around life. The task of philosophy is also to unfold the mystery behind creation and the creator. No doubt, it draws its data with the help of introspection, logical analysis and observation. It is still considered as a discipline based on metaphysical statements and propositions.

Philosophy is a term which is based on the concept of life and knowledge. It is an attempt to understand the world of experience in different perspective. "The nature and function of philosophy is itself a kind of philosophical problem over which there have always been controversies," says Reid. Philosophy is love of wisdom needed most in our life. A philosopher is the lover of wisdom who can see life steadily as a whole. Inspite of the differences of opinion about what is philosophy, there is an overall agreement on the meaning of philosophy. O' Conner believes, that it is a mistake to assume that philosophy is a sort of superior and profounder science. Metaphysics has emerged as a separate branch of knowledge to explain life and its purpose. Besides, it deals with certain issues around truth, knowledge and wisdom. Since time immemorial the mysteries of life and death are presenting challenge to mankind. It is only the philosopher who approaches this issue with a total outlook. Plato and Socrates have tried to deal with the question of life and living, reality and appearance and have thrown new light on these areas. Philosophy helps man to attain a clear and consistent conception of world system. The universe is the whole and its origin, function, destiny and end are the factors of the world system.

The scope and function of philosophy are no doubt, limited. The primary responsibility is to understand the nature of reality in all its dimensions. All the sciences started as branches of philosophy in a very general sense to cover all enquiries. In the past, philosophy was regarded as a specialised discipline relevant to education. This approach has been modified in recent years. Today philosophy is assuming a more operational magnitude. As a discipline it has enriched a number of areas of knowledge by providing a stronger foundation than any other branch of knowledge.

It offers a comprehensive outlook to serve as a link between the various isolated disciplines.

The moral and spiritual values and the relevant problems have been the topics for discussion in the area of philosophy. The basic assumption is that people must live in happiness with a purpose. With a view to ensuring this the following must be considered:

(a) The existence of the individual and individualism.

(b) Understanding the need for love, kindness and acceptance.

(c) Cultivation of capabilities and right frame of attitude.

Thus philosophy has also the following roles to enrich human life:

(d) Creating a self concept.

(e) Learning certain human relations.

(f) Inclusion of positive attitudes, human dignity, etc.

(g) Learning of cultural sets.

Besides, the philosophers have undertaken the challenging task of generating values.

It goes without saying that approaches to the study of education demonstrated the need for philosophy as a conceptual frame-work. Thus educational philosophy emerged as a concept for dealing with the philosophical issues and problems in educational perspectives. It is, however, viewed as speculative branch of study which attempts to get an overview of the entire field and putting various parts together into a system. It is no wonder that some describe the function of philosophy as synthetic rather than speculative.

Education is the core of almost all the social sciences. This is a purposive activity, a process and not a product. One can ask if education should have some ultimate objectives. This is a controversial issue and one fails to give a straight answer to this question. The basic query is whether education should have a philosophy. It does not mean that it should be bound by some set of values. Philosophy provides a vision and a wide perspective. One might ask if education can be thought as an independent autonomous function without any reference to any set of goals. To Dewey, education is life itself, and it is as dynamic as living. As we live, we learn and educate ourselves. This is a pragmatic view of Dewey. In fact, we need some frame of reference in which education has to fit into. No doubt, various schools of philosophy have emerged with their distinct bearing on education. It appears that education should be consistent with certain fundamental values in life. There exist truth, goodness and beauty as criteria. The question arises whether these dimensions of life, can be reached through education. It is obvious that goodness and truth cannot be divorced from beauty and happiness. Education for happiness is the ultimate concern of all.

Plato provides us with the psychology of education. Education is not mere acquisition of knowledge, it is the formation of mind. Knowledge can not be imposed from outside. Education is concerned with life. Athletic exercises and intellectual pursuits are all needed for the development of body and mind.

Plato does not forget that life has more than single purpose which a man may consciously pursue. As there are in man reason, spirit and desire, each of these must be developed by training and education. Through experience and education a human being grows towards maturity. Life becomes a perpetual striving for the fulfilment of his physical or spiritual need. To be able to fulfil this need adequately one must clearly understand what the need implies. The impulse must not be blind. It should be directed properly through education. There has been always a controversy over definition of philosophy. Yet, one should have a philosophy of life behind day to day functioning in this age of confusion. Life in order to have meaning and direction should be guided by philosophy.

Philosophy as a vision helps us to look at life and creation in wider perspectives. Metaphysics in the opinion of Ewing, helps one to make genuine discoveries of truth.

In short, philosophy of Education is the application of philosophy and its methods in the field of education. Education is a purposive activity towards the objectives determined primarily by philosophy.

It is a process of enabling one not merely to live but to live adequately. There are various aspects of education, academic, aesthetic, moral, physical, social and spiritual. Theories of education have been formulated and different values emphasised. It is not very difficult to trace the evolution of educational theories. Monasticism has laid emphasis on the orthodox moral values, while the importance of knowledge and learning has been emphasised by the scholastic school. No body cared for the child or the education until the school of naturalism made its bold appearance. Rousseau is the pioneer of this school and it was he who laid the foundation stone of "New Education" or 'paedo-centric' Education.

The horizon of education is gradually expanding. New education is tending to be psychological and at the same time sociological. The human values in education are gradually gaining recognition. The role of education has changed to a considerable extent because of a persistent human effort towards better adjustment of life. The modern movement in education is concerned with the child and its development in relation to his life and environment. It has embraced everything that comes on the way to the development of child. It has regarded humanity as the final object of its concern, and the human mind as a sole creative source. Man is the measure of everything according to the new school. There is some amount of idealism underlying the philosophy of new education. On the one hand there is man with all his potential needs while, on the other, there is total environment. Education has the function to aid in the growth of human potential in all its aspects. The entire outlook has undergone change because of the advent of new education. Every one has welcome it because of its close relationship to life. Today education can also be thought in terms of happiness and harmony. The concept of freedom has been wedded to that of discipline in the area of new education. Education for world citizenship has been considered important today. Democracy in education has been accepted as a mode of living. Both ethics and materialism have been combined and a compromise arrived at before the ultimate goal was pronounced by Dewey. Experience, according to new education, is a precious thing in life which cannot be separated from our existence. Our life is a treasure house where experience is precious. It is through our experience we feel and grow. New education believes passionately in the value of experience and spontaneous expression of the self. Dewey has no doubt, badly come forward with his new and progressive education. Yet the concept of education is shrouded in mystery because of the lack of precision in defining the purpose of education. The goal and direction of life are, of course, determined by human beliefs and needs. Some of these depend on judgements of values.

Today education has become experimental as a science in the laboratory of human life. The old notions and values are changing giving rise to new sets of belief and human values determining the nature of education. His environment expands or contracts as life and learning continue.

Society provides a social environment and education should help one to adjust to it. Kilpatrick and Russel have regarded education both as a force in life as well as a social control.

THE BEARING OF PHILOSOPHY ON EDUCATION

Philosophy, therefore, means looking at a question in its entire perspective. It demands self-consistency and comprehensive outlook. A philosophy of education, therefore, should take into account the conflicting values and notions of life and education. It deals with life, values and religion though it need not be associated with any particular creed.

NEED FOR PHILOSOPHY IN EDUCATION

In order to bring out one of the important points of contact between philosophy and education the issue of value and value judgements should obviously be discussed. In fact, philosophy provides a framework within which education and educational problems can be discussed. Education without any reference to philosophy loses its goal as the aims of education are mainly determined against the criteria set by philosophy. Besides, the philosophical perspectives help the teachers and educators to set the broad as well as specific objectives of education with reference to socio-cultural contexts. The philosophical basis of education is a must for any social science like education because of its dependence on the value of life and society. Of course there lies a controversy as to the role of philosophy in education. According to a particular school, education should be free from any dictation of philosophy and values. Particularly pragmatism advocates this approach with a view to building up the science of education on an independent basis. No doubt, there are certain questions of philosophy which have a direct bearing on educational theories. Any synthetic approach encouraging the combination of values and judgements is possible if philosophy is kept at the centre as a focal point. Possibly one might raise more fundamental question as to whether education is preparation for this life. By education, however, one means adjustment to the environment to bring a desirable change in habits, behaviour, thought and attitude. While philosophy tries to harmonize the different approaches towards life, the function of education is to help the pupils to adjust to the environment.

It is often remarked that every teacher should have a philosophy. A philosophy of education is often adequate to make immediate resolutions to conflict. As a matter of fact, the philosophical outlook has to develop in order to make education harmonious and self-sufficient. The philosophic method which is different from the scientific one, is not directed towards a solution of just a limited number of factors or variables to be controlled experimentally. A philosophical study of a problem may become very complex. Thus the data which educational philosophy draws into synthesis are often derived from a wide variety of sources. Indeed, religion which is closely akin to the philosophical enterprise is also interested in exposing the educational problems.

ONE OR MANY PHILOSOPHIES OF EDUCATION

While it is generally agreed that the unity of outlook is the legitimate objective of educational philosophy, the manifold details with which it deals may not reduce to a single principle of interpretation. There are some philosophies which succeeded in achieving a unitary point of view or synthesis. But other philosophies find unity in diversity. The educational philosophy of democracy has to promote the cultivation of diverse personality or cultures. Without any definite philosophy no educational structure can help the cultural development. Philosophy has got other responsibilities as well. In spite of the existence of a few schools of educational philosophy, the claims of educational philosophy to be grounded on an ultimate reality may lead to one single philosophy in education.

THE CONTENT OF EDUCATIONAL PHILOSOPHY

The difficulty we find in drawing a line of demarcation between the proper spheres of philosophy and science in education is not to be overlooked. Originally an advanced study of philosophy is based on common knowledge and gives rise to differences as well. As various sciences have evolved, a tendency towards specialization has been observed leading to the important subdivisions of educational philosophy. A controversy arises as to whether philosophy is at the root of education. There are three aspects which are principally concerned with education. They are: (a) theory of values, (b) the theory of knowledge and metaphysics, and (c) the general theory of reality. In examining the aims of education, the motivation of learning and the measurements of its results, are relevant. We are to deal with ethical problems and problems of value as well. Values are also important considerations in selecting the appropriate curriculum. The curriculum being the avenue for approach to knowledge helps us to understand the nature of knowledge. The nature of knowledge will not only influence the way in which the curriculum is organised, it will also help toward formation of the concept of truth. One will have to consider the nature of human elements as well as the world from which such problems emanate. Both will constitute the content of educational philosophy. Educational philosophers hesitate to admit of the importance of metaphysics. As such the need for metaphysics can hardly be overemphasized. A progressive education, therefore, admits of value of educational philosophy as a dynamic concept. They do not feel like accepting educational aim as fixed or final. They define education as the continuous reconstruction of experience.

Critics and opponents of progressive education can find themselves confronted with different issues of world. While recognizing the consistent world they reflect that there is much in the world that does not change. Thus greater significance to the enduring and changeless set up is emphasised. Consequently education is considered to have some definite pattern and goals which it seeks to realize.

3

INDIAN PHILOSOPHY OF EDUCATION

Introduction

Before formulating the principles and philosophy of education we should remember the following facts:

1. India is a country of villages with diversity.
2. India is a country of many languages.
3. India is a land of many religions and values.
4. India is a land of many prophets and spiritual leaders.
5. India has emerged as an important country or nation in the Third World and is also an advocate of peace and harmony.
6. India needs democratic principles in socio-political and educational life. She enjoys the largest democracy.
7. She has the progressive outlook and her desires to develop science and technology should be projected in every sphere.

All the above considerations should be projected while developing the philosophy of Education in India.

The curriculum and the co-curricular programme should be developed with a view to reaching the objectives set for Indian education.

The programme of evaluation should also be developed according to the objectives of education.

Evolving an Indian philosophy of education demands a study of Vivekananda, Tagore, Gandhi and Sri Aurobindo, with their relevance in modern India.

With a view to evolving an Indian philosophy of education, we need to understand the basic values guiding the life and education of Indian people. A close study of the history of education in India leads to the observation that different values have emerged at different times in Indian history. Yet one can hardly ignore the fact that Indian education remained insensitive to the needs and demands of the Indian society.

At times idealism appeared to influence education in ancient India while naturalism proved dominant in determining the educational environment for the total development of children's personality.

Traditional Indian education is naturalistic among adivasis and tribal people of India but the Western form of education prevailed among young Indians who were exploited by the British rulers and used as clerks or assistants. This system of education was far from being perfect.

Since India won Independence, attempt has been made to formulate a national educational policy. Various Education Commissions have been set up for reorganizing the educational system including the syllabus, examination system and method of teaching.

It has been considered essential to evolve an Indian philosophy of education in the light of the tradition and culture upheld by Vivekananda, Tagore, Gandhi, Sri Aurobindo and others.

India is known for her diversity in values and lifestyle. One has, therefore, to take into account all these Indian values and needs to finalize the blueprint of Indian education. A review of the socio-political trends in modern India shows mixture of various creeds and needs posed from time to time.

She has also imbibed a few western values. A new education has emerged as a result of this blend of cultures and values.

Democracy has finally taken root in Indian way of life. India in a world context presents the problem of reconciliation between various forces. The Western socio-cultural values may be in conflict with those of India. Yet India has absorbed some of the principles including democracy and pragmatism.

Idealism is replaced by pragmatism with the passage of time and democracy by the socialistic pattern of life.

In view of the currents and cross-currents in Indian society, an attempt to approach toward Indian philosophy of education should be made.

In fact, the needs and problems of India with reference to its aspirations have to be projected in the national policy of education today.

Every nation needs an educational philosophy for building up a sound system of education. India has passed through various stages of development during different periods. Since Brahmanic-education it has followed the monastic, scholastic, realistic, idealistic and pragmatic trends when values changed and new priorities emerged.

Recent development in Indian history have shown the need for setting up various Education Commissions to cope with the challenge of time. Yet we find loopholes and limitations in our educational system.

It is unfortunate that in spite of various experiments conducted in India at different stages after Independence, we find the problems of unemployment, youth unrest and national disintegration. All this shows disharmony and imbalance between the community needs and expectations as well as educational outcomes.

This is why a sound Indian philosophy of education needs to be developed, before long.

Criteria for determining the priorities of goals have to be set for planning and development of Indian education. Some important issues are:

(a) National integration

(b) International understanding

(c) Community and social awareness

(d) Indian economic goal and strategy and

(e) Cultural goals and values.

It goes without saying that mere idealism and scholasticism are not enough.

Conclusion

India is a land where values have emerged and influenced the cultural life of the land. It is observed that she was absorbed various religions and philosophies. Yet she has retained a unique style by blending naturalism, spiritualism and humanism.

With the changing time and socio-political trends objectives of education have changed. The ancient system of Indian education has a priority on spiritual aspect of human development while the modern science and technology with its impact on lifestyle and values have brought about a significant change in the area of educational philosophy.

The cross-cultural studies of modern values show an increasing tendency toward materialistic and self-centred outlook.

The world in which we live today is shrinking everyday, but every nation is busy in building, a wall of prejudice.

This is why we need to develop an Indian philosophy of education. The history of education shows how the different rulers have tried to use education for their political purposes.

In fact, Independent India badly needed a separate philosophy of life and education with emphasis on her cultural and traditional traits.

DEVELOPING AN INDIAN PHILOSOPHY OF EDUCATION

To start with we have to discuss what is typical of Indian philosophy. It is the history of Indian philosophy which will tell the stories of philosophers with their different propositions. As already known, India has passed through centuries which have witnessed the changes of outlook and faith. Right from the ancient ages of Brahmanic education we find different emphasis in terms of values and priorities. It is likely that the spiritual quest has become a fashion at certain age, whereas the thirst for knowledge dominated in the area of education for a while. Thus the monastic and the scholastic schools emerged one after another presenting the modalities of values for projection in the field of education. While these two schools dominated over Indian philosophy, the other schools developed as realism and idealism. Of course, realism could never be a school by itself as this emerged as a reaction to life. In fact, realism is an attitude rather than a school. Unfortunately there is a lot of confusion about the term reality. Reality, in fact, is a phase of life which is based on our experience and sensation. This is why the same reality appears to be different to different people. Subjectivity creeps in as a reality is perceived from different angles. In short, reality does not ignore the needs and demands of either individual or society.

As mentioned earlier, the need for building up a rational philosophy of education is imperative. This should be done in terms of values and goals for being reached through education. It goes without saying that India is known for her spiritual and idealistic outlook. It will be, therefore, quite usual to emphasize values in certain direction. Certain values are to be generated for using education as an agent for social change.

No matter what values or value promoters are selected for Indian philosophy of education, we can hardly forget that the world today is shrinking fast. This is why a fusion of values is bound to occur. On the one hand, we should look back for searching the permanent human values from tradition and culture of the country, while on the other we should look forward to future possibilities. Thus attempt should be made to retrospect and introspect for the prospect of a sound philosophy of education in new India.

ANCIENT SYSTEMS OF EDUCATION AND THEIR BEARING ON PHILOSOPHY

Buddhist Education

While the Brahmanic education was mainly based on Vedic concepts, the Buddhist education was more accommodating and open. It was the result of strong reaction against the rigidity and narrowness of the Brahmanic system. The door of the Buddhist monasteries was wide open for all castes and the austerity, laid down by the Brahmanic system was discouraged. The conditions for admission to the 'sangha' for receiving Buddhistic education were very simple. In fact, the main requirements for one's admission were that he must be free from certain diseases and he should neither be a slave nor a debter. The ceremony for the admission was called the 'upasampada' and no one could receive the 'pabbajja' ordination till he was eight years of age. There were strict rules as to chastity, poverty and abstinence from worldly pleasures. Respect for superiors was required from the 'novice'. Each 'novice' (samanera) was required to choose a 'bhikkhu' who was a full member of the order as his preceptor. As mentioned earlier, the pupil was bound by certain rules of conduct toward his preceptor who, on the other hand, had his responsibility towards the pupil. Among the centres of learning 'Nalanda' deserves special mention. Various courses of study were prescribed at different levels and they included grammar, arts, medicine, logic, philosophy and lexicography. In addition to these, certain special advanced course was also prescribed for advanced students. They included the 'Mahabbhasya' of Patanjali, the 'Bhartrihari Sutra' and the 'Bharatiya Sastra' as well. Grammatical study of the Sanskrit language was indispensable. Every student, from the age of six, had to study grammar until he was twenty. In fact, the value of Sanskrit grammar was recognised for the development of mental discipline. Emphasis was laid on discussion and debate, and not merely on lectures.

Although Buddhism encouraged a life of separation from the mundane world of desires, it did not advocate complete renunciation of the world. Unlike Brahmanic education, Buddhist education imparted some secular knowledge. It was broad-based and more humanistic in its approach.

The relation between the teacher and the student was close and cordial. Sometime the pupils learnt directly as a result of closer contact with the individual life of the 'guru'. Both the pupil and the teacher used to sail in the same boat in the ocean of knowledge. Thus the interaction between the pupils and the guru was more effective and less formal.

Regarding the school environment everything was so simple as much depended upon the spirit of co-operation and understanding underlying the Buddhist education. Lessons were usually repeated aloud and were recited in a singing tone. The alphabet was first learnt and was copied upon 'tal' leaves and the pupil began to write upon sand at times. There was no fixed building for most of the Buddhist schools which are usually held under some shade.

It seems that apart from the monasteries Buddhism did not provide any educational environment. Yet Buddhist education influenced the general mass of the people by providing opportunities for popular instruction. At one stage of the Buddhist religion the monasteries started undertaking instruction of popular nature. Gradually, however, the system underwent some change and an attempt was made to liberalise education in the light of fundamental human needs. No doubt, Buddhism has passed away from India, but it has left behind a tangible influence on Indian philosophic thought and religious ideas. Its curriculum, although meagre, became enriched from the borrowed materials and adopted from the Brahmanic school. The Vedas were replaced by its own sacred books. Thus the Buddhist educational ideals and practice were derived from those of Brahmanism.

Thus, the history of Buddhism traces back to sixth and seventh centuries before Christ. Although this was an extension of Hinduism. It has offered a new approach to life. The Buddhism as a lifestyle has its uniqueness as it attempts at salvation (Nirvana) through three types of Monastery.

On the other hand, the principal aim of the Upanishadic education is, therefore, to educate the mind instead of catering information. According to the Upanishad, education is a process of controlling the mind through self-realisation. Thus yoga has the same purpose of disciplining the mind for concentration.

Even the *Bhagvat Gita* offers much to mankind by way of guidance. It expounds the harmony between the diverse approaches to reality through knowledge, love and detachment. The *Gita* is the most comprehensive treatise with deeper significance for humanity at large. Its educational value is immense and enduring for the entire mankind. Man developed an inner spiritual nature through self-discipline and awareness in relation to reality. It is the question of the integration of our personality and the development of the divine existence which have been dealt both in the Upanishad as well as in the *Gita*. They have upheld the external values of life which should be fostered through education. In other words, the aims of education should be determined against the criteria of perpetual goodness, truth and beauty (Satyam, Shivam and Sundaram).

From the Upanishads we get more sidelights on the ancient Brahmanic education, where preparation for life was emphasised. Even serving the teacher and collecting fruits for him were considered as a part of education. Thus the Brahmanic education was more oriented to basic needs of life. The system also provided a broad basis for the growth of personality. It was both formal and informal as the pupils received verbal instructions at times in addition to directives for self-development through co-curricular activities. No matter whatever the structure of Brahmanic education was, the final objective of self-realisation, dominated over other goals. To establish the harmony between the inner self and the entire creation was another major aim of Brahmanic education. It was through the interaction between the disciple and the teacher that the process of education was completed. The teacher in the Brahmanic system occupied a civilized position of unquestionable integrity. His wisdom and learning were transmitted in course of this interaction and the disciple not only gathered knowledge of the subject-matter, he could make real advance in his spiritual life as well.

The pupil was under certain obligations towards the teacher. He was to remain with the teacher so long as his course lasted. In the Upanishadic texts there are references to cases where pupils wandered from teacher to teacher to complete a course. Certain menial services had also to be performed for the teacher.

This included fetching of water, collecting fuel and sweeping the place around the fire. Rigid rules were laid for the conduct of pupils and adherence to those was enforced. Regarding the approach to education one can visualise the importance of ritualistic pattern of Brahmanic education. *Sraddha* was considered as the primary means of attaining excellence in knowledge. Next came the importance of Samyama or self-restraint, which was given the top priority. (Sraddhaban labhate Jnanam, tatparah samyatendriyah). Regarding teachinques or methods of learning, the Brahmanic system emphasised the role of humility, of modesty, curiosity and questioning as well as service (pranipatena, pariprasnena, sevaya).

The course content under the Brahmanic educational system remained very flexible as it was designed to meet the needs of individual learners. It included humanities, science, vocational education and practical courses. In short, the curriculum was geared to the purpose of living as well as striking a balance between the conflicting values of life.

Regarding the technique of teaching, the question and answer method was popular although at times dialectical and other instructional approaches were followed. The pupils learnt through recital of Vedic texts, daily exercises and performance of duties as well as from examples set by teachers. Nature also contributed to the development of their aesthetic sense as well as healthy attitude.

The pupils were placed in life situations full of challenges and evaluated according to their ability to cope with those problems. There was no formal examination as the teacher (guru) used to test not only their theoretical knowledge but also the toal personality, skill and applied subject knowledge on day-to-day basis. Thus the teacher's recommendation was considered final before he was declared to have been successful in his academic life. Emphasis was also laid on the pupil's attitude toward learning, life and the superiors including teachers. Reverence for the teacher was the most expected conduct from every pupil. Conformity and obedience, modesty and manners formed the part of his duty and obligation. Thus in the Brahmanic educational system academic growth was not considered in isolation. The system encouraged every pupil to attain an all-round development of his potential in all directions so that he could emerge as a full man in his actual life. Regarding the subjects, there was a wide variety of contents catered to meet the intellectual needs of the learners. In fact, the subject-matter ranged from fine arts to medical science including music, arts, humanities, astronomy and social science.

4

HUMAN FACTORS OF EDUCATION

Education itself involves a number of factors as the ultimate objective is to bring certain desirable interactions. It would be a mistake if one takes a very narrow view of education. The modern concept of education is more concerned with the improvement of the total man in relation to his environment. As such, education as a social control has its responsibility. It is a telic process which brings certain change not only in human beings but also is the other factors like method of teaching, evaluation system, curriculum and total environment. If we analyse, it would not be difficult to see that the human factors are of vital importance in the entire set up while other factors are to fit in or adjust to the needs of the human elements.

The human factors of importance, according to priority, are teachers and parents who are supposed to be mainly responsible for the development of a child.

We could hardly expect to orient the parents for the proper upbringing of the younger generation for various reasons. The most outstanding of them is the want of healthy attitude and lack of consciousness of their respective roles in our changing society. The plan for bringing the teachers and parents together on various occasions might serve some purpose while a consolidated programme is badly needed for the development of a proper outlook among the parents in general. Home, is no doubt, the most important place where a child meets most of his needs and gradually gains self-confidence and security in constant association with the members of the family. The present educational system should, therefore, involve the parents in the programmes organised by the school authorities for the purposes of socialization. The role of the teachers is changing along with the role of the school as a community centre. It is felt that there should exist a very close tie between the child's home and school and the gulf so long maintained between the two should be bridged up by all means. Relationship between people involved in education is very important as much depends upon how human motives work in interaction with the toal group and environment. Today we are recognising everything except the human values resulting in the complete confusion among the students themselves and even teachers. It is rather disappointing that the human factors remain ignored if not neglected and the result is quite far from being satisfactory. The lot of the teachers and the students is still to be improved by provision of incentives, encouragement and recognition. The amount of frustration which the people suffer from proves detrimental to any progress in any direction. One wonders as to how situation would improve unless the human resources receive top priority.

The next important factor in education is the curriculum which is often misinterpreted. It is the totality of the experience which is important in the construction of a curriculum. Very often the rigid notions of subject-matter stand out and tend to build up small compartments. As a result, every subject specialist feels tempted to overemphasise his particular subject of specialisation sacrificing the total perspective. It seems that curriculum has been recently regarded as a very important factor for providing the necessary experiences for the preparation of life. At the same time the capacity of the individuals to assimilate knowledge at each stage should not be lost sight of, as otherwise the pupils would be subjected to the tyranny of the educational administrators. The present falling educational standard in certain areas may be partly because of the disharmony between the needs and capacities of the pupil on the one hand and the demands of the educational administrators on the other.

There is, obviously, a scope for misunderstanding on this point and much depends again upon how the knowledge is catered. It naturally raises a very important issue around another factor of education, viz., techniques of teaching. Quite a lot of materials could be presented to the students if they are done in an interesting and skilful manner.

With the advance in the methodology of teaching, it is emphasised that lectures and instructions should be supplemented by means of discussions and seminars or some other methods involving groups and individuals. Apart from that there is a question which has been so much discussed and that is examination. It is rather delicate to assume that examination is a necessity. If so, what should we evaluate? Is it the information acquired or the innate potentials or the acquired knowledge which we want to measure by means of examination? The answer is not so simple as it appears to be.

It is a fact that the examination system has to be geared to the objectives of education. If the aim of education is to develop healthy attitude towards life and skill for preparation of life, the system of examination has to take care of that as well. In this respect, however, our examination system is taking into account only one objective, viz., the academic growth, critical thinking or originality of approach. There is a tendency among the examiners to test what the pupils do not know instead of what the pupils know and this is basically a wrong approach. Very recently the term examination has been replaced by another term evaluation which takes into account all the sides of development of a person in his sojourn of life. Yet the problem remains unsolved. Lastly the Indian educational system has been passing through a period of a very unstable environmental set up emerging in recent years.

The field of education is thus wide involving a number of factors. Every factor is directed towards the improvement of the pupil's learning behaviour. There are certain factors which may be classified under 'human' and certain others as situational. Under human factors we can include parents, teachers, associates and even the neighbours. Under the other category comes a number of situational factors, like method of teaching, learning situation and classroom atmosphere, evaluation system, etc. The purpose is to orient all these factors to the need for development of the pupils.

The concept of a modern teacher is also changing. The function of a teacher is that of a friend, philosopher and guide.

The discovery of the potentials in each pupil is the most important function of a teacher because he has the task of unfolding those potentialities by gradual stimulation. Another important aspect of the teachers' role is the understanding of the pupils with reference to their needs and problems. The third role of a teacher is his participation in the community life so that the gulf between the school and the society can be bridged.

Teacher in Society and Teacher-Education

Teacher occupies a pivotal place in any social set-up. With the emerging social order the teacher's role has changed. He is no longer concerned with the traditional-teaching as he would be concerned with the education of the total child. It is one of his primary responsibilities to build up a new generation of leaders of iron hands, strong will and deep love for the nation and humanity. The teacher will have to enthuse this younger section of population with a spirit of devotion to serve the country and nation. Our nation looks forward to the selfless service of the younger generation with a view to maintaining its power and prestige. The teacher community would be required to generate that power inherent in the student population. Virtually they should be leaders of the young generation and not merely instructors.

Another important role of the teacher today is to promote the standard of community life in our new India. A spirit of social service should enthuse them to extend their function beyond the walls of the classrooms. They should come down to the villages of India to enlighten the poor and ignorant population with sympathy and determination. In other words, the teacher-community today should get actively involved in adult education and community service. Otherwise, the ignorant mass living in the midst of poverty and darkness would definitely impede the progress of young India. Rural education centres and rural universities should be set up for an effective operation. The band of properly oriented teachers should reinforce their activities in close coordination with the schools and institutions at various levels.

Teacher as Leader

What is urgently needed now is the determined leadership of the teachers of new India in building up a better, stronger and happier India tomorrow. In short, the role of the teachers of today should be quite extensive and varied. Teaching should be mainly an inspiration. With the emerging set up the responsibility of every teacher has assumed a very great significance for building up a strong and self-reliant nation of tomorrow. The teacher as a field worker has a wide area to serve, viz., the class, the community and the nation as a whole.

Builder of Academic Life

It has been held for many centuries that the teacher is the caterer of knowledge and one's primary task lies in building up the academic life of the students under the guidance of each teacher. Catering information has been criticised and suggestions have been made to improve the existing techniques of teaching for the development of the intellectual life in the real sense of the term.

Emphasis has now to be laid on the unfolding of the fundamental potentialities, e.g., critical thinking, reasoning and problem-solving capacity. With a view to doing this effectively the teacher has to be resourceful, well-versed in child-psychology as well as in the specific subjects, and keen to draw out the maximum of each child. It is now considered that collection of information in a field of knowledge does not help much in the actual intellectual development of a child.

Creating New Values

It is strongly felt that besides intellectual development, education has the primary responsibility of bringing about emotional maturity and developing sentiments for good, right and beautiful things and ideas. The place of 'Bodha' or sentiment, according to Tagore should occupy a prominent place in education. It is, therefore, almost imperative that a real educationist or educator should foster this spirit among the young children. The children should be taught to feel for others, to love their own country and people and to respect their superiors. What is lacking today is the emotional maturity, in spite of all academic preparation, even among the adults. This stands on the way to development of a healthy outlook in life.

The teacher's social activities are, therefore, no less important than other activities of academic nature. On the contrary, the social role of the teacher community has assumed greater importance during recent years. Attempt should be made to socialise education if not to humanise it. Problems of various dimensions confront the teachers and educators today and it would be a challenge to face them with self-reliance. The teacher community should restore the self-reliance needed for any reconstruction of our socio-educational structure. There should be a reawakening of the entire teacher community so as to inspire the younger generation utterly confused and bewildered about values of life. Unless the teachers accept this challenge with a spirit of dedication and national service there would remain little hope of any real change for the better. They should assert themselves for regaining their leadership captured by the people of other walks of life.

Teaching an Inspiration

With the emerging new social order the system of education is bound to change. It is, therefore, natural that new objectives of education have been formulated by the recent Education Commission. Secondary education in India is undergoing drastic changes and various problems are emerging. It is very often felt that the paucity of suitable teachers is an outstanding handicap in implementing any change.

The concept of education has also changed and so its role. Along with purely academic goals education has to cope with the changing needs of the growing society. The socio-economic factors as well as the political ideals cannot be totally brushed aside. With a view to meeting the demands of every kind, our nation needs regiment of qualified teachers with adequate potentialities. Unfortunately teaching profession is still not able to attract the promising young men who can inspire the young generation and instil in them desirable attitudes. Teaching is mainly an inspiration. There are needs for the teachers to get themselves inspired before they can inspire others.

There was a time when teachers were believed to be only born and not made. There are still people clinging to the old notion attaching great importance to ths scholarship of the teacher and undermining the value of teacher education. The reasons are not far to seek. This old notion can be changed if the impact of teacher education on the student population at various levels can be proved.

Inadequate Teacher Education

The existing programme of teacher education is inadequate for various reasons. It is peculiar that in spite of so many years' experimentation with teacher training schemes in India, the impact of the scheme is not very significant.

The teacher training scheme has not so far been able to take into account the various needs of our schools and community and the desirable roles of the teachers at various stages. It also fails to offer a solid grounding in the subjects taught in schools. Besides, the knowledge of the method of teaching and the various subjects provided in the training course do not cover the recent trends in education, some of the methods being rigid. The methodology taught hardly equips a teacher to face the complexity of typical classroom situation. They are mostly suitable for ideal classroom situation. The training course does not help much is developing an interest in the profession. Nor does it promote any other social growth essential for a teacher's success in his profession. The course also fails to develop a practical skill among teachers so as to ensure success in community participation. It hardly orients the teacher in the art of living a dedicated life

Teaching — A Life of Dedication

One can seldom deny the fact that teaching as a profession demands certain amount of dedication and spirit of service. This important aspect of education has to be kept in view while drawing up the total teacher-education programme.

India, since Independence has been passing through a number of odds to be partly tackled by means of education. The young generation of today should assume greater responsibilities in shaping the destiny of their nation. It is rather imperative at present that emphasis should be laid on the development of national consciousness and leadership among teachers to start with.

It is clear that the role of teachers is now varied and extensive. It is no longer confined within the four walls of the classroom. The teacher is, no doubt, a very important member in the society and the leadership is expected to emerge from the teachers.

Our teacher education programme should be adequate for meeting the new challenge. The traditional concept of teacher's training refers only to the needs of the school teachers and not beyond that. It is curious to note that such a notion is still persistent among highly educated people. This outlook is at present out-moded because of the increasingly felt need for development of skill in handling the human materials at any level. No matter whether one is a primary school teacher or a university professor, both are concerned with their pupils at different age levels. There is the question of motivation, intergroup relations and social interaction influencing learning and behaviour. If education is more than parochial learning, if it means real adjustment to life, the question of teacher-education at every stage would not be irrelevant. The knowledge of group-dynamics on the part of the teacher would prove extremely helpful for effecting any desirable change in experience, attitude and behaviour of the pupils.

New Dimensions of Teacher Education

With the heavier demand of society on education, the number of dimensions of 'teacher education' has increased beyond doubt. Teacher education should now cover a wide range of population including the college and university teachers. Besides, teacher-education should be more intensive and purposive. It should attempt at the development of a healthy attitude towards the profession, society and nation. It should inculcate leadership so as to help the teachers to inspire the young generation with new ideals. For example, the teachers should be so oriented through the teacher-education programme as to enable themselves to develop national consciousness among their students. This requires leadership and resourcefulness. Teachers would be required to draw up a plan of activities, a suitable curriculum and provide suitable media of communication through audio-visual materials and examples.

With a view to making the teacher-education programme effective both the nature and duration of the course should undergo drastic change. The course should be so designed as to create leadership in education. The following steps appear to be useful for the purpose:

(a) The curriculum should be totally revised so as to cover a wide range of studies in different subject areas, viz., Indian sociology, social psychology and rudimentary social sciences along with child and educational psychology.

(b) The course should be of two years' duration. The first year should be spent for orientation in the teaching profession. A major part of the teacher-education programmes should concentrate on development of proper attitude, national spirit and study of the national problems with their bearing on education.

(c) The course should be residential and there should be sufficient stimulation for a corporate life among the teacher trainees for opportunities of socialisation.

(d) Co-curricular activities and community work should form the major part of the first year's programme along with fundamental studies of sociology, social sciences, psychology of group dynamics etc.

(e) Such teacher trainees should be encouraged to do some social work during his training period and to continue it on his return to his school.

(f) Internal evaluation should be introduced with a view to attaching more importance to the development of a spirit of social service and at the same time national consciousness.

(g) Credit should be given for skills in arts and crafts, physical activities and leadership.

Need for Emphasis on Application

The whole first year should thus be spent as the formative period of intensive teacher-training in methodology. Every teacher trainee might be required after six months' theoretical orientation in method papers to choose his special field and the school where he would have to work at his own initiative and leadership with the headmaster and teachers like a regular member of the staff. The head of the school and the senior members of the staff will have to be entrusted with the task of assessment and a uniform rating scale may be devised for the purpose.

Emphasis should be laid here on the teacher's power of application of the self in taking initiative for activities, community participation and in his building up the relations with pupils and his associates.

In short, teacher education programme should be geared to national interests instead of being confined to academic or professional interests. Unless the teacher-community is oriented towards social objectives of education, the development of national consciousness among the young generation would be well nigh impossible.

A Controversy

A good deal of controversy still persists regarding the aims of education. There still remains a conflict between the academicians and true educationists. This may be resolved by making a pragmatic approach to our emerging problems through education. As a matter of fact, there should be no controversy today on the wider concept of education and its application to reality. As such, education at any level should come closer and closer to reality and our social and national goal cannot be segregated from our educational objectives. Teacher-education programme was being divorced from reality as no national interest was being served by the rigid system of training as well as evaluation. It is, therefore, high time when the whole scheme should be remodelled on a new plan so as to fit in the present context.

Development of the Personality of the Teacher

It goes without saying that example is better than precept. With a view to setting good example before the students it is imperative that the teachers should have healthy mind, spirit and personality. In reality, however, the younger batch of teachers has hardly any love and dedication to their profession. This is the starting point of all the evils creeping in the teaching world. It means that there is a lot of scope for improvement of the personality of the teacher particularly belonging to younger generation. It is, however, a difficult task to change one's personality consisting of so many complexes. The attitude of the teacher towards the student and the profession is of primary concern and much depends upon the teacher's attitude towards his own life. The disposition may be partly modified by the needs of the profession if the teacher has the keenness to do so. For example, a teacher can be very friendly and can take the position of a real partner in the same field. A smiling face adds to the grace of this profession.

The next important function of a teacher is to command love, respect and confidence. This can be done only by demonstrating the genuineness of interest in the student's welfare and benevolence. The changing time has necessitated to build up a bright image of a teacher different from that in the past. He will have to be more dynamic at the same time.

There are certain common codes of behaviour which every teacher should follow with a view to maintaining a certain standard in his personality manifestation. He should be polite in his expression on the one hand, while his personal interests should be sacrificed for the sake of his professional growth. Optimism along with cheerfulness would help to inspire the children. A teacher should meet their emotional needs and promote a healthy attitude. Thus a teacher should be mainly a source of inspiration and a fountain head for deriving stimulation. It is apparent that much depends upon the teacher's role and participation in classroom and community.

5

VALUE AND VALUE CHANGES

VALUES IN LIFE AND EDUCATION

Life is the expression of the infinite and it involves the process of gradual unfoldment.

Thus life is dynamic and it has a constant flow. As human beings we have to live to love and love to live. Man is the crown of creation and everything centres round his human existence. Humanity is thus the prime concern for education which should be geared to some purpose. One wonders as to what should we live for and how we can attain that. The concept of values is important for answering the question. Various assumptions about values are projected in life and education. These assumptions not only help the moral guidance but also the educational guidance. The criteria for determining the aims and goals of life and education are many. Often we mention about the three fundamental criteria, viz., truth, beauty and goodness. Keats has pointed out that truth is beauty and beauty is truth. It is obvious that without the values our life is like a drifting boat without any anchor. At present the mankind is facing a period of confusion, conflict and confrontation. The reasons are not far to seek. We have lost direction and values in this age of transition. No doubt, values are different and they may change from time to time. Yet the intrinsic values hardly change as they permeate through ages, irrespective of social and political contexts. Happiness is the goal of life and without harmony we cannot get happiness. It is, therefore, necessary to combine these for the well-being of humanity. Lastly one can hardly deny the need for instilling values in our individual and group life for attaining happiness.

There are ways of comparing vlaues but we may synthesize them profitably. In fact, there are three ways of comparing values. The first one is to do that in a normative way. In this sense things are either positive or negative and we have to choose set of values. In other words, values are arranged in dichotomy that is in terms of opposite, i.e., good or bad, high or low and so on.

The next way to compare values is different. Here the comparison is made on a different frame of reference. The concept of contrast is not the same as in the first case. Although one may think that such comparison tends to be arbitrary, it is not exactly so. The distinction is based on a more subjective criterion.

In the third place, comparison of values may take place without any reference to the traditional way of judgement. In fact, different values may emerge on different occasions. Their fulfilment is demanded by human needs in life. In short, values are of different types and they assume various dimensions in different perspectives of life. Preliminary survey of different values shows the relationship between needs and values. There are moral and religious values on the one hand, while social and cultural values are hard to ignore. Besides, there are values which are functional where the traditional approach to life is not followed. Peace, beauty, love, sansitivity are some of the dimensions related to values. No doubt, value beliefs have some bearing on actual values as they determine their nature and type. Very recently the need for teaching values has been felt both in the east as well as in the west. The question remains as to what values should be taught and how. No doubt, there are values and values and much depends upon the social and political need. Yet there are some fundamental values of life which are permanent through the ages, for example, love and compassion for mankind, truth and honesty, sincerity and integrity are the most outstanding values of human beings. In other words, there are certain human values which transcend all other values.

Time has come when we have started looking for these values for revival of our lost civilization. It is unfortunate that we are losing humanity and entrapping ourselves by greed and passion for power and wealth. We plan today sacrificing moral values for material gains. As a result, the identity of man as a rational animal is fading away. People like Bertrand Russell and Sri Aurobindo have shown serious concern for man's survival in the true sense of the term. His struggle through the ages for perfection will be meaningless if it fails to meet the challenge of the modern technological age. Money is the measuring rod of man's dignity and prestige.

It is often heard that the standard of education today is falling. One wonders as to why these standards are gradually declining. There is a strong feeling that education is loosing its impact on the mind of the learners because of the lack of moral values. It is obvious that learning without behaviour is meaningless.

At the secondary level of education teaching moral values is very important as childhood and adolescence are crucial stages of life. The curriculum should, therefore, include contents with moral implications. There should be in literature enough parables, stories and fables with enough moral values. Of course there should be no direct preaching as that defeats the purpose of moral education.

Therefore, the total programme of activities should emphasize the moral tone to promote the character development of the young generation.

It goes without saying that the entire young generation today is suffering from a feeling of insecurity and frustration. They have nothing to hold them, nor have they any inner strength to resist the evil. This is perhaps because of our secular education.

As regards organising the curricular and co-curricular programmes, every attempt should be made to orient the youngsters to the code of living geared to the purpose of spiritual education. It is, however, practical to elaborate the concept of moral education before discussing the methods of imparting them. By moral education we mean education for moral development.

Morality comes from a sense of values which are related to the meaningful life. The fundamental goodness, truth and beauty should be reflected on the canvass of life in such a way that life becomes beautiful, peaceful and harmonious.

Can we teach moral values? It is difficult to teach values in the real sense of the term. It is to be instilled and imbibed. In fact, indirect methods of imparting values should be developed with a view to making them effective. Audio-visual means for generating moral values have to be innovated.

There are few methods of instilling moral values in a formal way. Of them discussion, participation in cultural functions and sensitization deserve special mention. Story telling and listening to the life history of great people, often prove effective. Besides, recital of devotional songs and recitation of poems containing moral values are helpful.

Values particularly moral values are hard to instil because of the complex process of transmission involved. It is experienced that cultural environment enriches decency of outlook and promotes sense of morality.

It is, therefore, imperative that every school should create an atmosphere congenial to the development of moral standards. The ancient texts of wisdom including the Upanishad may be presented in their simple versions along with textual matters. Similarly legends and fables may be narrated very attractively. In other words, the literary values of the texts chosen for moral teaching should be kept in view. Both the curricular and co-curricular programmes should be designed to inculcate the moral values without imposing them on the young minds. The epics of India like the *Ramayana* and the *Mahabharata* have tremendous potential to attract the young minds and inspire the young generation towards goodness and truth. The fundamentals of religion are embedded in these epics and, therefore, they go a long way to the cause of generating transcendental values of life.

The teacher's role in the task of generating moral values is quite significant. They are the friends, philosophers and guides who can stir the minds of the young people, with new ideas, thoughts and philosophy. In fact, their life should be the example and their way of living should be the source of inspiration. It goes without saying that without good teachers, no amount of theoretical education would prove effective. Even the curricular contents may be mixed up with episodes of moral bearing for assimilation by students. Teachers should be resourceful to incorporate relevant materials to suit the interest and ability of the young people according to their needs. Assembly sessions may be characterised by messages from great people and short discourses. Birthday celebration of great people like Buddha, Chaitanaya and Gandhi or Aurobindo may be organised at regular intervals with an eye to the purpose.

Assumption about values are of great significance for education. These assumptions influence not only the curriculum but also direct the other factors in education. Even the aims of education are determined by the values assumed. Education is a part of life and the questions about values in education are of vital importance and are, therefore, inseparable from larger questions of values in life. If we assume that there are values, the question arises whether those should be compared and contrasted. While comparing values in a normative way we generally put positive things such as good and bad. We can also compare in a different way the pairs of values not opposed as good versus bad but as higher or lower. This is nothing but an attempt to have relative values against certain criterion. There is still another possibility of comparing values with one another without judging that some are better or worse, higher or lower than other. It often happens that different values emerge on different occasions presenting different frames of reference. Ultimately it proves difficult to compare the value of one kind with that of other. Yet this question arises in the field of education where different sets of values confront us for necessary selection. If we analyse the values we may classify them under a few headings:

(a) Values agreed by civilised people, as being basic to individual and social development.

(b) Values determined by democratic principles.

(c) Fundamental values of life.

There may be some conflicts of values, yet the aim of education is to strike a balance. The problem lies in determining the weightages of the individual set of values in the total heirarchy around goals of education. In spite of the controversy we can accept some absolute criterion, e.g., happiness and harmony. One of the recent trends is, however, towards pragmatic approach to life. According to this school of thought, education should not have any fixed and any absolute goal. Aims have to be determined in the light of the day-to-day experience and realization of the changing needs of our life and society. There has been certain conflict between individual and social aims of education. But this is nothing but a conflict at the superficial level. Besides, there exists an utter confusion in the mind of the educationist. One wonders if in India education should cling to the old set of values or one should welcome the new concepts of values with an open mind. If we look back we find a tremendous emphasis laid on the development of moral self at the cost of others. Self-realization and even self-deprivation were held in high esteem. But one's functioning is possible in a social context. Thus the individualistic aims like self-development or self-realization are being challenged with the emergence of new outlook in life. Vivekananda described the aim of education as a manifestation of the perfection already in man, while Tagore presented a different philosophy of education. To him education is more an enrichment of the self in respect of feeling. The idealistic concept of education is reflected in a Sanskrit proverb: "Ya Vidya Sa Bimuktaye", that is, the chief aim of education is salvation. Another school of Philosophy takes an extremely realistic point of view of education and emphasizes that education should primarily solve the bread and butter problem.

As the world is getting smaller, one cannot think of living in isolation. It is a pity that we have learnt to fly in air, dive deep into water, but we have not learnt how to live together on earth. This is the problem of all problems confronting us today. For the sake of safety of mankind one has to think how education can ensure peace and progress for better living. It is, therefore, imperative that education should be geared to the ultimate objectives of living with happiness and harmony. If education cannot meet this major aim, man would bring his own doom and destruction by his own misdeeds.

Some Fundamental Questions on Philosophy and their Bearing on Educational Theories

In short, the concept of philosophy has undergone different stages of evolution. Though it popularly refers to love, wisdom and knowledge, it gives rise to a number of fundamental questions. Its purpose is to help one to attain the wisdom of the world or the knowledge of the soul. There are few major concepts of philosophy. Philosophy is a synthesis of all the sciences. It is a universal science which interprets the results of the special science in a consistent manner. But this view suffers from many limitations. The truth of science and the laws of nature discovered by scientists are subject to change and modification from time to time. A comprehensive view of totality is, however, not attained by the scientific method of observation only. Some sort of insight is also needed for philosophy that critically examines the fundamental concepts of space, time, etc. In the opinion of Russell, philosophical knowledge does not differ essentially from scientific knowledge. Thus results obtained by philosophy do not basically differ from those obtained from science.

CHANGING PERSPECTIVES

It is human practice that our society has to motivate good behaviour and set principles to monitor the results of the application of these principles and to reformulate the principles to establish justice. Justice is considered among values as of paramount importance.

Values may be classified as moral values and competence values. Moral values are concerned mostly with the mode of behaviour and not so much with rational values that indicate end-state of existence.

Only certain kinds of instrumental values that have interpersonal focus are indicated by moral values. When violated, the violater suffers from pangs of conscience or feeling of guilt for wrong doing. Competence values are also instrumental values concerned with the aspect of self-actualization. Such values reflect a personal rather than interpersonal focus, and are not that concerned with morality. Any violation in respect of competence value arouses a feeling of shame about personal inadequacy but not so much of feeling of guilt. The difference between moral and competence values gives the feeling of behaving morally on the one hand and behaving logically and intelligently on the other. The latter appearing more competent than former, conflicts are experienced between these two subtle value concepts.

Values though separate as instrumental and terminal are functionally interconnected systems. Values concerning modes of behaviour are instrumental and those are applied towards achieving the values concerning end-state. Guiding ongoing activities is the responsibility of set standards which emerge from values. Conflict resolution and decision-making depend on value systems. Besides motivational functions, value systems have also functions to make life adjustive and defensive, for self-actualization.

Values answer some specific human needs interests attitude, traits, behaviour and social norms. None of these can interpret values in full. All these specific aspects may be in different order, according to their priority of choice, and requirement, for maintenance of style and behavioural adjustment. Each aspect creates a narrow sub-system of value in the larger value system of a person or a group.

Values in the perspectives of philosophy, psychology or sociology cannot be isolated. Philosophy, psychology and sociology are closely interrelated. The predominance of one characteristic develops from its relatedness to the characteristics of the other two.

Philosophical Perspective

A philosopher is bound by space and time and whatever he expouhds is subjective. Absolute neutrality or objectivity is impossible. Perceptions of reality determine his values.

According to philosophical perspective we are more concerned with the end-state of existence. We believe that we shall in the long run free from all sorts of fear, stress and strain. This end-state of being is 'Existence-knowledge-Bliss'. To reach this awareness of one's individual identity with the cosmic identity beyond duality is given the highest value by some schools. All modes of actions that help to reach this end-state are considered as instrumental values.

It involves a gradual process to reach this end-state of existences. According to these promises a value hierarchy is formed. This hierarchical value system presents a concept of interrelatedness of existence, between man and all other beings. If value orientation is achieved on the basis of such a concept, individuals and groups can overcome alienation, establish harmony in human relationship. They can also develop ecological balance. This philosophical view of value provides a metaphysical dynamism, generates in human mind a concept of indivisibility. The philosophical definition of value emphasises human preference to move from the state of alienation to the awareness of oneness of individuals.

Philosophically values are concerned with self and related to the constituents of the self, viz., the material self, the social self, and the spiritual self.

Psychological Perspective

Of late our attention has been drawn to the vital importance of values in regulating the affairs of man. We have been made aware by the progress of biological sciences that value formation also depends upon the biological basis. It has always been agreed that social scientists including economists, sociologists and anthropologists are influenced by the value system.

The biological control mechanisms have definite influence on human value formation. This provides us the rationale to accept psychological perspective as a force for value formation. Psychological perspective is caused by uniqueness of cultures, ethnocentricity, theological bias, social inhibitions and tradition. Value orientation can be made a lively affair if the relevant components inherent in these aspects can be identified, scientifically explained and allowed to be retained by people. Further, psychological excitement of depression can be caused by ongoing social events. For preferred value orientation a study of the effects so such events is to be made. A sort of value judgement should be determined, promoted or abandoned, as and when necessary.

The value trusts that democracy, socialism and secularism can create tremendous psychological excitement, and arouse value conflicts

For the purpose of value oriented education special stress is needed to give total exposure to the value contents on these three value terms with uninhibited mind.

Psychological perspective created for our children often leads to value conflicts between various aspects. For value oriented education we need to study in depth all these aspects and prepare a suitable methodology to inculcate the value awareness inherent in all such terms. We should allow our children to make their own decisions on them.

Sociological Perspective

Any study of values and value orientation from sociological perspective demands a thorough evaluation in various contexts with reference to professional, philosophical and human values. These values are not unique to social scientists. The first one is common to all scientists; the second is related to professional practice in all vocations. But the last one may be independent of social perspective. Regarding our study of social perspective greatest stress is needed to see the degree of our commitment of our self-respect (*Sraddha*) for human dignity. Our approach or study may be similar to that we adopt for other values. The three values are basically inseparable but to understand human behaviour on specific perspectives we now need to specially focus on the aspect of recognizing human dignity.

In social perspective perception of truth is related to variables like time, situation, events, relationship commitment and so on. On philosophical basis truth is looked upon as absolute, when truth is discussed as inviolable at psychological level. In societal environment social scientists can accept truth as only a relative value. According to metaphysical perspective truth as a value is eternal and enduring, but in sociological perspective this value takes the form of probability and temporal dimensions.

Professional ethics is concerned with moral values and quality of work-life. An answer to the question whether 'Honesty is the best policy' or 'Honesty is the best principle' will make the position clear. In sociological perspective moral value is relatively higher than competence value.

Value consideration in sociological perspective is related to socio-economic situation, class differences, cultural and religious bias and such other factors.

Man is ever concerned with the ethical concept of human dignity. It is universal to all cultures world over and an enduring one. Historical, political and ethical standards are concerned with the value of human dignity. Values of democracy, socialism and secularism (according to Indian Constitution) provide a unique sociological perspective for value formation. Particularly the value of human dignity related to democratic values is of the highest order compared to the value concept of human dignity conditioned by other than democratic socio politic-economic perspective. In India the sociological perspective provides for a value sense that help to solve the policy problems created by the immense value of human freedom. At the same time the value of socialism as understood by Indian culture, contains irrational ego sense of the value of human dignity and is persuasive to make individuals to behave harmoniously as a component of the society. The value of secularism also is to keep the political power neutral regarding any communal or theocratic pressure but not denying spiritual aspirations through free choice of rituals and beliefs (of course not according to dictionary meaning).

Value awareness of an individual in sociological perspective is conditioned by: on one side by physiology and molecular biology and on the other by society and ecology. The model is: (i) bio-evolution conditioned by values, behaviour and attitudes; (ii) education, religion and socio-economic conditions; (iii) social, economic and political conditioning; and (iv) environmental opportunities and limitations. Deterioration of law and order, large scale unemployment, economic unstability, etc., cause emergence of unconditional values.

Science, Technology and Value

Science and technology are the results of human search of absolute truth and application of its findings for human use. Science is a continuing effort for knowledge of lower degree to higher. Research is central to any effort in the field of science and it is governed by definite rules of intellectual conduct, which allows criticism and invites replacement of methodology. Science works through institutional systems. All these are value oriented actions. So science is never value free. Science cannot make any compromise with values like open mindness, regularity, appropriate choice of alternatives, devaluation of old concepts in the light of new discoveries and so on. To a scientist value of time is a resource which is eternal but never reusable.

Scientific results influence concepts of ethics. Science is not concerned with value judgement but it is the other name of the eternal urge inherent in a man to have knowledge and to know what is absolute; those are the values.

Science also inculcates the value of constraints and teaches us where to stop. It is the result of scientific investigations that can indicate what type of ethics should be given priority for survival of mankind as well as that of preservation and prevention.

Science being a research continuum it includes evaluative and normative issues as values. Values of science are preferred to value contents of superstitions. Too much emphasis on facts is prone to keep a group or community closed, but value search brings in changes, initiates development and sets the model of the liberal democracy.

Technology

Technology can be developed according to need, interest and attitude of people in power in search of increase of wealth in order to establish human welfare or guarantee security. Technological objectives are always dependent on value variables of people who own technological power and decide its application.

Technology brings in social value changes and motivates economic value search.

The instance of the problem of population growth can be taken as an instance of value-technology relationship. Technology has made it possible to isolate pleasure, fertility, and productivity. As soon as it has been possible to arrest fertility, chose the duration between productivity gap, the drive of pleasure value started taking the shape of a newly emerged spirit of freedom. The situation has been reinforced by the technology of medicines. The value of constraint was ignored as inhibition or superstition. But the process did not stop here. New problems and disaster have appeared, search for value of constraint has got restored once again. All these again motivate scientists and technologists to develop new technology.

Because of technological development there has appeared a new perception of nation-state concept due to shift of security value from territorial boundary of a nation-state to a remote defence boundary from the planet earth into the space. In such a situation the emergence of a new value awareness highlights the necessity of an enduring relationship not only of human beings but also of ecological balance.

Application of technology depends much on collective value awareness of mankind.

Science and technology seem to call humanity to build the concept of secularism and look forward towards spiritual concepts as preferred concepts for survival and better living. When we refer science and technology as concepts of values, our view opens up to the grand convergence of metaphysics and physics, the old time appearance of divergence fading out.

Value and Education : Inculcation of Values

Value education will be a total failure if it is considered as teaching of morality exclusively. One need not elaborate the question of inculcation of values; it is an effort to help pupils to develop and open a questioning mind. They are to undertake value judgement strategies concerned with varying situations related to family relationship and obligation, peer-group relationship in classroom and campus life, and neighbourhood situations. Cultural identity and diversity, ethnocentricity, health problems environmental issues, sex life, religions, interculturization, political commitment, and environment come into play. By undertaking exercises in such strategy packages young ones will develop adequate response capability to make appropriate decisions. It is value awareness that can only help decision-making. Educators also can help better with their managerial values in the sphere of education.

Inculcation of values in students is related to a process of learning instead of teaching. In experimental learning and intellectual perception, teachers or parents are the interpretors.

Inculcation of values in the perspective of value and education evidently raises the very important question whether a student entering the process of higher education will have his choice of programme of studies, or institution or faculty related to the values he holds. Whether a student giving high value on being a musician or artist can go for fine arts subjects in the curriculum? Or students placing a high value on humanities will have to choose economics or statistics as his subjects for the value concern of job market? Value priorities of a student may not be ultimate in his choice of a faculty or programme. Other considerations should be allowed as well. Education is a systemic process to help the potential of a student, to attain what he cherishes, to bloom in its fullness. There are, of course, innumerable instances to establish that the value choice of a student is not always based on mature-thinking, still the values he holds will deserve some consideration.

In the context of values and education the reciprocity of value-attitude behaviour is of considerable significance.

1. We must be aware that the value conflicts are more acute among the children and youth of today. They are more confronted by large number of choices than in earlier times. The alternatives presented to them are not only confusing but often extremely bewildering. The hardest job many children face is learning good manners without seeing any. The sophistication of modern society makes it more difficult for them to make the choice because of the complexity of our contemporary life.
2. Parents, guardians, teachers and leaders, because of their limited concern for the younger generation take steps: to impose 'adults' values upon the young, through direct moralizing. They think on the convictions that grow in them through their experiences. Instead of allowing the youngsters to discover their own values, they try to save them from any risk of making their choices of some less preferable values. It is a method of value transfer and not value inculcation. The young generation continuously gets exposures of conflicting values from different forums like schools or colleges, religious organizations, political platforms, diverse intellectual approaches through mass media and so on. They do not fail to discover the dichotomy between theory and practice. They feel hurt and fail to identify the values that will lead them to their cherished goal or motivate them to act in a way that will reflect their dignity and pride or position.
3. Value being a personal concept, there cannot be one single value for all to imbibe. On this logic any indifferent approach in respect of value transmission allows indulgence or even licence. The method fails to bring the desired result.
4. Value transmission is soon to be more effective through the approach of modelling. It is an approach through person to person relationship and the process is dependent on the concurrence between theory and practice in the life of the model.

5. The values-clarification approach gives relatively better result and it can be introduced from the primary stage of school education to the degree level. This approach creates an interest among the participating students, if the approach content is properly related to age groups and made subjectwise relevant to their life situations.

6. Value concepts can be brought in while teaching various subjects. The detailed methodology and pedagogy can be prepared through operational research on value education based on continuing fundamental research on values and our lives.

Teacher Education for Value Inculcation

In the awareness of an urgency for value inculcation, particularly on the perspective of new education policy, it appears that we should apply a two-way approach for programme implementation based on policy decisions. Firstly, steps are to be taken quickly to prepare teacher activists by orienting teachers in groups to a brief course to make them conversant with values and their implications related to behavioural science. The exercise may include the following topics:

(a) Definition of value.

(b) Classification of values.

(c) Identification of the source of values.

(d) To understand the complex nature of value-attitude behaviour.

(e) Value and social norms.

(f) Value changes-technology and other causes including migration and interculturization.

(g) Value religions and *dharma.*

(h) Complication in understanding raised by language difference and linguistic philosophy.

(i) Values and environment.

(j) Values and will-power development for human quality improvement.

(k) Exercises in cultivating will-power.

(l) Values and spirituality.

(m) Training of specialist teachers in graded course: diploma, degree at graduate or higher levels for creating an adequate academic team of personnel for pursuing value-education. Curriculum may be taken as a multi-disciplinary subject to reinforce not only teaching methods in other disciplines but also to achieve a high quality of education environment.

Our work programme needs to include ongoing research on values, value survey slow change of value awareness, environmental perception and relevant aspects related to values. Also continuous evaluation in respect of values through learning-teaching end-results is helpful.

6

AIMS OF EDUCATION

Everything including life has a goal. Life has its function which is related to its aims. Without goal and aims the direction is lost and without direction the functioning is not smooth. Therefore, for effective functioning aim is a must.

Life and education are interwoven in a meaningful way. Dewey considers education as life itself. Every moment of life is pregnant with possibilities. It appears like dew drops and reminds us of its transitoriness. Life is so beautiful because it is transitory. Education provides us with a sense of propriety, priority and perspective. It is also pragmatic as it changes with the ongoing life. A human being comes on earth, grows and lives for a purpose. Education is the process of realising this truth and reaching the goal. The question arises as to what is education and what are its goals. As mentioned earlier, education is both an art as well as a science. It is the art of living and the science of doing. We live to love and love to live with a view to enjoying his creation. The immortal self finds its way through education and culture.

Aims of Education in Ancient India

In ancient India, attainment of self-knowledge was the main goal of education. This spiritual attainment was emphasized in life. In other words, salvation or 'moksa' has been the focus of attention. In the Upanishads, self-knowledge has been acknowledged as the true aim of life and education. To spiritualize education has been the dominant concern in ancient India. Only in the later stages of Indian transition, social aims have been reiterated. Rammohan, Vidyasagar and others considered education as the tool for bringing social change and social reconstruction. In fact, aims of education are determined according to the needs of the society and culture. In ancient Greece, freedom was regarded as the most precious gift of human beings. This is why individuality has received maximum attention in the western countries including Greece. Man has been regarded as the crown of creation and self instead of society has captured the attention of the thinkers of the day. Gradually a shift of emphasis was noticed. Philosopher like Plato tried to seek harmonious development of the individual with an eye to social solidarity. Similarly Aristotle accepted as the goal of education the ideal of harmony between the individual and the society. To them cultivation of goodness, intellect and goodness of character has become the most important goal. Thus in spite of contradictions between individual and social aims of education attempts have been made for a compromise.

The passage of time has brought some changes in the concepts and aims of education, no doubt. But certain fundamental aims remain unchanged. Development of the finer qualities of heart and head has been recommended through the ages. Various schools of Philosophy have emerged. Realism, naturalism, idealism, humanism and pragmation have been propagated by different schools of philosophy.

It is obvious that education in all its perspectives demands certain direction and goal. It is obvious that the basic issue in Education revolves round its relation to life.

Human life needs development and promotion. This is possible if man knows who he is and what he wants. Self-knowledge is thus a vital consideration for happy living. In order to have a harmonious adjustment and functioning man has to discover reality in all its dimensions. The spiritual reality is not to be ignored along with the social, economic and other realities. Man should march in search of wisdom which provides insight into the spiritual world. The mysteries of life have to be unfolded with the help of wisdom and education. Education is thus a means to happy and harmonious living. The philosophical basis of Education looks for the inner values of life and wisdom. It is, however, difficult to define wisdom because of the deeper implication of the term. According to the dictionary definition, "It is experience and knowledge together with the power of applying them critically or practically." Thus wisdom is more important than ordinary knowledge.

As mentioned earlier, value serves as the criteria for determining the goals of Education. Philosophers have raised questions on different values and their importance. There is a lot of curiosity around what is good, what is true and what is beautiful. In fact, truth, goodness and beauty are the key points in life. That is why the poet has rightly expressed "Truth is beauty and beauty is truth". In the ancient texts of Upanishad we hear the echo of the same message, Satyam, Sivam and Sundaram'.

The social perspectives in Education are, however, different in appearance but not in reality. People and their interaction are the main concern of the social life. With a view to realising the goal of harmony in social life we have to adhere to the ultimate reality. One cannot deny that this creation is nothing but the reflection of truth, beauty and goodness blended together. The relation between man and a man, or man and nature is regulated in a spirit of harmony. Education helps in regulating this interaction between different parts of creation. Man as a strange organism has a number of propensities. He is the most unknown creature, still man is the crown of creation. Why? Because he has the mind and ability to build up the edifice of society where a bond of love and understanding strengthens the social fabric. In the world today we find a lot of disturbance in our social life and community. The reasons are not far to seek. The main task of education is to generate a deeper mutual understanding. As a rational animal, man is guided both by his instincts and intelligence. He has frailties as well as nobilities. Unless both these tendencies are regulated and used to serve our social purpose, a chaos is bound to prevail. Unfortunately education today is not helping mankind to attain this balance so essential for harmony and happiness. In the social context we find a lot of confusion about our goals and values. Needless to mention that basically man today is suffering from identity confusion. All kinds of deviant behaviour patterns are the outcome of this confusion leading to conflicts and disintegration.

Bertrand Russell in his book, *Education and Social Order,* has emphasised the role of Education as a tool for social reconstruction. Living together is an art and has to be learnt through experience. Education should be geared to that purpose and priorities are to be laid on the functioning of each individual in harmony with society. Today we have almost forgotten that we are the sons of the immortal (Amritasya Putras). As a result our values are dwindling. Matter today is ruling the mind. Thus we see that our life needs a philosophical approach as we cannot ignore the ultimate and absolute reality. Materialism is a reality, no doubt, but that is not all. It is the part which is gaining priority in modern life. Yet it has no conflict with the totality of experiences. One has to learn how to keep matter under mind and control the greed and passion around matter.

It is a fact that science and technology have made tremendous progress in the modern world. Yet man is suffering from want, poverty and illiteracy. This means that they are lacking in the proper direction. The gross injustice to a section of the people, the exploitation of the poor ignorant people by the rich are creating unrest and disintegration. This has to be handled properly and adequately by means of scientific education. Some believe that with the help of physical and social science the essential goodness of human nature would prevail.

A Critical Evaluation of the Aims in Philosophy

Different aims of education have been recommended from time to time. Yet there is a scope for specifying appropriate directions to be followed by education. It is observed that the educational aims are determined mainly to meet the cultural and socio-economic needs at a particular point of time. There are, of course, some fundamental goals which need to be reached through education. These aims are transcendental in nature as they are independent of the demands of any time or geographical context. Thus the human values provide a broad basis for determining some general aims of education. On a critical study of the trends in education, it appears that there are forces working behind the formulation of educational objectives.

1. Social forces.
2. Political forces.
3. Cultural forces.

The monastic school emphasized the spiritual values while the scholastic aims were more concerned with the academic and intellectual needs. A conflict started between the two schools resulting in an entirely different approach to life.

The philosophic traditions in India are, no doubt, rich and varied. Hinduism, Buddhism, Christianity and Islam as separate religions have contributed to the total Indian heritage. They have, thus, some bearing on education. The main forces working behind the formation of religions and cult may be traced back to the ancient history of mankind. It has been obvious that every religion like every cult or creed has searched for the truth underlying the entire creation. The unfoldment of the mystery has been the function of education. Religion or politics have been employed for satisfying human needs. Education is the major innovation for bringing a change in the outlook and attitude of man for better orientation to reality. It is interesting that certain fundamental values are embedded in almost every school of philosophy or religion. Educational thought is expected to orient itself to the fundamentals of all religions with a view to proving effective.

Culture is mainly sustained by its religious tradition while education deals with total life. The social function comes under the purview of education. In fact, in ancient culture the sacred Indian texts including the Vedas have provided adequate knowledge of the self as well as the Universe. They embody the wisdom and realisation of life beyond formal Education. For example, the Upanishads tend to probe into the area of self-knowledge and man's relation to his creation and creator. The Vedas offer clues to understand the vastness and variety in creation while the Upanishads shift the emphasis from the wonder of the outside universe to the self within. The *Bhagavat Gita* on the other hand, emphasises the joyful fulfilment of one's specific Dharma. Thus the sacred text points out the destiny of man in a different direction.

In order to understand this spirit of Hinduism one has to probe into the basic philosophy and its bearing on the educative process. The perception of life leads to the development of the philosophy of education. It is harmony which is the keynote to creation. In the east, the aim of religion is the realisation of the highest truth. This is possible through cultivation and spiritual discoveries contained in the ancient texts and the scriptures. The aim of education is not only the conservation and transmission of traditional culture but also the need for the renewal of experiences in the personal life. It is the special responsibility of the educator to generate the freedom of spirit.

The Upanishads speak of the highest knowledge called 'paravidya' as distinguished from all other knowledge termed "Apara-Vidya". Paravidya is that knowledge through which the ultimate reality is known. The fundamental vision of the unity of all life is acquired with the help of this knowledge. Unity is possible when humility, peacefulness. Self-control and equilibrium are reached as a result of total purification of the mind. It is no doubt important for us to reach the unity of knowledge in order to appreciate the growth of the educational philosophy. In Upanishads education reserved to aid the individual to achieve the extension of the self and its expansion into the absolute. Thus perception of life in the total perspective of the whole has been considered very important as one of the aims of education.

The principal aim of the Upanishadic education is to educate the mind as the creative self in man. It seeks to train the mind through the medium of knowledge rather than to fill the mind only with information.

The supreme knowledge cannot be gained by mere speculation. Realization is important for self growth.

The mission of the Upanishads is the recognition of dignity and freedom of the human spirit.

Realism and naturalism emerged as two distinctive schools in the hope that one would be able to live more adequately in harmony with nature and reality. Yet something is found to be missing in these two approaches. Idealism sprang from a growing dissatisfaction with the existing schools. There was still a felt need for permanent values in education. Idealism encouraged those seeking a spiritual shelter in the midst of currents and cross-currents of new ideas and thoughts on education. The nineteenth and twentieth centuries changed the character and life-style because of the scientific innovation and technological advance. Nothing was considered to be permanent and everything seemed to be changing. This brought out a new school of thought which was known as pragmatism where a new horizon waits at the end of each vista of experience.

Summary

The philosophical basis of education thus demands the determination of certain aims and objectives. Education is a life long process, and therefore needs some frame work for its operation. It is likely that the concept of aim is associated with certain values. On an analysis of the trends in education of the east and west, it will be obvious that the basic approach to life has contributed much to the objectives set for directing Education.

Before answering the question "What are the aims of Education?" One has to come up with a definite stand on the different values and ideals concerned with education.

No doubt, ideals are connected with wishes of some people. They pick up, objectives which by definition cannot be realised in practice. Peters[1] suggests that the features of the concept of aim indicate the specific social function performed. The word "Aims" conveys first of all some suggestion of an objective that is not too near at hand or too easy to attain.

---

1. Peters, Rs. S., *The Philosophy of Education*, Oxford University Press, 1973, p. 13.

The main points are —

1. We tend to ask about aims in the context where we want to get people to specify more precisely what they are trying to do.
2. Aims suggest the direction of the effort towards an objective that is not too palpable or close to hand.
3. Aims also suggest the possibility of failure or of falling short.

In spite of the controversy on the desirability of aims of education one has to accept the fact that various schools of philosophy have put forward some priorities in determining the objectives. Nevertheless life and education are inseparable and, therefore, the aims of Education should have reference to the values and needs of life. In fact, the knowledge of life is essential for formulation of the aims of Education. It has been observed that human life seeks fulfilment in various ways. Its needs are different. In addition to the basic demands of life including the physical, emotional and economic needs there are cultural and spiritual necessities. Besides, man as a social being has to learn the social skills for appropriate reactions to meet the expectations of the society. Thus it is not difficult to enlist the variety of approaches to life. While determining the aims of education Dewey considers the process of development in addition to the product of education. Home says, "Education makes an individual physically, intellectually and emotionally fit to adjust in the process of life. But the question arises as to whether the aims of Education should be directed only towards adjustment or it has further aims to meet". Nunn stresses on the development of the individual self. But how would this development take place if the concept of the self remains obscure. Thus the primary objective of true education should obviously be the knowledge of the self. As emphasised by the Upanishads, every effort should be made to help an individual to know and explore the dimensions of the self. Even the importance of the development of self-concept has been acknowledged by the western psychologists like Rogers and Edwards. While the purpose of education is to discover as well as to unfold the inner self, the need for development of skills, attitudes and total personality cannot be ignored. Whitehead has attempted to strike a balance between the extreme views on the aims of Education by saying that the only object of Education is the development of a complete life. It is interesting to observe that various ideas on the aims of Education have emerged as a result of the particular emphasis laid by the individual thinker. 'Pestalozzi says "Education is the harmonious expression of physical intellectual, moral and aesthetic aspects of life". As mentioned earlier, different schools of philosophy have projected different values of life on the area of Education and brought out their significance in special contexts. While the monastic school of philosophy set priorities in the spiritual unfoldment of life, the scholastic school emphasised the role of knowledge and academic excellence. Again we find the typical approach to life and education made by the naturalistic school including Rousseau. In the opinion of Rousseau, the purpose of education is to help the individual grow in complete harmony with nature without any interference from society. This view has faced criticism from those who consider the social environment as a part of life. No matter what the priorities are, the fundamental values of life can hardly be brushed aside. Here comes the importance of the basic qualities like love, honesty, truth and goodness contributing to life itself. This view is in keeping with the idealistic approach to life. Idealism is thus not a form of realism but it makes reality more meaningful. No doubt, there still exists a confusion around the apparent conflict between realism and idealism. The purpose of Education is to synthesize both the approaches by making the best of the two. Vocational Education is considered to be the out come of this realistic approach because the socio-economic aspects of life have gained prominence at the present age.

Thus it is quite obvious that the objectives and goals of Education are determined by the needs and demands of the changing time and society. Certain perspectives and frames of reference come into picture as determinants because of their bearing on Education. Education is not a concept for picking out any specific activity. On the other hand, it is designed to lay down criteria to which a family or society must conform. There is a confusion around the differences between education and instruction. It is accepted in general that Education has a more comprehensive role and a greater responsibility. This is why its connotation is extensive and is at the same time far-reaching. Of course, the controversy exists as to whether Education as a process should be normative or otherwise. As mentioned earlier, the general criteria of education are however, laid down by the different schools of philosophy. In spite, of the angularities projected here and there certain fundamentals remain acceptable to every school. While educationists proclaim that education is of the whole man, they are no doubt, enunciating a conceptual truth. In fact, education rules out narrow specialization and a purely instrumental approach to activities. It is interesting that life and Education are almost synonymous. Living is transformed into a quality of life which constitutes the basis of Education. In this connection the approach of John Dewey deserves special mention. The analysis of both education and its aim reveals the truth that life is the core of both education and its development. The intrinsic value of Education lies in its process of unfoldment. According to the ancient wisdom, truth, beauty and goodness are interwoven in a way. The development of heart has its tremendous implication for enriching and enhancing life and education. Turning to Prof. Peters' analysis we see that he has given us three conditions as mentioned earlier. Dewey has put forward some challenging comments on the views of education and its aims. He thinks that Education cannot be related to vocation and skills. This view has been shared by many who concentrate on the fundamentals of life and mostly ignore the mundane realities.

REVIEW OF THE OBJECTIVES OF EDUCATION

It becomes obvious that the aims of education are related to the values in life. It is felt that harmony, happiness and humanity are the key-words which should offer direction in educational planning. In other words, education as a dynámic process should be oriented to all kinds of values in life. While the values differ in various contexts, life remains fundamentally progressive.

In determining the aims of education one is influenced by the different kinds of values prevalent at that time. However, the aims of education are concerned with certain fundamental concepts of life. It is not difficult to trace the history of education with reference to the specific emphasis at different times. In fact education appeared to be wedded to certain goals and remained so until the emergence of a new outlook. It was felt by a number of philosophers that education deserves autonomy and liberation from the traditional aims. New horizons flashed indicating unending and unlimited boundary for its operation. Any value may be imbibed by the young learners who should be allowed the freedom to choose their priority and standard. Nevertheless, teachers have to be careful about the evil influence of politics and its persuasion in the interest of the sanctity of education.

The changing mode of life has contributed to new modalities of perception on values. It is striking to note that the values owe their origin to the basic concepts of life and influence the system of education designed to reflect certain aims. Unfortunately, values are fluctuating today as a result of confusion about life. In order to achieve clarity and precision in the realm of values we obviously need the metaphysical approach to life. Behind matter there is, spirit behind reality and there is ultimate truth. Those in charge of planning education should have far-sightedness as well as insight to evaluate educational objectives. This is very true and is quite in keeping with the Upanishadic thoughts on education. The concept of 'paravidya' and 'aparavidya' is thus relevant to the determination of the fundamental aims of education : "sa vidya ya vimuktaye" is the most significant statement ever made in reference to education. Freedom from bondage of any kind is thus the ultimate goal of every human being and so of education.

The educational standard is believed to be falling at present and a few seminars have been organized and studies conducted to determine its causes. It is observed that there is no significant difference either in behaviour, attitude or in performance of the so-called educated people and uneducated. The only difference is that educated people keep more information than those who are deprived of educational opportunities. Thus education cannot guarantee any excellence today in the area of sensitivity feeling or in attitude. The reasons may, however, be attributed to confusion and conflict around aims of education. No western values could be begged or transplanted in the field of Indian education. The typical needs of India and the traits of Indian culture have to be projected on Indian education in order to make it meaningful.

FURTHER REFLECTION ON CONCEPT AND AIMS OF EDUCATION

Professor Peters defines education as initiation into a worthwhile form of life. He emphasises the evaluative aspect of the concept. It is rather difficult to come to a totally uncontroversial position regarding the formulation of aims of education. The issue is a complex one as it relates to values and their development. Education is thus a process as well as a product. Roughly speaking two types of conditions have been suggested for the use of the term education. They are desirability conditions and knowledge conditions.

Turning to Peters' analysis of aim, we see that he has emphasised three conditions, each of which has been considered as a part of the concept 'education'. Nevertheless education should have certain quality and standard in order to be meaningful. As Warnock observes, "A good education must above all things, be directed towards the strenghening of the faculty of imagination". The practical question is whether the same kind of education with the same quality can be made suitable for everyone. The answer is obviously, in the negative as the concept of quality varies to a considerable extent.

In order to attain certain roles and standard one needs a suitable curriculum for its implementation. A curriculum needs to be not only catered to the varied needs of the learners, it should also be integrated into the system with the learning process of the pupils. The teacher in the system should provide not an integration of experience, but rather those experiences which would enable the student to achieve his own integration or organisation of experience. According to Dressel,[2] the integrative process strives to organise knowledge and experience in a meaningful fashion.

2. Dressel, P.L., The Meaning and Significance of Integration in 57th year book of a National Society for the Study of Education, Part III.

7

ASSUMPTIONS AROUND VALUES

Assumption about values is, of all assumptions, the most important one for education, as it affects the direction of education. As in life, so in education, the question of values persists through ages. Education is believed to be a purposive activity towards ends which are deemed to be good. While some aims of education are universally agreed upon, others are controversial. There is a wide divergence between aims and it is a challenging task to reconcile them with confidence.

Philosophy of education should, show the implications for education with reference to beliefs in values. The beliefs vary but they are not mutually exclusive.

Beliefs about Values

There are some educational values which we take for granted at first sight as desirable, depending upon our beliefs. The effect of such values on education is obvious enough. The practice and thought of education are affected by assumptions of many kinds. Practice is illuminated by thinking. Assumptions about values affect the direction of the moral guidance we give, they also affect the direction of the curriculum, attitudes and personality as well.

It is, however, worthwhile to compare values for the sake of a critical analysis. Perhaps we cannot finally settle the progress towards the truth which can be evaluated by judgement of values.

Our main concern here is with the values in education. Education is a part of life. Therefore, our questions about values in education are inseparable from larger questions of values in life. In short, values are embodied in education and educational practice. Value is a term applied to an actual complex factual state of affairs to which we attach the adjective 'valuable'. The normal use of the term is positive rather than negative. But this is too narrow a concept.

Three Ways of Comparing Values

The word 'value' may mean in the broadest sense any object or state of affairs which satisfies desire, gives pleasure or satisfaction of any kind. This is rather a descriptive sense of 'value'. It is a face value and in this sense there is no distinction between lower and higher values.

We may compare values in a normative way in which things, morally good, are opposed to things which are morally bad. Here we believe that we ought to cultivate one set of values and ought to avoid the others. Comparison is also possible between pairs of values in which they are not opposed as good versus bad. In the third place, we may compare values with one another without judging the relative merits on a relative scale. One value may be put side by side in a particular perspective. Thus the values of possessing and exercising skills may be put side by side with the value of health.

Types of Values Analysed

If we return to the first basis of comparison, viz., the morally normative comparison in which 'ought' is opposed to 'ought not', it would be desirable though formidable, to determine the priority of each value. In the widest sense, values are objects of satisfaction. But desires and satisfactions which are not morally supported cannot serve as a sound criterion. We do believe that there is an invariable connection between 'truly good' and what is most deeply satisfying to human beings. They are seen to be two faces of the same thing, a pattern and quality of total human living. It should, however, be noted that this accounts for a thorough search for a wider ground of human good. The particular idea or concept of ideas of what is good to do and seek must change along with other changes within the social structure.

Thus there are other sets of values besides moral, which cannot be lost sight of. Let us consider a few things which cannot be brushed aside in the contemporary world as unimportant in life and education. Some of the values are more immediate ones, relative to immediate individual and social needs. Others are less immediate and more general. Some of them are moral while some are religious. Some are both means and ends, and a few claim to be ends only.

For the sake of convenience they may be classified as follows:

(a) Values agreed as basis of individual and social living:

(b) Values broadly agreed to by educationists in western democracy;

(c) Values which are under dispute; and

(d) Values held to be important by special schools of thought.

Under the first heading, some of the basic skills are considered to be necessary for obvious social reasons. Then there is a need for development of personality in a democracy which may come under category (b) Besides, there are those which are almost projections of personal or group temperament. There are other value beliefs which are not so obviously connected with temperament and which yet seem to be influenced by it. One example is the emphasis in education upon intellectual development as distinct from concern with feelings and attitude. One can often sense in a modern school the emphasis on personality development and social awareness.

Justification of Judgements of Values

These are some of the many value beliefs involved in education. The question arises how we justify judgements of value and how we reason and argue about them. The conflict is not between values higher or lower. In fact, we are concerned with its multiplicity of values, making various claims upon us. Every now and then, we are called upon to make choices. On what principles do we choose when there is a conflict? Can we decide about values in a rational and objective manner? Can any one come up with single key to find a solution or is there a hierarchy of values ruled by some supreme ordering principle?

In short, "Is there any final truth about values based on our judgements"? The attack on the objectivity of ethical knowledge arose out of logical positivism. In fact ethical statements are neither analytic nor empirical and are thus unverifiable. An ethical judgement is not based on pure fact as it involves a certain kind of emotion. The various forms of subjectivism have made it clear how closely ethical judgements are related to feeling. There is a need for effective involvement as well as objectivity, but it is extremely difficult to achieve it. But this objectivity is not detached from the self and our progress from within. It is a sincere attempt to get beyond our own private limitations in one way. Yet, I am thinking more objectively. Secondly, it is the conception of what ought to be, which is subject to change.

The Problem of the Hierarchy of Values

With these preliminary questions it is worthwhile to consider some substance or content of competing claims between different values in life and education. The question arises as to whether there is any key principle which can give overruling guidance in moral and educational judgement and decisions.

Concluding Observations

The following theme may be followed for studying values and value-oriented education:

(1) Concept of Value and Value Orientation Form — (a) Philosophical, (b) Psychological and (c) Sociological perspectives;

(2) Science, Technology and Values;

(3) Value Education: Inculcation of Values; and

(4) Teacher Education for Value-inculcation.

VALUES AND VALUE-ORIENTATION

In the determination of human behaviour the most important factor is people's specific value awareness. One's choice of the course of action is dependent on the value alternatives. We prefer one course of action to another on our assumption that our choice will help to realize our values to a higher degree.

Changes occur in a person's value perception. For human quality improvement we are required to modify some of our values and identify the ways in which such modification can be developed. It is also required to have the ideal of soundness of the values to which we subscribe and build our value systems. This can be achieved through value orientation. Education is not merely a systematic process of transferring skill, it also imparts the rationale for value orientation and provides strategics for valuc clarification towards human development. Thus people's ability to respond to varying and demanding situations would develop adequately. We may however, follow a three-fold method to judge the soundness of our values: (a) by identifying the developments which constitute the realization of the currently dominating values we subscribe to, (b) by isolating factors which tend to preserve or determine such values, and (c) thirdly, by providing strategies and techniques for retaining the degree of such values.

In this context what is most important is to identify the values of a person or a society. The knowledge of the value structure, and the dynamics of value orientation is imperative.

Before proceeding further with the subject it is necessary to make an attempt to place some general definition of 'value' The simplest way to understand 'value' is the economic value theory that is exchange or market value of a commodity. It is not also difficult to understand that we value an object or a job that fulfils our 'needs' and 'wants'. Social value reflects an empirical content that some social groups may achieve to motivate social action. A value also denotes some idealism like patriotism, Leelfless service, environmental conservation, non-violence and so on.

Values mean the cherished end-states and the awareness of actions that directs human endeavour. Values also help to decide legitimate goals, which set in social actions. Values also indicate truth, good beauty and freedom and the inherent human drive for realizing these values. These are accepted as spiritual values.

'Value' indicates a persisting code or standard. It determines how people can order the thrust of their desire for various jobs, actions, ways of life, etc. It is a continuum of prescriptive and proscriptive forces having a sense of reliability, depending on culturally acquired or transmitted attitudes.

MAN IN EDUCATION

Human Nature

Man is endowed with a number of faculties. He has a soul, body and a mind. He possesses a number of faculties. He functions in a number of ways by exercising his cognitive, affective and conative domains. Besides, reasoning, thinking and judgement are his main assets. He is also guided by his feelings and emotions.

Man has his social and spiritual selves as well. He has his intelligence and power of adoptation. He explores, experiment, and manipulates the environment. Besides, he has the creative abilities as well. As a creative being man functions and shapes his environment. He has various roles and responsibilities.

MAN AND HIS PURPOSE OF LIFE

It is a controversial issue as the purpose is different in different contexts. Very often we hear about the spiritual aim of life. Man has come to this world mainly to fulfil his ambitions of self-realisation. It is also felt that this cannot be the only objective for a man in the society. He has got his social roles and responsibilities. So it is wrong for him to ignore this important part of life. Of course, there is a question of priority and he has to choose between various aims according to the situation and context.

Throughout the ages, man's quest for truth has been marked by the various events in the socio-religious history of mankind. Right from the Upanishadic age, we find different modalities of expression in the spiritual life and socio-political spheres. One wonders as to the preference of one to another.

Man has been described by Sir Alexis Carrel as the 'unknown'. According to him, he is the most mysterious creature on earth. Regarding the concept of manhood it may be said that it is a stage to the reached through persistent effort. It is not the physical appearance which is important in a man. It is his mind and spirit which are the main sources of his identity. The scientific basis of evolution does not explain the entire process of self promotion. Yet, the theory of evolution as propounded by Darwin at least shows the possibility of man's immense potential to develop and grow in all directions. In the *Life Divine* written by Sri Aurobindo, it has been pointed out that man may reach the supramental stage or enter into a divine life by means of meditation and yogic process. Similarly, mind and life cannot grow into their fullness except by the opening of the large and greater consciousness to which mind only approaches.

Humanity and manhood are related no doubt, but they are not the same. The finer sentiments and qualities of heart and head are considered to be very important factors contributing to humanity. One the other hand, manhood is a term which is more operational. It includes the idea of development and growth, which can be cultivated with deliberation. Man becomes more mature and determined to reach perfection by dint of his own effort. Thus the concept of man is multi-dimensional.

The cognitive growth of man is no less important than his emotional development. Both interact is a mysterious way to make the functioning more effective.

In order to explain the concept of man it will be better to cite certain examples. In the history of mankind we find all types of people. Some are bold, heroic, while some are timid and weak. In the same way we can classify people in different groups, according to their appearance, strength, quality, interest and attitude. We have found Buddha, Chaitanya and Gandhi. At the same time, we find Hitler and Mussoline. Thus, the man manifests himself in various ways and lifestyles. It is interesting that the characteristics of man may be fundamentally similar in all lands at all ages. Yet, the variation we notice among them reminds us of the diversity in creation.

Man is also known by his performance, as a tree is known by its fruits. Man is known by his character personality and a distinctive flavour. With all this he faces this life and places himself in a particular position for further development. No one rests at the same point as life is a continuous development. Therefore, we find different correlates of manhood, like environment, society, community and education.

According to the clinical psychology, man has a lot of imperfections within him. Yet he is the best in the creation. He is rational. The rational part of the man elevates his human existence and shows him the way to divinity. Nevertheless, his frailties and irrational self create a lot of conflicts within him. The Freudian concept of man is, of course, not very optimistic about human perfection. To him the primitive self cannot be denied and there is constant struggle going on in every human heart. The ego or the social self has been emphasized by a lot of psychologists for practical purpose. It is perhaps realistic to believe in the dynamic nature of man and the angularities of each human being. Thus it is extremely difficult to come up with a single notion of man because of the multiplicity of characteristics within him. It is unfortunate that man in spite of his continuous struggle has been at the same point for ages. No matter how much advancement he has made in the field of technology and science, his basic nature has not changed much. He remains a mystery forever.

Man stands as incomplete being in the life-long process of education. It is the task of education to build up the concept of man and develop in him the values for transfer from generation to generation. It is quite obvious that culture is like a flowing river which changes its course from time to time. Yet, it contributed substantially to human civilisation. Man as a unique part of the creation has a peculiar position. On the one hand he has his role as an architect of his future. On the other hand, he is subservient to the needs of the society, and thus, his responsibility is unending. His complex mode of behaviour suggests the scope for modification of his knowledge and skill as well as the attitude for better adjustment to community life. It is quite usual to think that there is a need for attention and recognition in human life. This is the basic requirement.Modes of behaviour which serve to satisfy his needs are very varied. They are built up in course of life.

As mentioned earlier the importance of manhood has been acknowledged at various ages by different cross-sections of people. The observations of a number of intellectuals have clarified the concept of man in terms of operational variable. It is not very uncommon to admit the narrowness of the logical frame of reference with its limits. Man's behaviour is developed through reinforcement. More frequently the reinforcement takes place, the better the pattern of behaviour. In education today we find that some desirable behaviour patterns also develop along with undesirable behaviour traits. The reduction of undesirable behaviour patterns can only be achieved through reinforcements of his good behaviour. It is quite usual to instil in the children the ideas of love and humanity from the very beginning in order to make a child a worthy citizen of the world. It goes without saying that the need for education is now imperative and the term education is used in a very popular sense.

If we sum up, we can observe the following:

1. Man should be at the centre of any educational programme.
2. The concept of man should be well formulated with reference to his roles and responsibilities.
3. The changing perspectives and the modern lifestyle should be considered at the time of educational planning for the development of humanity.
4. The methods of humanising education and socializing man should be innovated.
5. As man should be the prime concern in any educational programme, so our life should be the source of stimulation and education.

8

CURRENT TRENDS IN EDUCATION

Education has emerged as a separate discipline in recent times. It draws materials from a number of subject areas and is considered as an interdisciplinary approach.

It has developed in various perspectives with new dimensions. It has shifted its emphasis on child and its needs to start with. The process of teaching and learning has been analysed for evolving a scientific basis of education. The interaction model has gained its prominence among all and group dynamics have been introduced in classroom teaching. Teachers' role has been widened and the function of a teacher is not limited to classroom teaching. The emerging concept of child development has influenced education and child rearing practices. Teaching no longer means imparting instruction. It involves 'give and take' action and interaction. Exploration and experimentation have been considered as the main techniques of education.

Micro-teaching and macro-teaching have been introduced for diagnostic purpose to improve teaching. The various traits and characteristics of good teaching have been kept as criteria for comparing the qualities of teaching. Beside the concept of curriculum has recently changed. Providing knowledge and experience in different subject-areas has become the goal of framing a comprehensive curriculum. It is flexible and not rigid, total and not isolated.

Interdisciplinary approach has been introduced to integrate the areas of knowledge and experience. School has been regarded as a miniature society — a community centre.

Lastly, evaluation has replaced examination. It involves evaluation of personality, knowledge and performances by means of observation and testing. While education is a means of socialization it enriches the social and cultural life of an individual and society In fine, education has currently been more experimental than before. It is engaged in exploration of new dimensions and dynamics for the improvement of standard in general.

DEMOCRACY AS A CURRENT TREND IN EDUCATION

Education is a social process and this concept of education has been evolved gradually. The criterion for educational criticism and construction implies a particular social ideal. A society, which makes provision for participation in the good of all its members on equal terms and which secures flexible readjustment of its institution through interaction of the different forms of associated life, is democratic. Such a society must have a type of education which offers interest in social relationship and control.

Education has been considered as a means for complete and harmonious development of all powers with reference to the needs of a humanitarian goal. The national as well as social background has influenced the development of democratic concept of education to a great extent. On the one hand, the individual freedom has been granted for a fuller, freer and more fruitful association and intercourse of all human beings while on the other, a wider social aim for a democratic society has been kept in view. This appears to create some conflicts so far as the interfusion of these two goals is concerned. The conclusion is, however, bound up with the very idea of education as an unfoldment of individual capacity in progressive growth directed to social aims. According to Dewey, education as such has no aims. An educational aim must be founded upon the instrinsic activities and needs in a changing society. As a preparation of life, education has got to suggest the kind of environment needed to liberate and organise individual capacities.

Pragmatism and Democracy

To Dewey, there can be no ultimate aims of education as the imposition of certain aims on education might render the work of both teacher and pupil mechanical and slavish. So far as the sources of education are concerned, Dewey differs to some extent from his predecessors like Rousseau who says, "We receive from three sources — nature, men and thing". Dewey emphasised experience as a positive source. These experiences when brought together constitute education and stimulate living. Education has its function to create learning situation for generating and enriching experiences. To Dewey, "experience shared is experience enriched". He has also suggested method of sharing experiences. To Dewey, school is neither a family nor a state, it is a miniature society where the pupils learn together by common participation in a variety of learning situations. The philosophy behind the democracy is mainly humanitarian. It ensures equality of opportunity and freedom for the development of the whole man through happiness. It is, however, criticised that under the democratic ideals brighter pupils are sacrificed and opportunity is provided more for the less bright pupils in relation to their capacities.

On a critical review it will be observed that Dewey's concept of democracy in education has its limitations as well. Experience in education is the key word in Dewey's concept and it consists of the active relations existing between human beings and his natural and social surroundings. But this experience is hardly crystallised in a set up which does not demand any thing more towards the goal. Thus teacher, in Dewey's democratic concept, is nothing more than a part of the environment. His function is only to stimulate the group relationship for distribution of experiences. He has not a very distinct role so as to direct the activities of the pupils for gathering experiences and this leads to wastage in education. Efficiency has been presupposed in Dewey's democratic set up and rich human materials expected. In actual practice things are far from what were conceived by Dewey. So far as curriculum is concerned nothing fixed has been set except some broad categories for generating experiences which are the raw materials of education. This again demands high efficiency both amongst individual pupils as well as teachers. Thus school as a miniature society very often fails to provide those experiences as envisaged by Dewey. Nevertheless Dewey's concept of democracy in education has its outstanding merits. It has at least revitalised the stale and stagnant, rather the static concept of education as a mechanical process. No wonder that Dewey with certain amount of optimism has faced a challenging situation pregnant with all possibilities.

Democracy in Education

Democracy has become the slogan of the day in the field of education. It opens up a new road to the question of social organisation, to the question of freedom in school. It has emphasised the need for examining our cultural heritage and human values. Thus democracy besides, being a method is also a faith or a theory of value or social philosophy. Dewey puts forward his concept of democracy in education as a challenge to the rigid and conservative outlook. His democracy means a free healthy climate where full sharing of interest within a group becomes possible. It is thus a grand ideal, a way of life, a philosophical point of view hardly to be dispensed with.

Democracy is essentially a process of determining the values governing individual and social choices. It is a theory in operation and when operating, it becomes a norm of action. It is made of conjoint associated living where science, education and the democratic cause meet as one. It is obvious that the relation between democracy and pragmatism is a reciprocal one. Democracy is itself an educational principle or policy. It is a comprehensive plan for the organisation for individual and collective conduct. Thus democracy values experience and experimentation. Both democracy and experimentation are similar in many ways. One demands unending research and the other a continuous catering of interest.

The modern movement in education known as the new education rests upon the basic principles of democracy which accepts everyone as being one of the people. In other words, democracy as a principle believes in equality and freedom. It is a fact that there are certain imperfections of democracy. Still it contains within itself the possibility of progress. Living and learning go-together where democracy prevails. It is not enough that young people should have passively absorb the accepted values of life. They should also have direct experience through education. The variety of life situations should foster a spirit of democracy which evolves itself under congenial atmosphere. There are various facts of democracy, viz., political, economic, personal and spiritual. The larger the need for living together in peace, the greater would be the scope for democracy. The function of an educationist is to foster the growth of world democracy. If a school is to grow into a community, the first essential condition is the happy relation between the members of the school. Education is a process of nurturing this democratic ideal by promoting friendship and community spirit. It makes possible the emergence of truth, beauty and goodness, if there is no external pressure. Authoritarian outlook has every chance to hinder the progress of democracy, and as such the authoritarians are the worst enemies of the democratic way of life.

If one believes in democracy, he shall seek to promote freedom in and through the family and to help parents build personalities.

Thus education has a responsibility towards building up a system whereby the members of a community live together and can give the maximum service to the community. It is possible that democracy is not something that can be bestowed or given. It is essentially to be earned through knowledge and consideration, liberty and dignity of the individual man. Democracy does not, therefore, know where it is going but only feels its way.

Education is a means to the fulfilment of this dream, yet to be realised. Where democracy is an adventure education is the resource. According to Whitehead, "The primary objective must be to get pupils to acquire the values which underlie the democratic system. There is a great deal of philosophical and other work to be done here on what the precise content of teaching should be".

Whitehead says that there can be no successful democratic society till general education conveys a philosophic outlook. Democracy presupposes non-interference and rests upon the varying and changing values of life. It is related to pragmation and thrives on diversity. Education today is, therefore, more interested in dispensing with the rigid notion and authoritarian outlook. Full freedom should be ensured with a view to attaining the goal. This has influenced the various factors of education. The methodology and classroom situation have been reviewed in the light of the democratic goals and in short, the human factors in education have been correlated through democracy.

Where culture is the flower of civilisation, democracy is its fruition. As a principle, it has its appeal though as a practice it is not free from limitations. Nevertheless democracy finds itself reflected in various spheres of education. Teacher's function has been formulated keeping in view the ideals of democracy. He is regarded as a friend, philosopher and guide and he has the responsibility to act as a link between school and society. The curriculum has been so framed as to contain the elements of humanity and universal brotherhood. The role of community life in education has also been increased in the present programme. So far as the method of teaching is concerned, it is almost certain that pupils' experience has been taken into full account in classroom activities. It has been accepted that pupils can learn and profit more by sharing their experiences by way of discussions, than by any other means. This approach, no doubt, shows a respect for the individuality of each pupil expressed through modification of methodology on democratic principles. As regards, the last but not the least important factor, i.e., examination, it must be admitted that evaluation of the total personality of a child is the prime concern of modern education. It is the totality of a man which counts and in the present crisis one cannot think of education without any reference to world citizenship. Thus democracy as a philosophy has been accepted without much hesitation in the educational systems of the day.

Overview

Democracy, is thus a dynamic concept. It is very difficult to explain the term and clarify the modern concepts without its systematic analysis. The concept of democracy, has been changing from age to age or from place to place. In spite of the fact, it has brought about new modes of living. It has acquired vast popularity all over the world on the ground that it manifests equity, and social justice for peaceful co-existence in the fast-changing world of our time.

According to a number of writers, democratic ways of life can be traced back on the primitive age; it had its origin in the 'State of Nature'. There had been equality in the true sense only in those days and fraternal bond within the same tribe was quite natural. There are indications of peaceful co-existence and harmony with nature.

Even in ancient Greece, democracy was a form of government in which every citizen, had a direct share and positive role in deliberation and legislative processes.

With the passage of time, the medieval history stepped into Renaissance with the dawn of modern times. The products of Renaissance culture are obviously secularism, liberalism and individualism. All these forces naturally found expression in humanism, and this tended to bring about harmony and democratic ideals in social life and also in education.

"Humanism," according to Hans, implies "both a human and a humane" approach to educational problems. "It is human in the sense that human nature and human interests should not be suppressed; it is humane in the sense that the nature of the child and its growing mind should not be suppressed. This concept fertilised the soil for sowing the seeds of democracy. This indicates that social harmony and peace can be arrived through freedom.

Contradictions

In the words of Lowell, 'Democracy is an experiment in government; further, it may be a type of state and an order of society'. Maxey opines that democracy is not merely a political formula. It is a search for a way of life. It is the belief that such a way of life is the best way for all mankind. Democracy does not necessarily mean that all individuals are alike or equal. It tends to eliminate the apparent contradictory principles. Every member in the community may be entitled to attain the highest goal possible for him, through democracy.

Role of Education in Democracy

The success of democracy, depends upon the rational attitude of the group members or the common people which, in turn, depends upon the development of personal qualities of individuals. Education has, therefore, a definite role to play in this sphere. It tends to imbibe the art of good life through manifestation of peace and harmony. Democracy represents a philosophy of life or a way of ideal living in any social group. It stands for certain claims and opportunities that direct toward the way of a 'good life'. It is natural, therefore, that education must have some broad objectives and aspirations for the attainment of such a good life. The major dimensions of these democratic objectives are stated below:

(a) Liberty and Freedom;

(b) Equality of Opportunity;

(c) Protection of Human Rights;

(d) Decentralisation;

(e) Fraternity in Human Relationship and Peaceful Co-existence; and

(f) Unity and Social Harmony.

Analysis of Objectives in the Context of Educational Principles

(a) Democracy is to safeguard liberty and freedom of expression. It becomes baseless in the absence of this freedom. It helps to manifest the perfections in man. It further promotes liberty in the choice of one's vocation or courses of studies according to interest and ability.

(b) In the second place, democracy must ensure equality of opportunity for every individual. This may be achieved through abolition of class distinctions or social disparity and injustice. In any case, the fundamental goal of democracy is attainment of equality, and harmony at all levels. This objective asserts that education should be the birth right of all, irrespective of caste, colour, sex, rank or economic status. It further asserts that there should be free and compulsory elementary education up to a certain age, and free social education for non-literate adult and deprived population. Obviously, there should exist common schooling as against class-education.

(c) Besides, in democracy human rights are protected for growth and development. These rights are protected not only for fostering individual qualities but also for enriching social development. For this reason, importance of recognition of individual worth by fostering proper means of stimulation becomes so indispensable.

It is our common experience that any form of democratic organisation consists of heterogeneous social groups. So, diversities and disintegrative forces must be there. Each of these divergent groups has a unique social contributive property of its own. Some are intellectually advanced, some are physically strong, some are promising and prone to any type of adventurous activities while others are adaptive to various socio-political or cultural situations. Democracy nourishes the best qualities of all the divergent groups — big or small, advanced or backward. The main object of democracy is to establish a harmonious relationship amongst these various social groups and active unity in the midst of these diversities. An educational institution is also a democratic organisation in democratic countries. It consists of innumerable social groups of varing characteristics. However, the educational institution creates conditions leading to self development and self-realisation of its group members and unfolds the hidden genius kept dormant within these social groups. All these qualities, taken as a whole, constitute a unique corporate life, they develop a sort of concert or harmony and augment the qualities of the institution and of the society. So, diversities are the ingredients of social harmony and greater unity. This harmony and unity are achieved through democratic ideals of education. It is for this reason, great thinkers like Rabindranath Tagore, M.K. Gandhiji and Vivekananda assigned much importance on unity of mankind.

9

FREEDOM AND DISCIPLINE

Freedom is a word used in various contexts. It has different connotations. It is a condition of human living, a particular state of mind but it is not licence. It is a concept which is opposite to the concept of bondage.

It is sometimes used in a negative sense. Yet it may be positive. However controversial the term may be, it refers to certain values. Freedom in the first and the basic sense means freedom from restrictions, and all kinds of constraints. It also implies salvation which demies laws and conventions, fears and restraints. Even freedom ignores impulse inhibition. It is wonderful to have freedom which is, no doubt, enhanced by values. If life is a prison we are all prisoners. Is it then possible to have freedom? This is an intriguing question. Obviously freedom leads to happiness which comes from within. It is believed that complete detachment is the condition for freedom. In 'Geeta' it has been stated that the person who has the capacity to control his impulses has the potential to enjoy freedom. In other words, without freedom happiness cannot be won. This particular issue of freedom is rather complex. The questions of fact are mainly two — What are we free from? and What are we limited by? The more interesting question of value is what do we want to be free from, and why? In short, the question of freedom revolves round the concept of values. It is assumed that freedom is good itself. It is also true that freedom in its prime sense is neither good nor bad. It is a neutral fact. Thus freedom is a compound idea which stands for a number of conditions and states of mind. It is neither good nor bad but factual. The significance of freedom lies in its use. It can be internal or external. The primary notion of freedom from restraint has a reference to the ethics. The traditional concepts of freedom of will and the freedom of choice are somewhat interrelated.

The ideas of freedom and determination may be examined by the two questions as follows: (1) Are we free to choose? and (2) To what extent are we free to do so? Freedom to do this or that, to do or not to do is of great moral importance. If we are not free, the question of morality does not arise. Can this freedom be philosophically justified? Whatever may be the answer it is true that the freedom is a condition for discipline. We are, of course, influenced to a great extent, by heredity and environment, by temperament and character. If this is so then how could we be completely free? Does this mean that our freedom is limited? In fact, we are free to choose or not to choose within certain limits. We blame mankind for its inconsistency but we are to remember that there is a destiny or fate which play vital roles in our life. It is, however, too difficult to deny destiny but it is not impossible to create our own fate.

The question of freedom is thus related to other issues. Human beings have been endowed with reasoning which helps him to distinguish the right from the wrong, the good from the bad. It is a power, a capacity to judge the values for the right choice. A freedom is, however, not the same as liberty. We have our own limits and limitations, as discussed. Freedom from external and internal restraints and freedom of the will are not the same as liberty. Another dimension of freedom emerges as a result of the exercise of the freedom when in conflict. This can be discovered not only in moral living but through the acceptance of the discipline of learning.

To attain freedom is a supreme end of education. Freedom of a child is the first word of child-centered education. Without freedom personality cannot grow spontaneously, Kart held that all moral acts are not free acts. "Freedom is the truth of necessity," says Hegel. It is a compliance with a law, which is in conformity with our highest nature. According to Kant, in moral action the individual is obeying a law coming from the self. Within there is a categorical imperative. The transcendental freedom of Kant is not accepted by Harbert. Education would be tyranny if it did not lead to freedom. Freedom may be used as freedom from external strain or freedom of will or choosing freedom from conformity to order. According to professor Reid, freedom is mental detachment. Dewey mentions positive freedom which involves social guidance. Discipline on the other hand is related to freedom. It consists in the submission of one's impulses and power to a regulation. It is something some control applied upon the people for getting obedience. There is a misconception that freedom is opposed to discipline. As mentioned earlier, freedom and discipline are interdependent. Nunn says that discipline is not external, it touches the inmost springs of conduct. It controls and vibrates all our emotions and thoughts and gives perfect shape to all our activities. Freedom and discipline are not opposed to each other. Bertrand Russell says, "True discipline is not externally controlled but it is spontaneous and it leads to perfect development". John Dewey is also of the opinion that discipline brings social control. In short, freedom and discipline are two sides of the same coin. Freedom could not be used properly without discipline and discipline cannot be enforced without certain degree of freedom. Discipline, according to Herbert, is a continuous process which resorts to punishment. Freedom in a condition for effective discipline and discipline is the product of freedom. On a critical analysis we find that discipline can be considered as a concept in the sense of control. It may mean self discipline which is involved in exercising one's freedom and joy. One must be reasonably free from external restraint for maintaining the discipline without any imposition. There is also a literal sense of discipline, which comes from the word disciple. It naturally means submission, service and acceptance.

Discipline is connected with disciples, with pupils, with learning.

The art of discipline is the art of making disciples. The word 'discipline' acquires two meanings: (a) Restrictive treatment by teachers and (b) order among pupils achieved by this kind of treatment.

Thus the word has been changing its connotation from time to time.

Sometimes it means orderly conduct which is a social matter while in another context it implies moral values and correction. According to comprehensive dictionary meaning, discipline is an orderly action by instructing, them in the same way.

Another meaning of the word is the orderly conduct and action which result from training.

It is apparent that the word 'discipline' has become almost depersonalized. Discipline begins with a natural desire to achieve some goal in the realms of truth, beauty or goodness in personal or community life. The essence of real discipline is thus, not forced submission.

Discipline and freedom grow together. They are mutually interdependent. There are two kinds of discipline — One is positive while the other is negative. One refers to generation of best human impulses and their application. The use of the word discipline is, however, different from popular usage in which the word may mean either stern treatment or orderly behaviour. Discipline is thus a state of mind but order is a state of affairs.

Summary

The word 'freedom' is used in different contexts. Originally it comes from the word free and is a condition for living. Freedom is also the birth-right of every human being. Man is born free. Nobody likes interference. Thus it is a basic condition for effective functioning. "Freedom is a basic need," Kant says that all moral acts may not be free acts. There are limits to freedom. In short, freedom may imply both positive and negative concepts. For example, freedom from want and fear is more positive as a concept. Similarly freedom for self-expression has also a positive implication. Freedom in education has a wide connotation. This implies freedom of action on the part of teachers and parents, in school and classroom, at home and in the community. Thus freedom is a relative term. It goes without saying that freedom and self-control are not contradictory. Control of self is imperative for getting the full benefit of freedom. In other words, discipline enhances the scope of freedom. Discipline implies self-restraint.

10

CREATIVITY AND THE ROLE OF EDUCATION

The concept of creativity emerged in Europe during the period of renaissance and it was first formally used by the philosophers. The term was originally used to indicate the "great analogy" between the divine creator of the natural world and the artist with his power to create "forms which were never in Nature".

Today creativity is generally considered as the ability to make or bring into existence something new. It may be a new solution to a problem, a new method or device or a new artistic object or form. Sometimes it is also understood as a particular ability in action. Thus creativity is a specific ability. It has both a potential and functional side.

An enormous amount of research is being conducted on creativity in the West, particularly in U.S.A., but little conceptual agreement has been reached on what creativity is. When it is conceived by one group as a specific ability to create something new, others think of it not as an ability but rather as a psychological process by which noble and valuable products are created.

The third group considers creativity not as a process but as the product. Actually the definitions that are put forward to explain creativity ranges from simple problem solving to actualisation of self. In spite of all the differences of opinions about the nature of creativity, agreement is reached at least on one point that creativity is not a theoretical construct. It is a general traint which can be subjected to a variety of evaluative criteria.

To do justice to all the ideas and concepts associated with creativity there is a need to analyse and evaluate the perspectives such as (i) creativity as an ability or (ii) creative situation, (iii) the creative process, and (iv) the creative product. All these complete the facets of creativity as conceived today.

1. Creative Ability

A large number of research studies was conducted in U.S.A. and many other countries to identify the nature and characteristics of creative ability through inquiries into the activities of the creative people of distinction. The researches reveal that creative persons are people of high intelligence.

It was noticed that there is high correlation between intelligence and creativity up to certain level (e.g., I.Q. of 120-130) but beyond that, the correlation is not so high. That is, people of high I.Q. (above 150) are not found to be highly creative and highly creative persons generally do not possess very high I.Q. as the term implies. Eminent psychologist like Guilford conducted researches on creative ability and found that the intelligence tests constructed prior to 1950 do not consider all the components of creative ability. It was found that high creative ability does not always bear high positive correlation with superior intelligence.

A great deal of research has been carried out on the nature, incidence and cultivation of creativity, particularly, by U.S. psychologists (and later by Russian psychologists) since the World War II. It was believed that creative ability is normally distributed like intelligence and attempts were made by psychometricians to develop tests that measure creative abilities. Those involve test items such as multiple word associations, composition of fable endings, description of unusual uses or improvements for ordinary objects or implements. Power of novelty, is considered as an essential component of creative ability and is an inducement to action as established by psychological experiments.

Creative ability has the following characteristics:

(i) Creative ability involves production of new and original ideas.

(ii) It comes as a sudden flash.

(iii) Creative ability leads to perception of new relationship in a unique way.

(iv) It involves production of unique and useful things.

(v) It is often associated with tension in terms of such dualities as intellect and intuition, the conscious and unconscious, mental health and mental disorder, the conventional and unconventional, complexity and simplicity, symmetry and asymmetry, and psychological balance and imbalance.

(vi) Creative ability sometimes involves immature personality traits which may be an extension of a generalised receptivity to a wider than normal range of experience and behaviour patterns.

(vii) It leads to exceptionally deep, awareness of the self.

(viii) Creative ability turns those who have it to be more primitive and more cultured, more destructive and more constructive, madder and saner than average persons.

A research study into the nature and activities of a large number of creative persons of distinction reveal that a productively creative person is dominant, possessed of those qualities and attributes that underlie and lead to achievement of personal status, although not of a specially sociable or participative temperament, but demanding, aggressive and self-centred outlook. He is, permissive and verbally fluent, self confident and self assured and relativity uninhibited in expressing his worries and complaints.

Creative persons are comparatively free from conventional restraints and inhibitions and not preoccupied with the impression they make on others. Thus they are capable of great independence and autonomy and are relatively ready to recognise and admit self views that are unusual and unconventional. They are strongly motivated to achieve in situations in which independence in thought and action is called for. A creative person is not inclined to strive for achievement in settings where conforming behaviour is expected or required. He is efficient and steady in intellectual efforts.

2. Creative Situation

Creativity is not a fixed trait of personality. It is something that changes overtime. But there can hardly be any agreement in respect of specifying types of situation or life circumstances that facilitate or inhibit creativity. The reason is that it is unlikely that all persons will find the same situation equally conducive to creative effort. Falling of an apple from the tree on the ground could only move Isaac Newton's creativity to discover the law of gravitation. So many people jump into the full-to-the brim bathtub or cistern but it is only Archimedes who is creatively motivated to discover the laws of floatation. An inquiry into the life history of greatly creative persons reveal the widest variety of early circumstances and family situations which in different ways contributed to their growth as a creative individual. A nation-wide research study in U.S.A. on creativity inquired into the life history and important episodes of a large number of highly creative architects to identify the specific circumstances and situations which facilitate creativity and which retard it. The findings of that research study disclosed that the following situations and conditions fostered creativity in those architects:

1. An extraordinary respect by the parent for the child and an early granting to him usual freedom in exploring his universe and in making his own decisions.
2. An expectation that the child would not act independently but reasonably and responsibly.
3. A lack of intense closeness between the parent and the child so that neither own dependence is encouraged nor a feeling of rejection is experienced. In other words, the sort of interpersonal relationship between the parent and the child has a liberating effect upon the child.
4. A plentiful supply of models in the extended social environment of the child for identification and promotion of his ego ideals.
5. The presence of clear standard of conduct and ideas as to what is right and what is wrong, in the family and at the same time an expectation, if not requirement, of active exploration and internalisation of a framework of personal conduct.
6. An emphasis upon the development of an individual ethical code: the experience of frequent moving within the community as well as from community to community, country to country which provides richness of experience both personal and cultural and adds at the same time a feeling of loneliness, shyness, isolation and solitariness in childhood and adolescence.
7. Freedom to achieve skill and abilities at their own pace and encouragement and reward for the same by the parents and relatives in the society, and
8. Absence of pressure on the child to establish prematurely his professional identity.

It cannot be guaranteed that all these factors will be equally helpful to the development of creativity in persons, engaged in other occupations and in countries other than U.S.A. But it is undeniable that many of these are conducive to the growth of creativity in persons engaged in different occupations in all countries including India. A look into the boyhood experiences of Rabindranath Tagore reveals that most of these situations and conditions were prevalent in his early life and it might be that these helped his growth as a great creator.

3. The Creative Process

The creative process is the set of activities both mental and physical, involving our individual and social senses and leading to innovations, discoveries, inventions and creation in fields of human knowledge. It starts from sensing of a need or experiencing a deficiency and passes through the stages of exploration, clarification, preparation, formulation, experimentation and evaluation of what has been achieved through experiment. The creative process has the following distinct phases:

(a) *Preparatory Phase* : This phase of the creative process begins when a person after experiencing a need or deficiency is motivated to reach a solution. During this phase one acquires the knowledge, skill and technique associated with the need or problem through which he visualises the pros and cons of the problem or need.

(b) The second phase is a phase of concentrated attention in any attempt to solve the problem. During this phase attention is focussed solely upon the problem until it is solved. Some time at this stage there may be blocking of one's efforts to solve the problem and experiencing of frustration, tension and discomfort. One is led to such discomfort, tension and frustration for sheer self protection, i.e., protection of his service or occupation, prestige or dignity, etc.

(c) The third phase is a period of withdrawal from the problem. It is a kind of psychological going out of the field, a period of renunciation of the problem or recession from it. It is actually the inculcation period which often leads to insight for success or solution of the problem.

(d) The fourth phase of the creative process is the period of insight. Out of the distressing incubation period the hints for solution come like a flash. The flashing hint for success is the insight which is accompanied by exhilaration, glow and elation as the person involved in the process is confident of his activity at the solution without much tension.

(e) Next phase of the creative process is the phase of construction. From the promptings received through the insight in the earlier stage the person at work in the creative process reaches the solution of the problem or meets the need faced in the first phase or produces the thing. This becomes possible through the realisation, elaboration and communication of the insight that has been experienced.

(f) The last and the final phase of the creative process is the phase or period of verification. The things, objects, devices, or ideas produced in the preceding stage is subjected to evaluation whether the product is able to serve the purpose or fulfil the need experienced and whether it is economical and worthwhile to adopt the device or follow the idea which was just discovered or developed in the earlier phase.

Whenever the last phase of verification is not done or made instantaneously there is always the risk that the creation or the product may be challenged and nullified to make room to a new one. Thus Newton's theory of light was replaced by another theory.

Almost all these six phases are noticed in the creative process leading to a successful creation may be a musical improvisation or Einstein's theory of Relativity.

Actually the creative process is a complex set of cognitive and motivational processes involving perceiving, remembering, thinking, imagining, deciding, etc. Guildford studied creativity from psychological perspective and attempted to conceptualize the intellectual processes involved in it. According to him, associated fluency, ideational fluency, originality, adaptive flexibility, spontaneous flexibility, dedication and sensitivity to problems are the criteria in a creative process. In a creative process there are the periods of enhancement and inhibition of creativity encouraging or depressing the creator.

4. The Creative Product

Any thing that is experienced or made by man, for example, an idea, a performance, a work of art, a scientific theory, may be called in general a creative product. But in a strict sense, a portion of those products which meets at least to some degree certain specified requirements or criteria will qualify as creative products.

The criteria or specific requirements in content of which a product is judged as creative are *novelty* or *originality, adaptiveness, elegance* and *transcendence.*

(a) The first requirement of a creative product is its novelty or originality. But that is not sufficient, because it faces the question as to what extent it is novel or original, i.e., much of young child's experiences and many of his ideas will be new to him and in that sense creative to him; but these experiences and ideas are ones that practically every child encounters in course of his growing up. They are not creative products of the society in which the child lives.

Thus the creativeness of a product, when judged in terms of its novelty, originality or statistical infrequencies is always relative to a given population or products. The most creative products are those that are novel or original in the experience of an entire civilization or of all mankind. May it be Raphael's work or Gallileo's discovery of earth's movement round the sun.

(b) Mere novelty or originality of a product is, however, not sufficient to justify its designation as creative. There is a second requirement that it must be adaptive to the reality. It must work to solve a problem, serve a purpose, fit the requirements of a given situation and accomplish some recognisable goal. Unless it is adaptable in reality a product may not be regarded as creative product in spite of its originality. For this reason the discovery of the process of making artificial diamond from coal failed to win the reputation of a *creative product*. There is also the need on the part of an artistic creation to be adoptable to reality, otherwise it will fail to win the reputation it deserves. Artistic creation, no less than a scientific creation, involves the solving of a problem, e.g., in painting we find a more appropriate expression of one's own experience indiscovering to convey more adequately a particular mood or theme, etc.

(c) The third requirement is that a creative product must meet the criterion of elegance, i.e., it is beautiful or at least aesthetically pleasing.

(d) The fourth criterion of a truly creative product is that it creates new conditions for human experience and existence. In order to do this it must transcend or transform the generally accepted experience of man by introducing new principle that defy tradition and radically change man's view of things. Examples of creative products have in their time transcended and transformed the then existing constraints of reality. For example, invention of railway and automobile engines and that of aeroplane have removed or transformed the constraints of conveyance. Similarly inventions of much improved devices in surgery removed or transformed the constraints of sickness.

(e) The fifth requirement of a creative product is that the insightful solution that underlies the product should be realised, evaluated, elaborated and developed to the full. It must be communicated and communicable to others and thereby it becomes usable when these aspects in the society of the products are visualized. In other words, the characteristics of a creative product should be such that it can be produced in numbers from the prototype and these should be usable in meeting demands.

Lastly, creative products are manifestation of creative activity. In other words, there are tangible expressions or resultants of creative activity.

In each field of creative enterprises there are several dimensions peculiar to the particular product. These are to be subjected to the above requirements or criteria, namely, originality, adaptiveness, elegance, transcendence and usability to make or stamp these as creative products.

Creativity and Education

So far we have made an anatomical dissection of creativity that embodies in itself the process of harmonizing. Creativity produced highest models of human achievement and awarded eternal distinction to man which cannot perish with time. It is a spontaneous unrepeatable and sometimes unpredictable quality that transcends simple mechanism such as computer. A set of pertinent question comes to mind. Is creativity related to education in any way? Why do we need creativity? What are the implications of creativity in education?

Answers to these questions demand a clarification. In reality it is not a process of certification, though many people think it in such terms. Education is necessarily a man-making process by which he is transformed into the desired man needed for the society. It is a process of human resource development. This development becomes effective through acquisition and application of necessary knowledge, skill and attitude. If education is thought in such terms, there is hardly any creative person who is not educated. A dive into the life and works of great creators reveals that they acquired necessary knowledge and skill in their own fields and many other related fields. Though creativity is a latest human quality, it is encouraged, improved and developed to distinction by education. There may be one Beethoven out of a group of people having some education. Education is a must like the manure and water for the flowering plant. Otherwise buds will wither and drop and creative ability will rest and perish.

We need education for creation and fulfilment of life. We need creativity in education to extend and transcend beyond the routine work of life, to enjoy bliss and achieve distinction. It is creativity in education which turns the toil of living into the joy of life. The journey in education is a journey without end, and creativity is the unceasing source of inspiration and joy in that journey; it is the seed of life for the length of living and leaving.

The relationship between creativity and education is, therefore, close. The growth of creativity in an individual depends upon the nature and character of the creative situation. But people differ in their responses to the same situation and conditions and as such it is difficult to prescribe a particular set of conditions and situations in education for inculcation of creativity among the learners. The following conditions and situations were generally found to be congenial for the growth of creativity among children in the school system:

1. A tendency to stress freedom and autonomy of the child.
2. Substitution of self-discipline or discipline inspected from outside.
3. An openness to all ideas and a judgement in choosing out of them.
4. The adoption of a more playful attitude to study.
5. Engagement in imaginative play and inculcation of appropriate imagery.
6. Initiation to search for common principles in terms of which quite different domains of knowledge can be related.
7. Nurture of a feeling for analogies, similies and metaphors not only in learning materials but also in life situations.

11

OUR STANDARD OF EDUCATION

There is an increasing skepticism on the educational standards in post-independence period of India. In a democracy, standards cannot be considered apart from the dominant values of a society. The aspirations and goals of a country and a nation should find expression through its educational system. Sociologically, standards may be viewed in several perspectives. They may seem to reflect the dominant cultural values of society. In this connection some pertinent questions may be raised as follows: Is a present-day graduate better or worse than his counterpart two or three decades ago? Has the concept of the educated undergone some drastic changes during the past few years? Questions such as these obsess the minds of all thinking persons.

On a critical analysis it would appear that a lot of confusion still prevails on the concept of standard. What is educational standard? Kripal of the Ministry of Education, while attempting to define standard, raises a pertinent question: "Do we judge the 'standard' by performance in public examination, or do we judge them by their physical fitness, or by their conduct and character"? There is yet another way of looking at the question. One would possibly enquire in this connection, whether

(a) there is any national standard, or

(b) there is any international standard fixed up. If so, how do the present standards compare?

The following steps are involved in the treatment of the particular issue:

1. A comprehensive definition of education should be evolved.
2. The objectives of education should be formulated with reference to the values.

3. The basal factors should be determined and a set of criteria fixed up for the sake of evaluation.

Let us take one by one the various dimensions of the problem for a thorough discussion.

Definiton of Education

No other definition of education is more comprehensive than Dewey's. According to him, education is life itself and as such should embrace all the facets or values of life and society. This view is rather too wide and extensive. The result is an attempt to reach a practical definition within a limited framework. The development of the inner potentialities, 'the manifestation of the perfection already in man' has been accepted as a tentative definition of education. Swami Vivekananda has emphasized the need for 'manifestation of the perfection already in man'.

While Swamiji has emphasised the need for self-manifestation, our monastic ideal was geared to self-realization. Tagore expressed the need for self-expression and development of heart along with the development of head and hand. It is, however, extremely difficult to find out the weightages of the different values attached.

The concept of educational standards thus needs clarification. It is felt that the problem is multi-dimensional. Various aspects of the educational standard point out the presence of a frame of reference for the purpose of comparison or evaluation. Now the question arises as to what would comprise the standard.

(a) a definite level of excellence or attainment in certain subject areas;

(b) a norm in performance, in practical or theoretical fields;

(c) a standard of development in certain skills, interests and habits;

(d) a standard behaviour including attitude;

(e) a level of cognitive ability including critical thinking; and

(f) a level of affective development.

Standard is not the same as norm or the criteria. A standard is based on what is good and desirable with reference to certain ends which determine them.

It is felt that no single criterion can satisfy the needs of our society and life. There are some relative values and a few absolute values in life which should be kept in view, while evaluating educational standard.

Need for a Scientific Enquiry

There is a good deal of controversy over the concept of a general standard which implies the process of comparison of educational performance and behavioural pattern displayed by the students at various levels.

What should form the criteria? No attempt has yet been made to develop a tool or an index of educational standards. For lack of such common criteria, educational experts have emphasised one or more of such criteria as examination results and job performances, skills in performances, skills in expression, social competence, etc.

A number of questions arise in this connection:

1. Is it a general term which could be used in connection with all subjects?
2. Could we measure educational sandards in terms of our expectations?
3. Should there be a majority rule determining whether something is a standard?

There is a good deal of vagueness surrounding the term 'educational standard'. It basically implies the process of comparison of educational performance of students at a particular stage or level with some absolute or relative criteria.

The word 'standard', according to dictionary, means anything taken as a basis of comparison or model and originates from the German word 'estandart'. Dictionary of Education explains the word in the following statements:

1. a goal or level of education expressed either numerically as a statistical average, or philosophically as an ideal of excellence.
2. any criterion by which things are judged.

Thus, a standard to be a comparable criterion or norm, has to be relative and not absolute, tangible and not abstract, objective and not biased, clear and not vague.

The notion of general standards should, therefore, be discarded in all scientific discussions. The specific standards are objectively comparable and measurable while the general standards are not comparable for lack of any absolute criteria. Standards derive their value from the value of something else.

Components of Index

Having clarified the meaning of educational standards, it is now possible to suggest some procedure for calculating an index for the rise of standards in education. There will be three major issues to be considered for determining the standard:

(a) fixing a base line for comparison

(b) fixing terms of reference or determinants and

(c) determining basal factors.

It is, however, important that any comparison demands some base line in respect of time or space or any other variable. If we take two distinct periods for comparison, viz., pre and post-independence periods in the history of education in India, we may possibly compare the standards in spite of a number of external variables the interaction between which are not known. It is a fact that the same set of circumstances cannot persist owing to the dynamic social forces, yet the standards are comparable in terms of basal products.

Quite a reasonable demand for qualitative fundamentals for objective assessment may be placed for attacking this problem. For example, instead of going for examination results, we may think of standard in terms of fundamental potetialities, e.g., critical thinking, creativity, social sensitivity, and some of the basic qualities of head and heart. It is felt that the evaluation of the standard is rendered feasible, if the number of variables for assessment can be controlled.

Collection of Data

If we assume that our educational standards are falling, we should have the relevant data collected by means of suitable techniques at our disposal. The nature of data should, of course, have a reference to the educational objectives. If our purpose is to compare the academic achievements, techniques would be evolved accordingly. But how could we avail of the achievement means or averages of a particular section of population? Results are hardly dependable for such purpose, because of the changing policy of the educational authorities from time to time. Moreover, the percentage of passes of any class obtained by students are not clearly indicative of the standards.

If such are the problems in case of comparing academic achievement, there would be more complicated problems on the way to comparison of standards with reference to qualities of heart and hand. The techniques of collecting the data should vary according to situation and should consist of ratings, opinions, and questionnaire on the one hand and objective tests, on the other.

In the circumstances, no scientific enquiry has been conducted as yet to offer any conclusive evidence of the falling or rising standard. In a symposium organized by the Centre of Advanced Studies in Education, Baroda, it has been observed that standards very at different levels and there can hardly be any convincing results obtained except from the stray observations forwarded by the speakers belonging to various disciplines.

Some Concluding Observations

If we consider educational standards at various levels, our opinions would vary. Let us take the question stage by stage:

1. *At the pre-primary Level.* This is a stage at which education was mainly entrusted with parents and there was hardly any formal education for the children at this stage. During recent years, learning situations at this level have improved and greater amenities are provided, particularly in towns and cities. Yet it is difficult to say whether educational standard has improved or not, because here also the issue has to to be determined with reference to the values attached to the goals to be reached. If the aesthetic value is given preference to others, the standard appears to have gone up, as the children today are made more sensitive and alert to the environment by greater stimulations. So far as the academic standard is concerned, it is at least clear that attempts are now being made to stimulate the child's experiences in a more systematic manner. But the result is yet to be evaluated.

2. *At the Primary Level.* The first thing in collecting evidences regarding standards at the elementary stage, should be to select such schools where the student population can be fairly compared with that of the schools during the pre-independence period.

The comparison of the standards at the two periods is not an easy task and as such we could take into account some symptoms for locating the standard.

3. *School Curricula.* In the past, the course was stereotyped and objectives narrow. But now, with elementary education being conceived as the minimum essential education of the citizens of democratic India, the school curricula have grown both in dimension and in content. But one wonders whether things have improved in other directions as well. If we judge standards by the dimension of the

curriculum, one would be tempted to jump to the conclusion that educational standards at the primary level are going up. But is it based on scientific analysis of factual data?

If we take the academic value as the determining factor, we would be at a loss to come to a definite conclusion. Where is the evidence that academically the children at the primary level today are better or worse than before? As regards the development of fundamental potentials, it is rather very uncertain as to whether the width of the curriculum has contributed to the promotion of the standard. Observations, however, point out that the picture is not encouraging and the children today are gaining more alertness and sensitivity at the cost of thoroughness.

The reasons are not far to seek. The values in education are at conflict here as well. There are values ethical, moral, social and economic, besides academic. As we are still confused as to which value should receive prominence or priority, our educational programmes are failing to follow any particular direction.

4. *Standard at the Secondary Level.* Sri Prem Kripal has rightly pointed out that there is little clarity in the minds of people, and quite a number of observers think in terms of examination results, particularly in subjects like English. If we take percentage of pass as an index of standard, we fail to reach any definite conclusion. A study made by the Directorate of Extension Programmes in Secondary Education reveals that the results of most Boards of Secondary Education varied only slightly from year to year. It will thus appear that examination results do not furnish any reliable evidence of the standard in secondary schools. It has also been observed that failures in matriculation examination from the earliest years were largely due to poor results in English. So far as the other criteria are concerned one might think that pupils at the secondary level today are better informed of the outside world, more politically conscious and alert to environment.

Before enumerating some of the specific areas of deterioration, it would be worth while to say that there are some fundamental or basic aspects of educational standards which can hardly be ignored. For instance, an educated person must have developed in him

(1) an attitude of 'live and let live';

(2) respect for others' views and tolerance;

(3) a conviction that 'all human being are equal' in addition to

(a) general knowledge;
(b) proficiency in the application of knowledge;
(c) critical thinking;

and other personality qualities. Now this is again the question of values which would determine the issue. The question will remain unanswered until the criterion in terms of value is fixed up. This will remain a controversy as will be evident from few observations. Sardar Panikar, formerly Vice-Chancellor of the University of Mysore, observed that the standard of education in the country had not fallen as alleged by some people, but had gone up, while Sri Prem Kripal has indirectly supported the hypothesis that our educational standards are falling at certain levels in certain respects. So far as standards at university level are concerned, the same controversy would persist. The problems may vary in dimensions, but fundamentally most of them are alike.

There are various dimensions of educational standard. The continuous change in the composition of various factors of education stands on the way to any sound comparison. Curriculum, teachers, methodology, evaluation, etc., are changing in a dynamic set-up. In spite of the fact that all the changes are affected for the sake of betterment of standards, there is a growing dissatisfaction with the present educational standard. It may be that this feeling is partly due to emotional attachment with the impression 'when we were young'. But is it the only reason?

There may be another possibility that the modern age has highest demands on our education with the expanding frontiers of knowledge. In that case we will have to survey our various needs and evaluate the educational standard with reference to each of the needs forming the criteria.

This seems to be a better proposition. Instead of trying to compare standards at two different periods, it would be perhaps more worthwhile to investigate into our present emerging needs as well as outstanding values in life, and plan our educational programme to meet those adequately. It would be a wild goose chase, if we fail to control the variables of background before comparing on an objective basis. Whether our educational standards are falling or not, would thus remain a subjective and debatable question, unless adequate data could be collected and interpreted with scientific precision. There is, of course, a general consensus that we are gaining more and more in range and less and less in depth.

There is a strong feeling that students today are more informed and less thorough, more sensitive but less critical, mere distracted and less concentrating and persistent.

So far as the values of life are concerned, the picture appears to be blurred by so many images. It appears that the present student population tends to be less introspective with varied interests, more pragmatic and confused and less interested in knowledge for the sake of knowledge. These are, however, some of the general impressions formed by a particular group of thinkers.

It is indeed a gratifying phenomenon that 'old order changes yielding place to new', but it reflects a fluctuating tendency. When one sits to examine that oft-quoted statement beginning with 'old is gold' on the one hand, and 'new is noble', on the other extreme, it leads us nowhere, if we merely continue to relish the past glory and condemn the new change. Similarly, it is equally stagnating if we close our eyes to the past and fail to evaluate the change with reference to the emerging values of life. The values of life are unfortunately at cross-roads as it is essential to determine the values in order of priority before undertaking any other exploration of this nature.

12

PEACE AND EDUCATION

Peace is the living principle of nature as well as mankind. It is all about the living organisms we care for. If we look at the nature we see all distortions and calamities ultimately end and tranquillity comes back. In our human life as well, we see that peace is inherent in us. It is affected by some outward disturbances, ignorance of some human beings and misunderstandings among a few individuals. Peace is a discipline, it should be practised in the life of every human being. Education is there to help mankind to find out what we are for in this world. It is harmony and peace. According to Dean Gooderham Acheson, "Peace is positive, and it has to be waged with all our thought, energy and courage". Children need education for peace to develop right attitude of life. To quote Albert Einstein, "Peace cannot be kept by force. It can only be achieved by understanding. It is essential that the student acquires an understanding of and a lively feeling for values. He must acquire a vivid sense of the beautiful and of the normally good. The school should always have as its aim that the young man learns it as a harmonious personality". Our learned teacher, Dr. S. Radhakrishnan states that "Education for peace should encourage the exercise of these qualities—adventure in the world of spirit, the tradition of tolerance, the instinct of live and let live, these are deeply ingrained in us. Men are born for love and friendship and not hatred and war.... It is the task of education, to create in us a love for the new world of peace and fellowship". In this reference we should mention the name of R.P. Masani who suggests that the teachers can use materials for fostering world loyalties, a sense of moral values, the dignity and freedom of the human spirit. Teacher education, as Mohammad Sherif Khan states, is "teachers' training plus the theoretical framework and philosophical foundation in a field of education". To quote Medougall, "Teachers make their effect more by what they are than what they do" Pandit Jawaharlal Nehru says,

"Peace cannot suddenly be deserved from the heavens. It can only come when the root cause of trouble are removed" We know, avarice, ambition, envy, anger and pride are five great enemies to peace that inhabits with us.

Objectives Necessary for Education of Peace

1. The teacher should develop in students appreciation of importance of co-operative living, atmosphere of social confidence, hope and securities.
2. The teacher should help students to develop an understanding and skills for corporate feeling and feeling of social purpose, to guard against separatist tendencies of language, religion and province.
3. The teacher should nelp pupils to develop insight into the functioning of group activities and social services for the welfare of the community wherein they live.
4. The teacher should help students to develop awareness of use of Panchasila in educational set-ups.

PLAN OF PROPOSAL FOR PEACE-EDUCATION

I. Instruction materials through subjects taught in school, need to be rightly selected, organized and presented following certain basic principles such as:

(a) These should be selected in accordance with the purpose of education for peace and harmony.

(b) Care should be taken that children get their first picture of the past heritage and culture from historical tales and prejudices inculcated at their early ages.

(c) Social science should have to be supplemented by social philosophy and social ethics for peace.

(d) The meaning of secularism should be explained on proper perspective, i.e., "Secularism requires us not merely to tolerate, but to understand and love other religions."

(e) Science education should be based on the realization that nuclear weapons should be turned into the service of peace and human welfare.

II. Group discussions and Debates on Peace their values in Life. Certain activity-oriented plans should be organized such as:

(a) Necessity for developing habits of exchanging opinions and thoughts among age-mates of various provinces, countries and nations in favour of peace and harmony.

(b) Guidance should be given to participants to develop an attitude to speak and listen easily, sympathetically and without fear.

(c) Critical analyses should be made among pupils about damages of a narrow nationalism. Encouragement should be made for realising the importance of pen-friendship.

(d) The teacher should endow pupils with a purposive-enfranchisement of the mind, freedom from prejudices, and fanaticism, to develop right outlook for harmony and peace.

III. Audio-visual aids in favour of Peace and Harmony should be provided to students to develop better understanding of national and international cultures, historical facts and world's progress for which certain specific measures need to be adopted by teachers such as:

(a) Books and films for children and adolescents should be carefully prepared, selected and scrutinized before giving to their pupils for developing awareness of peace.

(b) Care should be taken that there must be no wrong informations about other nations or other cultures and countries or misdirective ideas against peace.

(c) Radio and television programmes should be selected so that children may realize the value of peace and harmony. Peace programmes must have scope for vitality, wide imagination and perpetual vigilance; need of fellowship, common ideals and definite purpose of human peace.

IV. Daily prayer that portrays about peace and integration is essential for school children.

Whatever may be, Language of prayer, the contents should convey "Meet together, talk together. May your minds comprehend alike. Common be your action and achievement. Common be your thoughts and intentions. Common be the wishes of your hearts, so there may be thorough Union among you."

— S. Radhakrishnan

V. Field experiences in some selected areas should be provided to pupils for better understanding of peace as follows:

(a) Interest-groups should be organized by students, e.g., clubs and societies to discuss freely on Peace.

(b) Publication of magazines should be arranged on peace movements in our country and abroad.

(c) Community education project should be organized to motivate peace approaches.

(d) Inter-school and inter-college unions should be organized to write dramas on peace and to stage such dramas co-operatively among students of various countries.

(e) Camp-living should be provided to lead corporate life.

(f) Parent-teacher meetings should be frequently organized to discuss on harms of war movements, terrorism and their horrors to provide healthy care for children, motivate them towards peace and harmony.

VI. Seminars and workshops on Peace and Harmony should be arranged so that children, under the guidance of their teachers, may have scope for doing following activities right from their school days:

(a) Extempore lectures on peace and its effect on human progress.

(b) Mini literature on peace programme may be prepared and published by students as classroom projects.

(c) Exhibition of paintings on the value of peace and horror of war may be arranged by pupils by themselves.

(d) Some projects on Peace and Harmony, may be organized by adolescent pupils under the supervision of teachers.

VII. Some innovative researches on peace and harmony may be encouraged among the high school students.

In conclusion, let me state that our teacher-education programme should pay more emphasis on developing right attitude among teacher-trainees. They should realize what Dr. Radhakrishnan means: "All systems of education aim at the education of the whole man. The main line of work in the teacher-education system, I hope, should be more dynamic and peace-oriented."

THE MOST NEEDED EDUCATION OF THE DAY

The first task of an educator or any enlightened citizen of India is to provide scope for developing the excellences that each child has. These excellences are mainly innate in the child. They are only to be lighted up by giving him appropriate environment. In the words of Swami Vivekananda, "Education is the manifestation of the perfection already in man''. We have been mishandling our children and do not provide proper environment for the growth. We lack in our sincerity.

Even after 35 years that the Constitution of independent India came into force 66 per cent of the people of India are literally illiterate. The democracy of our country has thus remained a misnomer. The politicians are exploiting the illiterate mass to gain their vested interest, thereby turning the franchise of the people to a mockery. They are banking upon the illiteracy and ignorance of the mass to fulfil their political ends. Thomas Jefferson, one of the founders of the U.S.A., remarked, ''If a nation expects to be ignorant and free, it expects what never was and never will be''.

Peace is a boon of affluent democracy. For this we need educational institutions which aim at culturing excellences among the people. Every child has some excellences. They are to be cultivated and cultured by the society for meeting the real educational needs of the country. We cannot be a prototype of China or Russia or U.S.A. We can be only Indian with Indian excellences cultured, thereby turning us out to be a prominent up-to-date nation of the world. It does not mean that we shall not imbibe the good cultures of the foreign lands. The power of imbibing of good cultures is a great art. Excellences, though mainly innate, are also to be gathered from inside the country as well from outside the country. Thus only we can have education in its true sense.

National or international peace can come only through citizenship education. This education is much more than acquiring skill. A skilled person may be an engineer, a technician or even a thief or a murderer. But an educated person has the regional, national and international understanding, through which he brings social and super social goods. He can criticise all problems sanely and squarely, and act accordingly.

Self-concept is the basis for assimilation of education. Self-culture and self-education provide self-enlightenment and can lead to the attainment of ultimate realisation of self. This only leads to proper understanding of others. This can be had only through moral education in its real sense. Man and man are brothers when they are educated, even though their views may differ; but they are enemies, when uneducated, since they cannot stand the difference of views of others. Thus peace of mind is disturbed. Peace can emanate only from the right type of education. The League of Nations or the United Nations Organization may be the first step for establishing the peace of the world. But the nations are sure to break away, if they are not very willing partners. The veto-right of the big powers hampers peaceful solution of international problems. Hence this should be abolished from the UNO.

Atomic energy, electronic discoveries, medical advances and space explorations are boons to human knowledge and achievements. If these are utilised for human development and peace, they can do a lot of good to the people of the world. They can control the population explosion giving an eugenic advancement, better living conditions and international understanding.

The cultural activities of Santiniketan and the culture radiated by our great poet, educator and philanthropist Rabindra Nath Tagore or by the great dancers and musicians like Udai Sankar, Rabi Sankar, Timir Baran and Bare Gulam Ali and the artists like Nandalal Bose and sculptors like Ramkinkar Bej will be leading to a great extent to the establishment of harmony and international peace of the world.

The proposed National Cultural Centre or "Centre of National Integration" at Santiniketan is a step forward toward the attainment of national and international understanding by the people of India. According to Sri Janajit Roy's views expressed in his article "Making Tagore's Dream Come True" published in the magazine of the Telegraph dated 15 September, 1985, the centre will conduct studies on the theme of synthesis of India's spiritual, philosophical and ethical thought and the development of India's art, architecture, music, dance and drama to illustrate the cultural unity of India. We heartily welcome the establishment of this centre.

REFERENCES

1. Collected Lectures of Dr. S. Radhakrishnan, *Education for World Understanding.*
2. Shrimali K. L., *Human Relations in Teacher Education.*
3. Mohammad Sharif Khan, *Teacher Education in India and Abroad.*
4. P. Gurrey, *Education and the Training of Teachers.*

PART II

SOCIOLOGICAL FOUNDATION OF EDUCATION

1

INTRODUCTION

THE SOCIOLOGY OF EDUCATION

Education is an activity which goes on in a society, and its aims and methods depend on the nature of the society in which it takes place. Education is a means of organising the individual self and the social self into a disciplined stable and a meaningful unity. Mannheim on the other hand does not regard education solely as a means of realising abstract ideals of culture. According to him, education can only be understood when we know for what society and for what social position the pupils are being educated.

Sociology is the study of society. The chief concern of sociology is the social relationships of mankind. Thus it includes topics like social structure and organization, the interaction of social groups and the means of social control.

Thus sociology of education studies the relations between education and society.

It is obvious that the study of educational sociology can make a valuable contribution both to sociology and to society.

The separate use of two terms educational sociology and sociology of Education might be maintained in order to preserve the distinction between the two types of emphasis, viz., one upon the sociological problems — their bearing on education and the other on the educational problems with their bearing on sociology.

Educational sociology is the study of the interaction of the individuals and cultural environment which includes other individuals social groups and patterns of behaviour. It is the science which describes and explains the institutions, social groups and the social processes.

As sociology contributes to education, education offers sociology the direction toward progress through experimentation. The system of education provides situation in which experiments are possible without offending values about human beings. The sociology of education is thus an analysis of the sociological processes involved in the educational institution. The right approach emphasises the need for studying the group-processes and social interaction within the educational institution.

Karl Mannheim has outlined three courses for inclusion in the teacher-training programme as follows:

(a) Sociology for the educator;

(b) The sociology of education; and

(c) The sociology of teaching.

While sociology of education is mainly concerned with the study of the social phenomena within the school for improving the social climate and social life of the institution, educational sociology has its main task of using education as a social control. It aims at applying the sociological principles to the administration and process of education, as it is concerned with shaping the child's behaviour in the light of the community need. It describes the group process to which individuals are subjected and the influence of one group upon another to provide an understanding of the context within which the aims of education are pursued.

In other words, sociology builds upon the knowledge of many fields and relates it to the social environment.

SOCIOLOGICAL FOUNDATION OF EDUCATION

Sociologists regard education as a distinctively social phenomenon. Thus a sociological perspective of education is important. While sociologists are primarily concerned with building a body of verified knowledge about education in social context, they are also concerned with the problem of applying their findings and conclusions in the field of education. Thus education needs a sociological foundation for its meaningfulness in social contexts.

A number of sociologists used to think of educational sociology as a field which would offer clues to the solution of social problems. In fact, education was looked upon as a process involving the function of improving society. The works of Good[1], Ellwood[2] and others[3] lay emphasis on education as the means to progress in society. They expressed the ideal that school might succeed in teaching the pupil to exercise social control for ensuring promotion of culture. Another concept of educational sociology was developed in the social perspective of education and it was hoped that it would help in determining the social objectives of education. Thus an attempt was made to arrive at a social philosophy of education to be based on an analysis of society and the needs of people in society.

Educational sociology has been defined as the application of sociology to educational problems. Brown said in this connection that "The educational sociologists utilize all that has been learnt in both the fields and adds them to a new science by applying sociological principles to the whole process of education."[4] He also adds that it is particularly interested in finding out how to manipulate the educational process to achieve better personality development.

While educational sociology was looking for its popularity because of its confusing nature of content, sociology of education has emerged as more relevant a subject for prospective teachers. In recent years, greater interest has been shown in the analysis of the educational system as a pattern of social interaction and thus a different role for sociology in relation to education has been conceived. Emphasis is being laid on the nature of human relations within the school and the social structure within which the schools operate in the community. The patterns of interaction in the educational system are, therefore, receiving greater attention.

Education means different things to different people. It is a process as well as a product. Thus it has a definite role in the society. It is no wonder that education means something very important to a sociologist. Educational sociology is particularly interested in finding out, how to manipulate the educational process to achieve better social and personality development.

---

1. Alvin, "*Sociology and Education*," Harpers, 26 (1926), p. 25.
2. Ellwood, C.A., "*What is Educational Sociology*?" Journal of Educational Sociology (September 1927), pp. 25-30.
3. Kinneman John A., "*Society and Education*" New York, Macmillan, 1932 p. 49.
4. Brown Francis, *Educational Sociology*, Prentice-Hall, New York, 1947.

Educational sociology is interested in social behaviour as it includes anything in the field of sociology which could be related to the learning or socializing process. According to Brown, the educational sociologist not only utilizes all that has been learnt in both the fields, he also joins them in a new science by applying sociological principles to the entire process of education. It is also viewed that educational sociology is more a technology than a science. According to Dodson, "Educational sociology is interested in the impact of the total cultural milieu in which and through which experiences are acquired and organised". Educational sociology today lays emphasis on the analysis of the role of education in the community and society.

SOCIOLOGY OF EDUCATION AND SOCIAL FOUNDATION OF EDUCATION

In short, sociology of education is the scientific study of the social processes and social patterns involved in the educational system. This assumes that education is a combination of social acts which deals with analysis of human interaction. Education draws attention from a sociological point of view. Thus in the sociology of education emphasis is laid on education in relation to social perspectives. The social interaction and socialization within the school and community gains prominence in the sociology of education.

1. Educational sociology has been considered as an area which would provide the basis for social progress and social change.
2. Educational sociology is also supposed to provide specific aims for education.
3. Educational sociology deals with the entire process of socialising a child. It aims to study the patterns of social interaction and Social roles within the school and society. Thus a scientific study of the human relations in education is one of the objectives of sociology of education. It also deals with the social processes and patterns involved in the educational system.

Sociology also deals with:

(a) The relationship of the educational system to the process of social and cultural change.

(b) The functions of the educational system in the process of social control.

(c) The relationship of education to the social class of status system.

(d) The relationship between the school and the community.

Thus the need for a comprehensive study of the human relations in the educational system is receiving more and more attention in recent times.

With the rapid expansion of social science, sociology has included a vast area of social phenomena.

2

WHAT IS SOCIETY?

Introduction

Society is an enduring group of living beings carrying on all their activities in common. It is a dynamic body consisting of a large number of people under the same basic circumstances. It is just like a complex web of relations and various forces and factors go into its making. In a society, therefore, there exists a common ideal or belief, some mutual understanding and a common frame of reference.

Society is the creation of man. It is one of the monumental achievements of human beings. It is something more than a multitude of people as it contains different bodies but one mind, manifold expressions but one ideal.

Same basic factors of society : There are certain basic factors which comprise society. They act and interact and operate in a sort of dynamic equilibrium. These factors provide for the growth of society and social life. Population is the set of people, who build up the society. In course of living together these people undergo a process of adjustment to the environment. Natural environment including contour, rivers, seas, deserts, mountains and plains is another important factor comprising society. The people comprise the dynamic forces which operate in a particular field, i.e., environment. Besides, there are resources, viz., minerals vegetation, animals and the like which play their part and contribute to the development of society. Man meets his basic needs by getting suitable food, clothing dwelling and other amenities of life by dint of continuous efforts. Much depends upon environment. The habits are also influenced by environmental factors. Different lands represent the world communities. They build up definite patterns of living, culture and taboos according to the local conditions.

The physical environment sometimes provides man's physical needs and sometimes hinders the growth. The occupation and the living conditions are often guided by this geographical factor. It will be observed that people living in deserts are often restless and rootless and nomadism is the normal mode of their life. On the other hand, rivers foster in man a centralising tendency. According to Gidding, some degree of total aggregation is an indispensable condition for the evolution of society. This is known as a population which may vary in kind and density. Population, though one of the important factors of a society, is not all. Location has got a large part to play. The local conditions vary to a great extent and lead to diversity. It is location which offers clue to adjustment.

With the changing time man is changing in interaction with his local needs and conditions. Localisation of industry is one of the most recent trends in sociology and this is nothing but natural. Besides population and location, communication deserves special emotion. This is one of the important means for mobilising resources according to human needs. It is a wide term which may convey the various ways of social intercourse and transport. This is an attempt to adjust and bring a dynamic life. Today when living has become complex and needs increased, our world has become too small. Communication is being speeded up in order to keep pace with the changing time. Social structure changes but there remains sudden fundamental character in every society and social order. It is human nature which works as the dynamic force in every community.

In the present society man is trying his best to conquer nature and to dominate over the various forces. But how far he will succeed, will depend upon his know how to bring harmony between man and the machine.

Family

A family is a place where the child grows and unfolds its potentialities. In other words, much depends upon the family stimulation, love and affection within the family. The mutual trust, respect and cordiality among fellow beings, in the social environment shapes the personality of the family members. In India when fellow-feeling and humanitarian outlook were held in high esteem, family life was more integrated and conducive. Everyone enjoyed the joint family system where they could share their joy and sorrow. All the members used to live together in the same family in peace and happiness.

Mutual trust and tolerance formed the basis of altruistic motive. So Indian culture was that of mutual co-operation and love, giving rise to a humanitarian outlook. With the growing impact of western culture on our society we have become more self-centred and less tolerant. The economic factors are, no doubt, responsible for such a change but there are other forces which are equally responsible for this difference in outlook. As a result, the Indian culture is under conquest gradually giving way to the foreign influence in changed circumstances. On an analysis it will be seen that a large number of factors have to be considered for forming a proper estimate of a culture.

The following is the list of such factors:

1. Miscellaneous factors including income, occupation, education, language, habits, type of residence, spending habit, etc.
2. Lifestyles, clothes and dress, eating and diet, physical habits and means of keeping health, attitudes to marriage and sex, techniques of bringing up children and patterns of family life.
3. Leisure pursuits — reading, radio and television programmes, sports, entertainment, means of artistic expression, etc.
4. Beliefs and value systems, moral attitudes and standards, religious beliefs, political views, social ambitions and aims in life.

The modern family is a group of interacting personalities in which each member has a specific role. Family is an important unit in the society because the child's personality and its development depend to a great extent upon its size and organisation. Today with the changing society the patterns of family life in India are also changing. The interaction between one member and another, the obligation and responsibilities assumed in family today are not the same as in the past.

The family patterns change from place to place and depend upon customs, standards and ideals, folk-ways and culture of society. Family is an expression of the richest fulfilment of human need among people of every race and nation. It is as old as man himself. Society and school should go hand in hand preparing healthy citizens. Democracy in education has carried a message of hope and goodwill and admitted of the equality of human rights and opportunities. But this is a concept very difficult to be translated into action. In spite of the best attempt to remove disharmonies there are disappointing pictures every where in our country. Even now, education is a luxury to many who exhaust all their energies and time for making their both ends meet. Besides the conditions of our schools are in majority deplorable. There is hardly any parent-teacher co-operation, and scope for recreation and relaxation on the part of the children. It is, therefore, natural that our educational programme does often fail to create interests among children. Joy and freedom are only to be found in the dictionary. Particularly in the urban schools there is no breathing space for the children.

The interrelation between society, philosophy and educational theory

Before going to show the interrelation between society, state and philosophy in education, it would be worthwhile to describe the social implication of education. The significane of the social dimension of educational philosophy varies according to conception of how individuals should be related to each other. Some societies notably those in democratic state recognise the differences among individuals. It may also be wise to narrate the nature of society itself. Since society is contractual it would not be unfair to think that it goes as a result of mutual interaction between individual and social interest. Education, according to Bertrand Russell, has much to contribute to the welfare of society. Here education has an independent role to play. Similarly society is one of the important agencies influencing educational activities. Education has a close relationship to society as they interact on one another. As society is guided by educational ideas, so education is influenced by the social forces. Education as a social control has the power to bring the necessary changes which are deemed desirable from time to time. Like society, state has also certain influence on the educational programme. State as a social control is far more effective than any other factor of society and is thus in a position to bring new impacts. Some time, the needs of the state are to be fulfilled through education which can foster a spirit of nationality in the young generation of the country. Thus society, state and education are interlinked as they have got the same objectives, namely, the happiness of man. For the promotion of international understanding education may be profitably employed and the world citizenship may be rendered feasible. The question then arises as to the importance of philosophy in the sphere of education. It has been already admitted that society has the highest role as it represents the people and their culture. The taboos and customs are sometimes modified according to the changing attitude of people towards life. It is admitted on all hands that education is also conditioned by economic factors. At the same time one can hardly ignore the influence of philosophy on our daily life and education. In our discussion on educational values, it must be remembered that philosophy is also reflected upon the educational principles or policy. For example, the democracy in education has brought a new era in the world of education by pronouncing the principle of equality of opportunity. This principle of democracy has, no doubt, been inspired by the philosophy underlying humanitarian outlook. It asserts that every individual should be treated as an end. The concept of freedom and joy in the field of education is also another outcome of this new outlook. The rigid and traditional view-point has been replaced by this new concept as propagated by the modern thinkers in this field. In short, education is an active process which functions in a most dynamic manner for better adjustment in the interest of the common cause. Today education has gained a distinctive status of its own because of its high potential.

FACTORS INFLUENCING EDUCATION

The concept of Social Role

A person learns to behave in his cultural group and develops in a society. The roles depend on the different statuses he occupies as he grows up. Some roles are of a special kind which a community assigns to all its members. Another type of status is achieved by the efforts of the individual who reaches a position in his group. The social group thus helps in setting up a general standard of behaviour expected by the community as a whole. It should be mentioned in this connection that appropriate forms of behaviour are also laid down to suit different social occasions and the individual response according to situation. The concept of social role can also be extended to group membership of all kinds. As the social interaction increases, the child begins to learn his role in different groups and to absorb the varied patterns of behaviour. His prestige and success in the group will depend upon the group values. The wishes and attitude of the group are impressed upon the child by the degree of approval and disapproval of his actions. Each group will have its various techniques for maintaining discipline. It is sufficient to point out that the approval of the group is one of the strongest incentives to right behaviour. The child who will not fit into any group develops some more or less serious problems or disturbance in personality. The child learns the ways of his society along with any desire to change them by the growing concept of his role in social groups. The groups to which he can give his full loyalty and in which he achieves status through his efforts are of great significance to his development. Whatever may be the group formation, some social learning of the following kinds can be observed to take place: (1) The struggle for leadership and.the shifting nature of this role. (2) The need for roles and training the individual wishes for the good of the group (3) The expression of the child's needs for some emotional response from his playmates. (4) The need to belong to a group and the struggle to be accepted by the group. (5) The opportunity given for co-operation and learning the team spirit. (6) The first experience of inter-group opposition or a rivalry by the other groups and possibly a conflict with the family over codes of behaviour learnt from the group.

It is in adolescence that the need develops for more organised groups which are conventionalised and have a more permanent purpose and tradition. In whatever form it takes the value of social interaction to adolescence, the following are the needs which group life may be expected to satisfy. (1) The adolescent has a great need for a social group experience and to experiment new relationship with others of his own age. (2) Some such group experiences can take place in family, school or work groups and voluntary membership of a group of different kind may fulfil other needs. (3) The need to mix with members of opposite side or sex is not insignificant. (4) A group or club of which a boy choses to be a member may also be run by the member. (5) As a part of the group a young person learns to accept responsibility. (6) The adolescent needs for adventure are of a legitimate kind. (7) Adolescent learns a great deal from each other. The function of youth in society has been considered from a sociological point of view and co-operation of a youth in a changing and dynamic society has been regarded as very important.

Social Interaction in the School

A school carries on an organised life of its own as a social group within the society around it. A school is some time referred to as a society but it would be better if we call this a community since its members have many things in common. The school as a society makes the following definite suggestions which are summarised as follows:

(1) That pupils themselves should take some share in making the school's programme. (2) That a greater number of pupils should take

responsibility. (3) Minor organisations should be left to the pupils. (4) There should be closer relation between the school and the society outside. Thus a school should stimulate a healthy social life and promote the social understanding.

The social interaction is influenced also by family life which is the first and the most intimate group to which the child belongs. We are concerned with nature of the family as a social unit. The functions of the family have been classified in various ways as follows: (1) In giving and receiving affection, the value of the family circle as a source of love and security cannot be over emphasised. This continues to be a major function of home life. (2) As the function of proper reproduction a family unit must adjust the birth of children. The size of the family has a considerable influence upon society. (3) The family known as the unit of production has to supply its own needs. Agencies outside the home have gradually taken over more and more economic function. (4) The family used to take full responsibility for protecting its members. Now the state has taken much of the responsibilities. The family still gives the protection or affection which leads to the kind of emotional security which cannot so far be acquired in any other way. (5) Education is also being taken over more and more by the state. The tendency has been to raise the school leaving age at one end and the lower age of entry at the other. (6) Recreation and relaxation which the home used to provide are the chief sources of leisure and stimulation in occupation. Children and parents spend less of their leisure time at home. The sport, the ease of transport, the outdoor activities, the desire to travel, the independence of women have all contributed to this change. The cinema takes people out but these have limited effect. (7) Each member in the family has a clearly defined status and each status has its role. Thus human relations within a family are very important.

Parent-Teacher Relation

The family life of a pupil is also stimulated by the parent-teacher relation. Since the school is tending to share the function of the family, it is necessary to provide frequent opportunities for contacts between parents and teachers.

Outside Cultural Influences

As discussed previously, the influence of group membership in transmitting the culture of our society is remarkable. The most important source of influences (external to the small group) is the mass-medium of communication. This consists of cinema, the radio, newspapers and magazines. All these are media of communication in an industrial society in which we live. All the features of our life and the interests of people are being brought to public notice through these mass-media of communication. The printed word has influenced on the mind and the impact of the modern printing press on universal literacy is great. The influence of cinema on the children leads to dissemination of cultural values and habits. Thus with the changing time our culture is also being influenced by the various scientific innovations and attitudes of the people. The social role is, therefore, an important concept where the various institutions like school and club, family and church, cinema and press, interact and shape the future generation.

Culture Concept and Social Institutions

As defined by Ralph Linton, a culture is the organisation of learned behaviour and the result of behaviour whose component elements are shared and transmitted by the members of a particular society. A culture pattern can be taken to mean the ways of behaviour associated with any permanent need or function in the social life. It is also represented by material objects which are included under the results of behaviour.

3

SOCIETY AND ENVIRONMENT

SOCIAL FACTORS AND SOCIAL ORGANISATION

Environment provides the basis for the growth or social development as society is formed as a result of interaction within a geographical boundary. Population is one of the factors of society although its size, structure and organisation vary to a considerable extent. Environment influences people in a number of ways. There may be different types of physical environment, social environment and cultural environment. The climate, natural resources, the nature of the soil influence, the distribution of population, the food habit and even the habitat chosen by people. Besides, the type of surface of the land has a bearing on the personality of the people in respective areas. For example, people living in hill areas are more painstaking than those on the plains. Similarly those living in islands are more outgoing and courageous than others. Thus the nature of the physical environment has a distinct bearing on the body and mind, the habit and personality of people. Even population is distributed differently according to the physical environment, industrial growth and natural resources.

Like physical environment, social and cultural environment also determine the attitude and outlook of the people in a society. Certain communities are socially backward because of their inability to accommodate new ideas and values. Exposure to the outside world and varieties of culture leads to broadness of outlook. It is interesting to observe that certain communities are very rigid and conservative while there are communities with greater adaptability. It may be relevant in this connection to mention that certain monuments of civilization have been built up on the banks of the rivers like the Ganges and the Nile. Thus the contribution of river to the growth of culture and civilization and the Egyptian culture are examples, no doubt.

In addition to physical environment, certain other factors are related to the development of a society. Among them the cohesion and morale, the nature of interaction between members of society, the values, common faith and belief deserve special mention. In order to bring a cohesive pattern of community-life certain goals and common ideology would be essential. In addition to the physical or geographical factor the interaction among the members of the society determines the pattern of the social structure of a society. Of course communication and culture help the process of social interaction. Thus among the factors of society, cultural values and norms, interaction and means of communication play prominent roles. Besides, the social units and social groups form the internal structure and generate the forces.

Needless to mention, that social environment is created as a result of interplay between the people and the socio-cultural factors. This kind of environment contributes to the growth and development of a society. The last but not the least important type of environment is the cultural environment, as it provides the guideline for formation of values and norms in a social context. The richer the cultural environment, the more conducive it becomes to the growth of personality. A civilisation is enriched by the affluent cultural environment for obvious reasons.

Factors of Society

Society is like a complex wave of relationship between various groups of people. There are certain factors which comprise a society. A geographical boundary, within which people live in interaction with one another, is essential for a stable society to build up. But more important factor is population or a set of people with common interests or goals. Even a natural environment including rivers, sea, deserts influence the social structure and the social function. The composition of the social classes and the distribution of population depend mainly upon the available natural resources as well as transportation system. Communication media serve the purpose of interaction at various levels. Thus the entire social fabric is the outcome of so many threads running into one another for adequate functioning.

In addition, there are social units around which the social activities are continued for the promotion of the set objectives. Of all the units family deserves special mention because of its vital importance. Family is a place for socialization where the child grows in a sheltered situation. It provides a background for transfusion of social values. In fact, the role of family in a child's development is quite significant. There are other social units which go to the making of a society. They are religious institutions, social organisations like club, educational centres including schools and similar social units.

The factors mentioned above, no doubt, condition education as they influence the growth and distribution of population, social mobility and social structure. Even the social stratification depends upon the economic status of people as well as their educational achievements It is interesting to find out relationship between the growth of as well as the cultural decline. In a changing society the media of communication play an important role in bringing social change or social progress.

The social forces are the result of social interaction. They produce social changes as well as create conditions for social progress. Among the social units certain sub-structures develop more communication channels and individual values. Social classes including castes are the outcome of the economic and cultural disparities found in a social structure. They create conflicts and dissatisfaction within the unprivileged section because of the stratification. In certain tribes or sections of the society we find less mobility and more rigidity. Even today most of the aboriginal tribes tend to cling to the old values and resent any change even in a desired direction. For example the depressed classes in India were very reluctant to accept the value of family planning and population control. Similarly among the American Indians there still exists some resentment against modern technical education. With a view to generating public opinion and new values the roles of mass-media and recreational agencies are tremendous. The social organisations, economic and industrial institutions can contribute substantially to the cause of mass enlightenment and national integration.

The Individual and Social Organisation

The social relations are developed by the way people behave with each other and by their membership in groups. There are many ways in which an individual interacts, sometimes through co-operation and at other times through competition and conflict. It is observed that interaction follows an established pattern. The individual's interaction and his group memberships are mainly determined by the way in which he solves the problem of day to day life. There is a variety of social relations built up through friendship, leadership, partnership, citizenship and host of other relations. Some social bonds are strong while others are delicate. Marriage remains a relatively strong and stable bond. Moreover, the strength of a relation depends on whether it serves the needs of the individual.

The social structure consists of a number of roles defined as patterns of behaviour associated with a distinctive social position, e.g., that of father, teacher, employer, etc. The ideal role, however, prescribes the rights and duties belonging to a social position. Most roles are more complex than they appear to be. Yet it is necessary to specify the social position with which it is associated, as the individual is subject to conflicting pressure and strain in course of his functioning. Some of these strains arise as a natural consequence. The role conflicts may be observed in various areas in industry and military life and so in education. The individual gains much from his involvement in social organisation. There are many types of group interactions which determine a particular social group. In fact, mere assemblies of people without interaction do not constitute groups which differ greatly in character, purpose, mood and cohesiveness. Some groups last longer, while others are relatively momentary. For example, the most enduring group is the kinship group which involves only the immediate blood-relations. Similarly there are territorial groups formed on the basis of their residence and interaction. Thus community is a large unit while neighbourhood is a group of common locality whose members share not only the feelings but also the advantages and disadvantages. Like territorial groups there may be interest groups which are formed on the basis of common interest. There are other classifications on the basis of the nature of relationship. They are primary and secondary groups. The intimate groups are face-to-face groups which are enduring. The family is an example of the primary group as it is very close and intimate as a social unit.

Secondary groups are impersonal groups where relationships are less enduring. However, many groups fall between the ideal primary groups and the extreme secondary groups.

Thus not all small groups are primary as the primary relations among the people, living and working together, form the criteria. On the other hand, primary groups can be formed in spite of the largeness of the size of the population forming the group. In short, a high degree of cohesion under sense of unlimited commitment may form a primary community. It is interesting that the nature of interaction varies from group to group. Love, friendship and intimate relations grow in a congenial setting fostering a close relationship among the members. In this connection it should be mentioned that primary relations are not necessarily good at all times. What is more important is the personal satisfaction derived from the interaction and a feeling of belongingness. Particularly during adolescence when the child faces a life of storm and stress, the need for socialization is almost imperative. He has to develop the coping mechanism within himself to face the hard realities of life in day-to-day struggle. The child has to learn to live with problems, deprivation and depressions in the hope of overcoming them. Socialization offers the key to living in conformity with the social demands as well as ethical standards. Unfortunately education today is pre-occupied more with catering information than with the development of intrinsic qualities of head and heart. If we expect our new generation to take the responsibility and leadership in future society tomorrow, adequate preparation should be planned through educational activities accordingly.

The Family and Education

The family is one of the most important units in a social fabric. It is concerned with face to face relationship within the primary group it belongs to.

Edward Weztermorck held that the family was not necessarily rooted in marriage and that marriage is not an institution arising out of the family. There are two main types of family, viz., the extended family and nuclear family.

In short, the family is the world's oldest and most basic social institution and can be considered as either a social institution or as a social group. As a social institution the family is a system of norms guiding interaction among persons related by blood or marriage. As a group a family refers to relatives under one roof. In short, the concept of the family as a social institution is a sociological concept that focuses on norms rather than people.

Functions of the Family

Recently responsibilities have been shared by many other social institutions. Family has still retained its two major functions: (a) Producing and (b) Socialising children.

The family also performs the functions of regulating sexual behaviour, determining social class and providing emotional support and affection. Among the functions of the family, socialization of children deserves special mention. The child learns cultural patterns acceptable to the society. Socialization is the cumulative result of experiences. The child learns to participate in a society by observation.

The actual functions of the family enumerated by Murdock are mainly sexual, economic and educational. In fact, sexual family is a special agency for providing the affection to ensure the emotional stability and security so much needed for a happy and successful living. According to Talcott Parsons human personality is made through the socializing process promoted by families. Both father and mother have distinctive role and instrumental functions. While the father helps in establishing instrumentally the desired relations to external goal objects, the question of the expressive affairs of the family system and the integrative relations among its various members, remains pertinent.

Thus family is an institution which permits safeguarding the interest of the child during its period of biological immaturity. Socialization and initial education, are the means.

The functions of the family are different. As described by Ogburn, the functions are mainly: (1) affectional, (2) economic, (3) educational, (4) recreational, and (5) religious. Becker also lists the following functions of the family: (1) production of population, (2) protection and care of the child, (3) socialisation and education of the child, (4) reaction, and (5) affectional interaction. From the above two lists of functions, it is obvious that family has got a close bearing on the life and education of a child. The role of the family in the social adjustment of a child is too great to be ignored. In the present society, family life in India is gradually losing integrity and harmony. This may be partly owing to economic factors. But there are many other factors responsible for the change in the family structure, e.g., (1) marriage age and rate, (2) conflicts between the family members, (3) employment of the women, and (4) the encouragement of extreme individualism.

As days are passing the number of broken homes, divorces and separations are increasing even in our country. As a result, the child development is adversely affected. The spirit of tolerance and sacrifice is fading away and the smooth functioning of a family is also affected. With this family background a child enters into school and faces problems of adjustment. He cannot see things and conditions favourable for his social and intellectual growth. This is one of the main problems leading to the problem of backwardness and juvenile delinquency.

The School

Education takes is significant role in every human society and the school has a unique function to carry out. It is school which can transmit effectively the cultural heritage from generation to generation. So the school has a significant role and responsibility.

The School as a Social Institution

Education takes place in all human societies. The school concept has developed eventually as a social institution for transmission of cultural patterns and cultural heritage. In fact, the school has a greater impact on community life because of its direct involvement with culture. It is a major force in shaping the cultural pattern according to be needs of the community. As a social institution it helps the process of socialization by fostering the social values. The school not only creates a favourable situation for interaction among individual members school is a miniature society. It also generates a climate for the development of in-group and inter-group relations. In the words of Ruth Strong, "The social cosmos of the school is the children's own world. The processes of affiliation, identification, group action and interaction are among the primary means of social development for all children".

The teacher is the most important person in determining the extent to which the in-group feeling is developed. He can create a learning situation where the students roles and participation contribute to the development of social awareness within the groups. Thus the dynamics of human relations find their expression in a variety of social situations. The teacher is the key person to lead his pupil into active membership in a fraternity to which he himself belongs. He is, thus, in a position to serve as an important link between the community as well as the school. Nevertheless the role of the teacher is not as easy one as it involves a number of difficult functions. In the words of Alexander, "The calling of a teacher, as so defined, is one of infinite difficulty. But it is also infinitely significant. He is commissioned to form and fashion both human society as a whole and the individuals of whom that society consists."

Socialization

Socialization is a process which continues for the entire life-span of an individual. It is the way, culture is transmitted as it humanises the biological organism by regulating behaviour. At different stages of human life different modes of socialization are observed. An infant grows as he interacts with the environment for enrichment of his biological existence. Socialization is the outcome of man's adjustment to his social environment. It inculcates basic disciplines and produces a degree of conformity. It also instills aspirations and teaches social values and their supporting traits. Socialization may be the product of spontaneous human interaction or it may be deliberate and planned. An individual is socialized by a number of agencies including the family and school.

Socializing the child is a must for his development. The social response of the parents is based upon needs and values already formed in a particular culture and society. It goes without saying that socialization helps to create a self image and an ego.

In conclusion, one may say that socialization and education are not different. Both involve life-long process. They take place at various stages of human development. Socialization of the child is no less important. The child's father presents as authority figure particularly in Indian families and takes the role of the captain of the ship. While a child grows he becomes aware of his expected norm of behaviour. He learns to comply and conform to the norms set by the family community and society. Besides, it is important to have acceptance, respect and appreciation for the development of personality. Giving and receiving love help socialization. Similarly reward and punishment, praise and reprimand contribute to the process of socialization. All the members of the family, play-groups as well as associates have significant roles in the child's socialization.

The school environment is, no doubt, a source of socialization of the child as it inevitably produces a degree of conformity through discipline, reward and punishment. The teachers serve as agents to effect this process of socialization while the pupils interact and develop values of their own. The classroom provides learning situation promoting socialization through mutual help and co-operation competition and conflict. Similarly the co-curricular activities organised in the school contribute a lot toward the child's maturation and growth in terms of socialization. In fact, the child emerges as a social being and learns to step into new world of friends and associates, teachers and other members of the school community. In short, the push and pull, the plus and minus, confronted by a child in a school climate provide a strong foundation for social development. The child in course of his growth receives stimulation from his environment in his own way. Thus school environment socializes children by its control and discipline, its nourishment and nurture. The child learns to react to the people around him appropriately and grows emotionally as well as socially. His parents help him to build up self identity by giving love and affection and providing a basis of security. The father's role is significant in the process of building personal identity.

In the social context of modern India we find a dwindling or decaying relationship between members of the same social unit, viz., family and other organisations. The sociologist and the educationist should see that the relationship between the members of the community is sustained.

Social Institutions

Social institution is the result of man's long endeavour to organise group-life. Any social system demands interaction among groups, and individuals and the social order. Among the social institutions the family deserves special mention, as it provides the shelter and a congenial climate for individual development. It gives a sense of belonging to life. Parents see the children taking up their role and responsibility for placing them in the life of the community. While a social institution provides a systematic way of meeting major group needs provided by culture, family serves as the cradle for nourishing individuals in the continuous process of adjustment. Patterns of family life differ widely although all the families have certain common roles as follows:

(a) Seeing a child reaching maturity,

(b) Socialising him in group-life, and

(c) Providing a cultural background to meet obligations for training.

The modern family is more than a number of persons living in one house-hold unit. It is a group of interacting personalities in which each member has a definite although varying role. These roles are never static as they change both with different situations and with different culture. Thus in a family the in-depth personal experience and the interaction between members create a bondage or familial cluster. The family as an institution assumed certain responsibilities enforced by community, but today those roles and responsibilities have become more formalised. Basically the family doesn't depend upon legal sanction, it lies deep within the customs, standards and ideals — the folkways and mores of society. In short, the family is an expression of the maximum fulfilment of human need among people of every community.

4

CULTURE

Concept of Culture

Every society has its own culture or social heritage. It has been used with various meanings. The concept of culture was discovered recently as its significance has been realised more than ever. Culture has been defined by E.B. Tylor,[1] the English anthropologist, as "that complex whole which included knowledge, belief, art, morale, law, custom and any other capabilities and habits acquired by man as a member of society". The concept originated with anthropologists but has been later on developed further in many other ways. As commonly used in the social science, culture refers to a social heritage. It is the distinctive way of life of a group of people and their complete design for living.

Thus the idea of culture has a rich intellectual background as it refers mainly to ideals of enlightenment and refinement. This humanistic view of culture emphasises creativity and excellence. "It is transmitted socially by communication and gradually embodied in a group tradition of which the vehicle is language." Thus, the definition, given by Ellwood[2] is more specific. The idea of culture is used in the perspective of the entire society including aesthetic and moral attainments.

Anthropologists of the nineteenth century used culture and civilisation almost in the same sense. A line of demarcation was gradually discovered. The term 'civilisation' retained its evaluative connotation while culture referred to the total way of life of people in general.

---

1. Tylor, E. B., *Primitive Culture*, page 1, Brentanas, 1924, N.Y.
2. Ellwood Charles, A., *Culture and Evolution*, page 9, New York, D. Appleton Century Company, 1927.

A few observations on culture may be relevant at this point:

(a) Culture is free of value-judgements. It is mainly descriptive.

(b) The social influences on human nature and human achievement are projected in culture.

Thus, it includes ways of living in different contexts and the entire range of human activity. Anthropology emphasises a comprehensive view of culture instead of differences and distinctions. It assumed that humanity may be achieved through any sustained social experience. Culture has also been viewed more as a symbol in the realm of values. For the purpose of understanding culture two types of symbols should be taken into account. They are referential and expressive. The expressive symbols have a special significance for culture as they are connotative while the referential symbols are just words or objects having specific reference.

Culture is a design, the composite of guiding values and ideals. Hence it is not difficult to discover the interdependence between culture and social organisation.

There are mainly two forms of culture. One is the material, while the other is non-material. The material culture consists of the tangible forms such as dress or any object that man has created for his own use. The development of art, new amenities and gadgets indicate the cultural progress of people. Thus the material aspect of culture includes cultural instruments.

The non-material culture is another form which is intangible but has a greater impact. This is noticed in, beliefs, attitudes and behaviour pattern in a society. Thus culture tends to be pervasive touching every aspect of life. It includes social activities and involves institutions. Like an individual a culture comprises a consistent pattern of thought and action, within each culture there may be sub-cultures. People living under one culture area will be similar in many respects. In India as well as in the United States there are many ethnic sub-cultures. The ethnic groups tend to be unique by their difference in dress, food-habits, as well as languages. Some sociologists mention about youth sub-cultures. In fact, there are cultural uniformities and cultural variations and sociology is interested in seeking explanations for those. In recent years there has been a great deal of interest in the study of cultural similarities and cross-cultural traits. The cross-cultural index is used by students and researchers in comparing the ways of life of people in various cultures. It is interesting to see that the cultures vary and at the same time they have something in common. Sociologists are intrigued by the problem of diversity in culture. Among the factors contributing to the variations: (a) Migration and isolation, (b) The geographical factor, and (c) Individual differences deserve special mention.

The study of the nature of culture reveals that culture is pervasive and at the same time cumulative. This is transmitted by teaching and learning. Thus the inter-relation of culture and the educative process is apparent.

The Impact of Culture

It is obvious that culture creates a world by providing a context within which individual inter action takes place. Culture is an important determinant of thought and feeling. The impact of culture as a variable depends upon the particular aspect of culture involved and the related circumstances. People participating in culture in different degrees are more or less responsive to values and norms. Cultural norms are based on cultural values and they develop according to situation. There are rules that define approrpiate and inappropriate ways of thinking. Mores are also rules for thinking, feeling and acting as they have moral significance. The folkways and mores are the routine ways of doing things developed through trial and error as people struggle to meet the needs of life. In other words, mores are those folkways identified with group-welfare and group-survival.

Sociologists use the term norms or cultural norms to include folkways and mores. In fact, a norm is a standard to guide and regulate proper and acceptable behaviour within the groups. Usually violation of norms, prescribed as a must, calls for some kind of punishment. These norms vary in degree of explicitness as some are spelled out very precisely while others remain flexible. It is interesting to study the components of culture and fit them into some classification-scheme. Clerk Wissler, a noted anthropologist, made such an attempt, but Wissler's outline was not comprehensive and elaborate. Education was excluded from his list, although he listed the major areas of socialisation.

It is culture which influences future developments. For practical purposes culture traits have been used in terms of culture complexes. Anthropologists, today, are interested at present in studying the culture-patterns like trait complexes. Thus the patterns of a culture are important for distinguishing one society from the other. Such patterns of culture are known as ethos.

In short, culture is a collective term for all behaviour patterns, socially acquired and socially transmitted. A recent definition of culture is that given in the book on Educational Sociology by Francis J. Brown, he defines culture as "the total behaviour pattern of the group conditioned in part by the physical environment both natural and man-made but primarily by the ideas, attitudes, values and habits which have been developed by the group to meet its needs".

Cultural Traits

Cultural trait is the simplest unit of culture. It may be material or non-material. Personality is shaped to fit into a culture. Similarly culture shapes us to fit into a particular way of life. It even moulds our ideas and beliefs concerning the world around life. Parts of a culture which everyone must learn are called cultural universals. Cultural specialities are parts of culture, while cultural alternatives are those aspects of culture in which one has a choice. As already mentioned, culture traits are combined into culture complexes. Like trait complexes and norms are interrelated to form culture patterns. The patterns of culture vary from area to area. For example, American culture patterns are different from oriental culture patterns. Like culture patterns there are culture areas over which a given type of culture prevails. Similarly there are ethnics of cultures and some other types of sub-cultures including occupational sub-culture.

In short, an interelated chain is formed around central trait which is either an abstract or a concrete entity. This cluster of traits forms a culture complex. Thus, culture traits are not only inter-woven into larger patterns but are also characteristic behaviour patterns of constituent groups. The size of a culture area representing the portion of humanity depends upon the particular trait complex used as the basis of differentiation. There are many ways in which the cultural change takes place. Diffusion, acculturation and other methods are involved in the complex process of cultural change. Diffusion means the acceptance of cultural patterns from other groups while acculturation is a result of adoptation and eventual assimilation of one particular culture by a group.

Cultural Change

Cultural change takes place as a result of acculturation or diffusion.

Acculturation is a term which is used as a synonym for socialisation. Like all cultural acquisitions, socialisation and acculturation are used almost in the same sense. Culture changes as a result of inventions or discoveries, industrialization or political revolution. Similarly improvement in communication and transportation leads to cultural change. Any cultural change consists of the modification of existing material culture and the adoption of new patterns of behaviour. Thus the dynamics behind the cultural change need to be studied for the proper understanding of the process of cultural influx. Cultural changes are prompted by the dissatisfaction of people with the existing situation. Migration, war or conquest influence diffusion of culture. Diffusion may take place even without the deliberate attempt on any one's part.

A glance at the history will show that culture changes at cross-roads at a particular point of time. For example, Egypt, Palestine and Arabia have undergone a dramatic cultural change in recent years. The factors which contribute to the diffusion of culture traits are as follows:

(a) Accessibility of communication and transportation;

(b) Migration, war and conquest;

(c) Prestige of the lending culture;

(d) Cultural preparedness of the recipients of culture;

(e) Utility of new elements in culture; and

(f) Appeal of new element.

Diffusion takes place with and without deliberate attempts. It becomes purposeful when diffusion is organised. Purposeful diffusion is ever on the increase as we are living in such an age when education and publicity need deliberate planning. For example, the United Nations as a special organisation, is seeking to defuse culture in a planned and purposeful way. In fact, this is the great age of purposeful diffusion.

It is obvious that social change and social evolution are not the same. Similarly cultural change does not necessarily occur through evolutionary process. Cultural change may be classified under three categories. Material culture changes fast. Culture evolves gradually. The evolutionary concept of social change is also undergoing change. It is now believed that a man is capable of defying the laws of evolutionary change. This is known as a telic process involving the intelligent and planned direction of natural and social forces toward the achievement of a purpose. The rate of social change is uneven and the variability of cultural change characterises different groups, e.g., families, communities, etc. Variation in the rate of change also exists in different aspects of culture. For example, the material culture changes more rapidly than the non-material. It is observed that certain aspects of culture remain unchanged. In fact, modern culture has emerged after a lot of changes within the socio-cultural context. A rapid change in one part of the culture, however, requires re-adjustment in the various correlated parts of culture. This is known as the social or cultural lag which varies according to nature of the cultural material. It is desirable to minimise this cultural lag through adjustment. It is the unevenness of change in the forms of culture or lack of balance which is responsible for social problems. The task of education is to assist members of the society to face the cultural world realistically and to direct its development toward higher human goals.

Factors Resisting Change

There are certain factors that resist cultural change. They are negative as they impede the progress. The following deserve special mention:

(a) The overlapping of generation,

(b) Cultural inertia,

(c) Vested interests and

(d) The degree of isolation.

Usually resistance to any change is the result of a fear of change. People get used to the existing state of things and show inertia. Similarly any kind of vested interest including financial, personal or group benefit stands on the way to a desirable change. Besides, cultural isolation may be the result of close community, lack of outside contact or predjudice and bias. It is often experienced that the backwardness of a community persists because of the rigidity in outlook of its members, who are close minded and less amenable to change.

Changing Patterns in Family-Life

It is interesting to observe the origin and development of the family in different contexts. The three aspects of the history of family have definite bearing on educational psychology. They are: (i) the child-parent relationship, (ii) the husband-wife relationship, and (iii) the shifts in the function of the family in its interactions with other community-groups.

In different cultures the child-parent relationship assumed different patterns according to the expectation of the community and family. Moreover, the belief and customs play a vital role in the area of treatment of the parent toward son and daughter or vice-versa. For example, in India a son is considered as a special gift of God. The line of dynasty is maintained and the father gains heaven. So in Indian context the sons gain prominence and more attention than the daughters.

It is also observed that certain cultures encourage the dominance of father and the whole family and the children are supposed to follow the dictations of the father without any question.

THE SCHOOL IN RELATION TO CULTURE

The modern world with its complex social structure and cultural heritage presents the fact that culture accumulates. The school generates education and culture. It transmits cultural heritage and develops values. The school reflects the culture of the community or the nation, but it is a major force in changing the cultural pattern.

The school reflects the culture of the community or the nation. It is a major force in changing the cultural pattern. The school provides the basis for extending the boundaries of understanding.

5

SOCIAL FORCES AND SOCIAL CONTROLS

The Nature of Social Control

Social control is a collective term for those processes planned or unplanned, by which individuals are taught. Persuaded, or compelled to conform to the usages and life-values of groups, social control occurs when one group determines the behaviour of another group or when the group controls the conduct of its own members or where individuals influence the responses of other.

It operates at three levels:

(a) Group over group;

(b) Group over its members; anu

(c) Individuals over their fellows.

In short, social control refers to the attempt to intluence others in accordance with some previously developed ideal, goal or purpose.

The Development of the Concept of Social Control

Social control is both old and new as it also exerts in the most premature forms of human life.

The socio-cultural forms are of primary importance as they decide the directiŏn in which social control operates.

Process in Social Control

Social control involves a complex social process underlying intricate social relationship. The analysis of social relationships and social orderlines may be approached in terms of what are called socio-psychic processes involving thought and feeling which arise in interactions among persons in organised group-life. All social controls are dependent upon communication which is fundamental to all social processes. There are various methods of communication including all the ways by which meaning is transferred from individual to individual.

While perception and experience play vital roles in the socio-psychic process in social control, mental set and the context in which experiences occur for the individual contribute to the entire process of social control.

Education as an Agent of Innovation

Social forces are the result of social interaction which is a process. This is mainly based on the different groups of associations and varying degree of inter-stimulations. The result is the evolution of different social controls. Personality is dynamic whereas environment is to be modified according to the needs of the changing time and society. Besides the individual action, there is a question of group mind and interaction. As a result, social customs and codes are framed not for individual interest but for the interest of a community. The interaction between individual and community interests sometimes leads to conflict. It is admitted that society consists of an aggregate of individuals carrying on activities within a particular geographical area. This involves a system of relationship in which the activities of each individual supplement those of every other individual. This is essential for the functioning of a society as, it implies inter-dependence. Functional integration takes place with reference to the unity of a group or of society as a whole, as a result of a number of mutual and supplementary functions. In other words, the social roles that comprise a society are dependent on the various inter-group relations, Sociologists, however, recognise three bases of classification of the social interaction, viz., (a) In terms of the number of persons involved, (b) on the basis of degree of intimacy, and (c) Social processes of all these. The social processes will consist of adjustment, opposition and co-operation. These take place at various levels and a complex process of interaction goes on. Social interaction is, therefore, a multipolar process. It may take place between an individual and a group and between groups.

This concept of social interaction is of importance and is related to social force and social controls. There is mobility of population, impact of culture and other factors. These have given rise to a number of social forces. There are some who believe that public opinion and religion are the two great social forces or controls having considerable influence upon society. The social forces are the product of man's volition and they contribute to group interaction. These forces are not the outcome of one or two individual directives as group mind has a large part to play in the formation of the social forces. When they become effective, they prove to be of importance as social controls. On an analysis it will be clear that the social controls can be enumerated as follows:

1. Education as a social control.
2. Religion as a social control.
3. Public opinion as a social control.

Forms of Social Control

There are various forms of social control including non-violent means, e.g., art, literature, religion and education.

Education as a Social Control. Education has assumed a great responsibility with the march of civilization. In the days of yore, when everything was in a state of flux, education was functioning mainly in the shape of instruction. It was more allied to preaching as in the field of religion, but it was realised that education should mean the spontaneous development of human virtues and potential. The task of education is to create opportunities for the unfoldment of those innate abilities and sensivity to the right, good and beautiful. It is through education that attitude can be changed and so the human behaviour. The modern thinkers believe in the autonomy of education. According to them, education should have an independent status irrespective of the individual needs and interests. It should have a reference to the fundamental and permanent value of life and thus should not be at the mercy of politics, or any other external pressure.

Every country today is confronted with the problems of stratification and disintegration. The basic instincts seek their outlet when no sufficient scope for their sublimation exists. Education should prepare the mind of the public for the right type of thinking and behaving in a society. It is essential because of the increasing tendency of maladjustment in every sphere of life. It should act both as an incentive as well as a control. The anti-social behaviour should be very carefully handled by means of proper education. The different social agencies should be well organized, co-ordinated and properly motivated. This is possible only when education is granted sufficient freedom for its functioning. Education starts from the cradle and continues up to the end of life. It is a continuous process and is closely correlated to life itself. This is why education can easily sublimate the basic instincts and develop the healthy attitudes of the people at different stages of their lives. Through schooling, broadcasting, publicity, propaganda, press and other individual means, education can achieve its end and can prove as an effective social control.

Religion as a Social Control. Education first started from the church. The church had enough influence on people and public. It was the centre of cultural activities and religious instruction. Religion had a control over the society, but gradually the churchmen lost their hold because of their tendency towards propagating dogmas. Nevertheless, religion had its appeal because of its value in life. In spite of a good deal of conflicts between different religions, there are some fundamental values common to all.

Religion at first dominated over the feelings and as such it proved as a social control.

Religion can be described as the ethical code for adjusting human behaviour. It serves as a frame of reference for those who find it difficult to adjust. This is why the role of religion is very prominent.

It is a major force in sustaining the cultural pattern of the group. It stimulates the highest aspirations of mankind and translates those into individual and community behaviour.

It tends to establish and perpetuate certain values within the total culture. In a majority of countries, state and church have influenced each other. One provided authority, and the other spiritual sanctions. The stability of the social order and the security of the state demand the religious solidarity of the people. It is a great force which acts on the mind of the people. As a social control, religion has hardly any parallel. The issue of religious instructions may bring conflict but every citizen would like to have one religion or other. It is a vital force in our culture and the school should have a regular programme of moral discourses. As a matter of fact, religion being an important part of culture forms an essential feature of life. There may be controversy about how religion can be used as a social control. It is a fact that in our daily life we cannot completely avoid religion so ingrained in our culture. By observing rites we conform to the dictation of religion. Religious sentiments prove very effective and strong, even for those who are not educated. It helps to form a group mind and guides human feeling and action. As such, religion should be regarded as one of the best social controls.

Law as a Social Control. The variation in state legislation and in judicial decision is great because of the circumstances. The difference among the states has to be taken into account. Law has a practical disciplinary value for obvious reasons. Man is not by nature always rational. He requires some dictation and guidance through legislation. It acts as a deterrent against tendency towards anti-social behaviour. There was a time when people used to decide their own fate and give out their opinion. But now-a-days it is not so forceful unless it is put in a very organised way. With the rising democracy public has been much conscious of their rights and individual judgement. So their opinion cannot be completely ignored. There have been cases when people have been more afraid of public opinion than of law or state.

India today is passing through a transition period and there have been conflicting views on the right principle to be adopted in various fields. Unfortunately enough, public opinion has not been fully organised at this stage because of the want of proper education among mass. So there is a danger in depending too much upon public opinion as a social control. Nevertheless, its influence will be there. With the growing individual consciousness people feel great difficulty in adjusting themselves to the state ideology at all times. They try to give vent to their feelings, thoughts and desires. For this, there is often a state of conflict at different levels of society and public opinion has got its limitation. Besides these social controls, there are other forces working as controlling agents. For example, films, radios, advertisement and folklores have their influence on the mind of the people. They, therefore, can be used as social controls.

Public Opinion as a Social Control. Although the term 'public opinion' is a coinage of the late 18th century, a number of approximate equivalents may be traced to much earlier periods.

The struggles of 17th century England represent the step in clarifying the nature of function of public opinion. In the absence of a carefully set convention a great deal may pass as public opinion which in reality is merely the publicly expressed opinion of an individual or a small group, and is thus essentially personal in character.

Public opinion today is a great social control which often forms stronger than any other control.

What is a public opinion? As public opinion is necessarily the opinion of the public, the term 'public' must first be explained and analysed.

Public is a group so large that all the individual members may not be in direct contact with one another. The interaction between them, though not of a direct kind, get collectively effective in the sense that their attitudes, opinions and behaviour converge to a large extent.

The members of the public to whom advertisers, editors, authors and politicians appeal through posters, books, radios, newspapers, movies, etc., are not in one place. They are scattered all over the country. Modern means of distant communication (e.g., books, newspapers, movies, radio) have made the spread of ideas and attitudes possible.

Public opinion is a deeply pervasive organic force, intimately bound up with the ideological and emotional interplay of the social groupings in which gregarious individuals have come together. It articulates and formulates not only deliberative judgments of the rational elements within the collectivity, but also the evanescent common will, which somehow integrates and momentarily crystallizes the sporadic sentiments and loyalties of the masses of population.

Formation of Public Opinion. Analysis of the particular forces and processes, which are instrumental in shaping homogeneous group attitudes and pressures, calls for emphasis upon:

1. General level of socialization and the cultural media of expression prevailing in a given period;
2. The racial and national characteristics of the group;
3. The framework of political, legal and economic institution within which the process operates; and
4. Particular set of objectives towards which it may be working.

The term 'public opinion' should not be taken to imply that all members of the public hold one single opinion. Studies of public opinion have shown that on any subject at any time there are diverse opinions held by different sections of the public. Public opinion simply refers to that mass of ideas which people have expressed on a given issue.

The public opinion is not a reasoned judgement and there the word opinion is quite appropriate. It is desired that public opinion should be national but it is not always so. It is rather an attitude which people take in relation to an issue. It is usually emotionally charged, and involves beliefs, accepted principles, convictions, sentiments and firmly rooted prejudices. It is characterized by processes like personification, rationalization, etc. It is often determined by the desire to maintain the existing order of things to which the people are accustomed.

So, the formation of public opinion is obviously a complex process. The pattern of its formations is also different for different communities.

In a community, the contact between the members is direct although their minds can act in common. Hence the public opinion in a real community should be more definite and more stable.

There are two main types of public opinion, static and dynamic. The static one (not necessarily rigid) manifests itself in the form of traditional customs, modes and usages.

The dynamic one which is predominantly rational in character is built upon the cultivated arts of persuasion and systematic publicity. It draws upon definite historical events on comtemporary happenings as the material for its propaganda and agitation. This type of public opinion flourishes in the crowded streets and squares of the city, where the life of the masses unfolds under the pressure of common intercourse and exchange of opinion during the daily routine of association.

Change in Public Opinion. It is only in rural communities that the public opinion is relatively stable. But, condition of living changes as people's habits, opinions and attitudes also change. The means of ideas in a society have no longer great stability.

Modern means of indirect communication, e.g., motion pictures, newspapers, radio, etc., have made it possible to stimulate the thinking of large number of men and start the process of the formation of public opinion.

6

SOCIAL STRATIFICATION

Inequalities are intrinsic as the very genetic make up of man. Even if environmental conditions were capable of eradicating the major inequalities in human nature, the very fact remains that men must play a variety of roles. So vital or unimportant in society they would create social distinction and status differential.

Caste, broadly speaking represents a social class system in which membership is determined. In fact, there is little vertical mobility. The three upper castes formed from the Aryans were known as the twice born, because they had gone through the process of natural and physical birth and that of spiritual initiation. The four broad divisions do not by any means constitute the total complexity of the caste system.

Taya Zinkiri maintains that caste is neither class nor colour, neither occupation nor religion. He also observes on Indian Hindu Caste system a unique system of social stratification.

In fact, the ultimate sanction of the Hindu caste system is the religion and the concept of Karma. It has been assumed that castes are similar to the statuses of Europe. Of course the manifold subcastes of Indian society particularly those living in village communities are linked very closely with the economy, its division of labour and its necessary production.

Economic considerations above all, determine the class system and there is a certain correlation between the social class and the occupation pursued. Individuals in any society seek an identity with the class structure through continuous struggle for improvement of their position: Class has become associated with standards and modes of behaviour, patterns of expenditure and consumption.

Stalcup defines social class as "A level in society made up of people who consider themselves equals due to similarities in family background, level of education, occupation race and attitude toward social issues''. Attempts have been made to classify occupation according to various criteria. Time has arrived when it is impossible to be precise about the criteria of class. It is less useful to talk in these terms. Groups of people may best be described by means of their role and function in society.

SOCIAL CLASS AND EDUCATION

Emile Durkheim maintained that there were as many different kinds of education as there were social milieux in any given society. Equality of opprotunity cannot be provided merely through Acts. In spite of an increasing attempt to provide conditions for equality of opportunity in education the existing social stratification inevitably presents a variety of conditions. Homogeneity and diversity are both essential ingredients in any society and any educational system.

SOCIAL MOBILITY AND EDUCATION

Social mobility is basically the movement of individuals or groups of individuals from one social position to another. Such a movement may be up or down between the classes in any social hierarchy or stratification.

Sudden appreciation of a property or power accrued to certain families, development of skill or success and achievement may lead to upword mobility. It is interesting to note a greater emphasis upon upward mobility than upon mobility downwards.

The important question now arises concerning the relationship between education and social mobility. A controversy obviously exists as to whether education acts as a sort of agent for social mobility.

THE INDIAN PERSPECTIVE

India is now in the grip of transition and the caste system is gradually losing its hold. In reality, we find a new form of startification emerging in modern India.

It is a mixture of class system and caste system. We also find the gap between the upper and lower classes increasing day by day. The growing disparity is creating a lot of discontent and conflicts — between those who have and who have not.

In fact, the middle class contributing to the cultural heritage of India is fast withering away. The majority of people belonging to this group is facing a hard struggle for survival.

Upward mobility is only a dream for most them. There has been a growing tendency to amass wealth in an unscrupulous way for improving the status. In spite of the dwindling caste barriers in Indian society there is still some resistance against inter-caste marriages. Dowry system is still prevalent as a social evil.

SOCIAL STRATIFICATION AND SOCIAL MOBILITY

Social stratification is the result of social inequality. The major dimensions of stratification are power, prestige and wealth. Individuals or families in a group or society constitute a social stratum if they rank equal on a particular dimension of stratification. For example, families with income within a certain range form the same income stratum. Thus stratum is meaningful as a term only when it has a reference to the specific dimension of stratification. Some sociologists use the term social stratification in the sense of formation of fairly distinct social strata. A typical society is considered as a pyramid of ranks with the different social layers. At the bottom of the broad base lies the lower class while the narrow peak represents the upper class population. Nothing is more likely to influence the individual on the social history of a nation than the system of stratification. The nature of social stratification may vary from society to society. It, no doubt, affects the relationships and achievements of individuals and groups. Social stratification has also been called a system or institutionalized social inequality. There are obviously various forms of this stratification. For example, the caste system is based upon a rigid form of stratification, whereas in the class system the boundaries between the strata overlap as they are quite indistinct.

The bases of stratification have also to be considered for a clear understanding of the modes of interaction between the members of the society. A number of factors determine where an individual or family fits in the class-structure of a society. For example, in a caste-ridden society social status is determined almost exclusively by birth. The child of a Brahmin in India is the Brahmin for life. Similarly in every society some jobs enjoy more prestige than others. Besides wealth and income, education, prestige and privilege influence the determination of the stratum in different societies.

Social Stratification in India and the Role of Education. Two functions of education have been distinguished in respect of differentiation and selection leading to stratification. A differentiating function is held to be more pronounced in societies with a rigid system of stratification, whereas the selective function is considered to be more emphasized in open class societies. It is recognised that formal education plays a vital role in dealing with the problem of social stratification by effecting social mobility. As an agent of social change education brings more flexibility of outlook and enhances the socio-economic status of individuals even at the bottom of the rigid system of stratification. In India, today mobility is observed in both the directions vertical and horizontal as a result of education. The caste system no longer holds the same ground because of the occupational mobility. The Brahmins take up various vocations without clinging to study, teaching and scholastic pursuits. Similarly the so-called sudras move up at present on the social ladder by improving their education and economic status. Thus rigid system of stratification known as the caste system has started dwindling. In fact, modern India is passing through a stage of transition in respect of values, faith and belief. The cherished values and goals are changing mainly because of impact of the western system of education and culture. The world is shrinking everyday and the specific boundaries of each culture are giving way to the new wave of ideas and ideology.

The unprivileged community so long kept in ignorance, is waking up with the dawn of emerging political consciousness. The scheduled caste, the tribal communities, the various aboriginal groups have been neglected in the past. They have been deprived of their legitimate rights of freedom of expression, education and security for ages although, they could contribute a lot to national prosperity. Similarly women in India have suffered because of the dominance of men over them. The inequality of opportunities of self-expression between people belonging to different strata and different sexes has impeded the national progress to a great extent. However, the recent education commissions have favourably considered the unprivileged classes for providing greater apportunities in the field of education and employment. This is, no doubt, a timely move in the right direction.

The stratification which exists, today, in India needs to be handled very carefully as there are certain sensitive areas demanding delicate treatment. Ignorance, poverty and prejudice which are common in the down-trodden class in India, should gradually be done away with through educational and social planning.

The traditional social structure is being influenced by major changes in the educational planning and new system of education. A gradual dissociation of occupation from caste is the result of the new emphasis on dignity of human labour. Obviously there still exists a dichotomy between manual and non-manual occupations. Although low castes are found employed more in manual occupations than in non-manual ones, the real status of a caste is not always congruent with its economic status. Of course when a caste becomes economically rich, it seeks to better its position in the caste hierarchy leading to upward mobility on the social ladder. It has been found that Western Education, particularly in India, has been one of the means of achieving upward mobility outside the framework of the caste system. Inter-caste marriage is gaining more grounds in recent times resulting in certain degrees of mobility in the social structure. Similarly the growing recognition of individual excellence irrespective of caste is contributing to social mobility as well.

Educational opportunities are still not equal as the quality of education varies according to the financial resources of the parents.

It is observed that most of the well-to-do parents tend to send their children to special schools providing western style of training and education while the municipal and local board schools are filled up by the children of lower classes and low-income groups. This, obviously, creates a form of stratification by encouraging a system of hierarchy. In other words, class-system within the framework of education is observed with all its evil consequences.

In modern India when the entire value system is in a state of flux, it is expected that significant social changes will take place as a result of the interaction between education and society. Shaping a new society with emerging values is the task of education no doubt as orienting education to the social needs is inevitable.

Social stratification which seems to be inevitable in groups is one of the most constant features of social life. Thus social stratification refers to the ranking of social positions in terms of the amount of certain desirable things associated with these positions. In most societies the most important desirable things are related to wealth, prestige and power. Thus stratification occurs in all groups. From families to entire societies within each community or a society, social classes are created by the process of ranking positions.

The importance of the social stratification in modern societies can hardly be overlooked. The problems like poverty in the midst of plenty and conflict between ethnic minority and majority groups are examples of stratification problems.

One may question, ''Is social stratification inevitable? The answer is yes. As long as efficiency and control are valued in any society a form of hierarchy is bound to exist. As a variety of roles is certain, status differential would emerge. Even if inequalities are not consistent with the very genetic make up of man, caste in India represents a social class system in which membership is determined at or by birth. The four broad divisions, viz., Brahmin, Kshatriya, Vaisya and Sudra don't by any means constitute the total complexity of the caste system. Of course the Hindu caste system is closed one. It is a stratification fixed for all individuals by the nature of their birth. Thus it is unique among the systems of social stratification.

While social class in our society developed, economic considerations were of prime importance in establishing new classes. Class has become associated with standards and modes of behaviour. Several classifications have been attempted by different sociologists.

Behind each from of stratification one may find some criterion or criteria which may vary from context to context. Academic excellence, intellectualism prestige and power in addition to economic status provide the basis for most of the stratifications. For example, the class structure followed in European societies is as follows:

(a) Ruling groups.

(b) Intellectual group.

(c) Service Class.

(d) Ruled Class.

It is, however, interesting to observe the following groups or strata within the Soviet society as identified by Inkles.

1. Ruling elite.
2. Superior intelligents.
3. General intelligents.
4. Working Class aristocracy.
5. White colour.
6. Well-to-do peasants.
7. Average worker.
8. Average peasants.
9. Disadvantaged worker.
10. Forced labour.

7

THE CONCEPT OF SOCIAL CHANGE

The idea of social change came from the desire for betterment. There are many theories of social change. Ogburn pointed out that social changes originate in the invention by some individual of a new way of doing something or of something new to do. Hart says that social change is linear and accelerative and the direction of change is invariably toward increasing efficiency or effectiveness. But the inadequacy of this theory has also been demonstrated.

Social change comes about through the working of home process that is built into society, some inherent social process.

The a-social nature of social change has been assumed by many. Social change emerges directly out of the society.

Robert E. Park says that change comes about as an incidental consequence of the interaction of numbers or people.

Change is inevitable in society and life. There are reasons for any type of change. Social change presupposes some dissatisfaction with the existing state of affairs. There are conflicts responsible for the changes. Many factors, internal and external, contribute to any type of change. We are living in a period of rapid social change and it is often difficult to understand the reasons. While we find the external change, we also realise its implications. The principal sources of such changes are likely to be either (1) Changes in the physical environment and (2) Changes in the social environment or any other event and influence.

1. *Changes in the Physical Environment.* Changes in the physical environment leading to social change may be classified as those which arise (1) independently of human action, (2) as a consequence of the cumulative effect of the reaction of man to his environment. It is usual that changes in the physical environment leading to social change arise from interaction of man with his environment.

Besides changes in the physical environment, there may be changes in the social environment. A changing social environment has to face new problems for solution. Closer communication between societies inevitably stimulates diffusion. While diffusion tends to be continuous, culture traits do not spread regularly in all directions. Diffusion involves more than the simple addition of cultures which are nothing but organised systems. A trait complex which is part of one culture has to be adapted to fit into a different cultural setting.

2. *Internal Factors Effecting Change.* There are factors external as initiator of social changes, but at the same time there are factors internal having some influence on the change. Invention is a basic unit of social change and culture traits stimulate invention. The larger the culture-base, the greater is the possibility of social change.

It is an admitted fact that culture is directly related to the amount and intensity of contact. It is, therefore, obvious that any change is bound with a number of factors. India today has faced a new problem after her independence. The previous set of ideas is becoming obsolete. The economic, political and cultural life of India is undergoing gradual changes.

It is almost certain that man is dynamic in nature and he wants changes. The state of dissatisfaction when intensified leads to a change. This love for a change is inherent, natural and instinctive. Various type of conflict act and interact and help to develop a feeling of need for a change. In order to make any progress, this change is essential.

Technological bias is highly responsible for the instability of a society at this age. There is nothing very stable because of the ever-changing outlook of life. Social change is sometimes a great stimulation for improvement. But too many changes abruptly brought may prove to be disastrous. There should be some amount of social security as well among the people as no culture can thrive in an ever-changing society.

3. *Education and Social Change.* Social change is a complex affair, a resultant of so many factors joining together and influencing each other in varied combinations.

Natural climate and conditions are effective in determining the social conditions. Thus with the change in the natural environment social life undergoes change. Similarly by exploiting natural, agricultural and mineral resources man has altered his environment and thereby his social life and institutions.

Migration is another instance whereby people move into new environment different from those to which they have been used. The size of population of a nation or a group has a distinct influence on its social and cultural life as well.

But the fastest social changes are brought about by scientific and technological inventions. Social change thus takes place under different pressures. For example, the press, the radio, the aeroplanes have brought the world closer by breaking the regional barriers. Through industrialisation, the typical character of rural community is fast changing. Family structure has already undergone a radical change in recent times. The joint family system is fast breaking down and new individualistic outlook is ushering in.

Factors which bring social change may be classified under the Following:

(1) Environmental factors.

(2) Influx of population.

(3) Socio-political upheavals.

(4) Technological factors.

(5) Ideological factors including value system.

It is interesting to observe that the social changes take place in a mysterious way. Apart from the environmental factors, psychological factors also operate and work slowly but steadily. Education itself is a great force working behind any social change in a desired direction.

Socialisation is one of the important functions of education. The concept of democracy and world citizenship should be fostered through education. The teachers could inculcate the value of citizenship and good living through curricular and co-curricular activities. What is mostly needed is the development of leadership right from the initial stage. Teachers have to work as friend, philosopher and guide for creating in the young generation a spirit of service and co-operation, self-confidence and healthy outlook.

4. *Agencies of Education for Social Change.* Of all the agencies, family, school, church and club deserve special mention. Some of them are not very formal while a few are formal. For example, school and church are mainly formal agencies of education while the mass media of communication, like public opinion, radio, or press are basically informal agencies.

Various human organisations contribute to socialisation and social change at various stages of life.

As mentioned earlier, family is the first unit of social life having to meet the physical and emotional needs of the children. Each member of the unit has a special role and a sort of status. Social experience in the family in early childhood proves effective as a basis for the development of personality and culture. It is family which aids or subverts the larger social process through effective or ineffective social-control.

Ogburn mentions seven functions of the family in the past. These are : (1) affectional, (2) economic, (3) educational, (4) protective, (5) recreational, (6) family status, and (7) religious status. But the functions of the family never remain constant. They change from time to time according to socio-economic structure.

With the growing impact of industrialisation, the role of church or religion is also undergoing drastic change. Most of the religious ceremonies are being replaced by social functions and losing their initial force in upholding the moral and spiritual values. New forms of spiritual congregation are coming into being with our changing outlook and social order. Missions and cultural centres are trying to keep up the spirit with increasing modifications of their programmes.

Various group organisations like Y.M.C.A., Youth Welfare Associations, Red Cross, M.R.A., N.C.C. and cultural institutes have also distinct roles in contributing to socialisation.

School is itself a miniature society and has a unique position in controlling the social interactions. As cultural patterns of the society find their way into the school, so the educative forces of the school exert active influence towards social control and change. The processes of affiliation, identification, group action and interaction are among the primary means of social development. They produce an evolution of society that is formed by each new generation entering school.

8

THE SCHOOL AND THE COMMUNITY

A community is an area of social living marked by some degree of social coherence, locality and community. They form the basis of community. Members of different groups share various conditions of life with varied interests. All social relationships may be found within a community.

There are primary and secondary groups in a community. There are diversified groups of people young and old, male and female with different skills and abilities living together as neighbours.

It is a face to face primary group in which many of the major functions of life are carried on co-operatively within the group itself. Primary group is a small group where people know one another with a sense of belonging. The role of the community is (a) to inculcate in its children the attitudes and values in addition to folkways and (b) to set the total pattern in which the school as an institution functions.

Thus the climate in which the school functions is set by the community.

Communities vary in the degree of their stability. Every community is bound to feel the impact of the changing elements in our culture.

The school tended to become the focus of community interest. Steps have been taken to establish and maintain school community relationships. The school-community relationship develops gradually on the basis of social interaction which is not a one way process. The school should be flexible to continually readjust its programmme in the light of the changing needs and services of the community. Similarly, the community has its responsibility to shape the curriculum and extra-curricular programmes according to changing demands of time.

In short, school community relations should be based upon a few basic principles including that of flexibility, adaptability, expansion and responsiveness to national and world-needs.

The following principles would serve as criteria for the evaluation of any programme in progress:

(a) Education is a social process in which the child shares the community consciousness. As community life is the sum total of many agencies, individuals and institutions it can be enriched by increasing the interaction and organization in which the school plays a vital role.

The community must understand, appreciate and support the varied and difficult responsibility of our schools. Similarly, education must seek to modify community patterns of behaviour through close and constant interaction. As already mentioned, the role and function of the school should be determined in the light of the needs of the specific community backgrounds of the child.

The school should develop a programme of activities and services to extend, refine and integrate human experience for all age-groups and at all levels. Changing the behaviour of individuals is not enough, education must seek to modify community patterns of behaviour through close and constant interaction with the total culture of the community.

It is obvious that the school functions in the community with a view to contributing to the total culture. There are other agencies including church and club providing opportunities for development in different directions. The school enjoys a unique privilege because of its unique position. Although the school has a dominant role, it cannot reach all the goals. It needs help and co-operation from other agencies, so that it can effectively contribute to harmony and happiness for humanity at large.

Broadly speaking, education is not limited to the classroom; it is a continuous process of interaction through the family, the playgroup, the church, the vast number of organizations, the community, the nation if not the world.

EDUCATION FOR NATIONAL INTEGRATION

The word integration implies harmony and synthesis. It involves a continuous process of accommodation, assimilation and adjustment.

A close understanding and mutual respect are essential for reinforcing the bond of integrations.

National integration refers to any nation within the world today. India has been known as a land of diversity. Yet there is a unity and oneness between the various states and cultures. There is a tie of amity which binds all the parts together. Unfortunately a lot of confusion has disturbed the ethnical balance in recent years. Some how, the inner spirit of unity and harmony has lost its strength in the midst of changing values of life.

To start with, integration as a process needs elaboration. No doubt, it involves interaction between minds and entails the process of accommodation, assimilation and adjustment. Thus mutual respect and understanding are essential for strengthening integration. Psychologically the process of integration is dynamic and continuous. Of course the fluctuation occurs from time to time in the field of interaction between different people because of their differences in outlook, attitude and values.

It goes without saying that the intensity of integration depends upon the nature and direction of the forces working behind the process of interaction.

While psychological forces work behind shaping the form of interaction on the way to integeration, the social and cultural forces also influence national integration. The present state of confusion over the problem of national language and education-policy has given rise to the present controversy and conflict. As a result the regional bias is prevailing sacrificing the national interest.

It is unfortunate that national leaders today are failing to inspire people to set top priority to our national interest. States instead of the entire country are gaining prominence although states cannot flourish at the cost of nation and national welfare. Every State like Punjab and Bihar is claiming a separate identity and self government in contradiction with the Indian Constitution. In this way our future prospect is getting more and more gloomy. Time has come when revolution should be brought for bringing a total harmony in our national life. This can be done through education and cultural enterprises. Every educational institute should take a definite role and responsibility to instil in the minds of the young learners a desire for unity in diversity. Besides, every attempt should be made to generate national awareness through mass media of education. Even formal education can be geared to the purpose of promoting national solidarity. All the factors of education including curriculum, teacher and school environment may be employed for the purpose.

It is quite realistic to approach the problem of disintegration from a pragmatic point of view. Prejudice and ignorance are at the root of national disintegration. Lack of mutual respect and understanding lead to disharmony. Thus a constant flow of goodwill and human commission is necessary for keeping the spirit of harmony in tact.

NATIONAL INTEGRATION AND EDUCATION IN INDIA

It is logical to state that the objectives of education at different levels are to be drawn from the two main sources of (i) the needs and aspirations of the people and (ii) the needs and aspirations of the learners. Dr. Arora[1] has re-emphasized it when he put forward the case of 'Societal needs' in the matter of curriculum planning. In a different context, Mahanta pleaded for the assessment of the needs of the people and the requirements of the nation and also for a sharp probe into their aspirations.[2]

Dr. Arora, in his attempt at identifying the 'needs' of the present-day Indian society, has drawn freely upon the recommendations of the major Indian Educational Commissions and Committees. He has referred to the ideas and thoughts of a few 'great educators' of the land, the deliberations of a number of 'Teacher-Organisations' and the findings of some educational researchers, when he has come to conclude that for 'curriculum' planning, we should consider the following four major 'needs':[3]

(a) Promotion of national integration;

(b) Acceleration of the process of modernisation;

(c) Eradication of the social inequities; and

(d) Removal of the moral injustices.

We may fruitfully recall here the suggestions made by the A.I.F.E.A. (All India Federation of Educational Associations) in their seminar on 'Education', held at Hyderabad in 1975. The A.I.F.E.A. discussed the

1. Arora, G.L. Societal Needs and School Curriculum Bulletin of the Curriculum Group, N.C.E.R.T., New Delhi-16, September 1982.
2. Mahanta, D., Indianisation of our Education-W.B.H.A., Calcutta-73, (1981), pp. 126-133.
3. Arora, G.L., Curriculum Bulletin, September 1982, *Ibid.*

theme 'Education', for the needs of India, today and tomorrow''[4] and suggested that the following points should be duly considered by the future curriculum-makers:

(1) The long-term development plans to be launched for the growth of the nation.

(2) The enterprises to be undertaken for the generation and furtherance of the new economic order.

(3) The measures to be taken for the awakening and spread of 'National Consciousness'

(4) The policies to be followed for the establishment and consolidation of the new socio-political order.

(5) The work programmes to be implemented for the eradication of 'ills' like poverty, illiteracy and injustice.

The UNESCO in their fourth Regional Conference (1978) on 'Education and Economic Planning in Asian Countries,' recalled the recommendations of the International Commission on ''Lifelong Education'' (1972) and suggested the following major areas of emphasis in the educational reform of the developing countries.[5]

I. Democratisation of educational opportunities to the optimum level and, as such, arrangements for providing educational services much more diverse in character.

II. Community involvement in education with necessary scope for decentralisation of educational programmes and administration.

III. Appropriate articulation of 'Education' with 'Productive 'Work.'

While the first two areas could urge us to the strategy of 'collective movement' for a 'nation-centric' education-system, the third one would directly influence the 'structural change' and the 'curricular reform'.

Anyway, we may all agree that our education system should be better adapted to our national realities, in the form of national needs and aspirations, and that it should duly reflect the national ideals and goals that would evolve from the new Constitution of the nation. We

---

4. A.I.F.E.A., Souvenir Education, Today and Tomorrow, 1975.

5. Bulletin of the UNESCO Regional Office for Education in Asia and Oceania, Number 20, June 1979, Unesco, Bangkok, (1979) p. iii-v.

may also agree that for the sake of national identity we should work out a common structure and devise a basic framework of the school-curriculum that would embody the broad principles and policies of our national life. The amendment to our Constitution which has placed 'Education' in the 'Concurrent List' may pave the way towards that. Necessarily, this will entail a critical review of a few of our national policies and the corresponding educational programmes.

One such policy is the policy of national identity and national integration with a truly significant implication for the education system. The divisive forces of religious fanaticism, communalism, casteism, regionalism, provincialism and linguism have occasionally been raising their ugly heads to kindle and spread the deadly fire of separatism and thereby to disturb the veritable existence of the nation. Dr. Arora has rightly listed 'National integration' as the first and foremost 'need' of the country.[6] Whatever we may think out to be the true concept of such 'identity' and 'integration', our experience of the last three decades would clearly indicate that we have to devise a new way to our 'identity' and plan a new move to our 'integration', no matter if we are to fight against heavy odds to that end. Particularly, the young generation that constitutes the strongest force of the nation must be helped to imbibe a new 'Indian outlook' and to assimilate the new 'Indian Values' of democracy, socialism and secularism.

Ours is a multilingual country; and in a multilingual country, the language policy that is followed is normally, the most important constituent of the desired 'identity' and 'integration'. The language policy, followed so far, has resulted in the three-language formula of the education-sector, during the last thirty years. We should, however, recall that the three-language formula was only an add interim measure for the first ten years of our 'Constitutional Adventure', i.e., from 1950 to 1960, and that we were required to review it in 1961. Unfortunately, however, that three-language formula has been allowed to stay unmodified, even after 1991, although it has in no way proved its worth for the intended task of national integration.

Some may be tempted to suggest that we have perhaps hung too long on a formula of dubious value and it is time for us to review the whole issue and formulate a new line of action. Moreover, it is evident that the real spirit of the three-language formula has mostly been lost sight of or deliberately neglected in many of the states, with the result

6. Arora, G.L., *Ibid.*, p. 3.

that the said formula has not only proved itself un-congenial to the cause of our national identity and national integration, it has of late turned into a positive handicap. Further, the young pupils, specially those of the disadvantaged section of our population including what we call the 'first generation learners' are being increasingly overtaxed when they are compelled to learn the three components of the language. There three 'major' languages to learn as first, second and third languages are too heavy by way of supplemental language-development. The consequence is that the educational progress of the majority of our school children is seriously hampered.

Even a crude analysis of the results at the school stage will show that about 80-85 per cent of the pupils have failed in English, the so-called 'second language' in most of the States.

All these, and a few other side-effects would force us to suggest that the three-language formula should perhaps be dropped and a two-language formula be introduced in its place.[7] The two-language formula would obviously consist of the 'Regional' language as the 'first' language and the 'Official' language, as the second language. There may be provision for learning a third language, but only on an additional elective basis. Of course, the issue of the 'Federal' language of the Union should be settled immediately, in order to reduce the scope of any further disturbing situation. In an earlier article on 'National Policy on Education', it was submitted that the 'Federal' language of the Union should be so developed as to serve satisfactorily as the common language of thought and expression for the people of the country, as a whole[8]. And if so required, it should transform itself into a veritable 'Lingua Franca' for the 'States' of India. Moreover, it should also improve itself to become an adequately equipped vehicle of 'modern science and technology' that now pervades our expanding socio-cultural life. In the 1972 Annual Conference of the All India Federation of Education Associations held at Varanasi, it was pleaded that the Federal language of the Union be newly named as 'Bharatiya Bhasa' the language of Bharat (that is India). That change in the name is likely to create a favourable atmosphere of emotional acceptability.[9] Hindi, the official language of the Union, can very well be acclaimed as the

7. Mahanta, D., Our Education in the Making, W.B.H.A., Calcutta-73, pp. 131-134.

8. Mahanta, D., National Policy on Education, Bulletin of the West Bengal Headmasters Association, Calcutta-73, March 1981, pp. 3-9.

9. Mahanta, D., Our Education in the Making, *Ibid.*, p. 133.,

national language or the language of India (that is Bharat). A vigorous 'Campaign' may immediately be made to that effect and simultaneously, we should make an all-out effort to translate the Hindi language (i.e., Bharati Bhasa) into a real link-language of the country, through liberal incorporation of 'rich' vocabularies from other major Indian languages, just in the same way as the English language does to enrich itself continuously. In other words, our 'Bharatiya Bhasa' should also try to develop itself in such a way that it can, in the near future, claim to be compared with the richest languages of the world. Such a conception of our 'Federal language' would easily reinforce the new spirit of the democratic, socialistic and secular Republic of Bharat. If the choice of Hindi as the official language of the Union was dictated earlier by the decision about 'Bharatiya Bhasa, the federal language of the country should now be taken to consolidate the sense of 'Bharatiyata' (Indianhood) and thus to give a new tone to the intended goal of an integrated, unified nationality and to boost up the 'morale' of the people to that end.[10]

Of course, change in the language-policy is not the end all of an 'alternative solution' to the pressing problem of national integration as there are other vital issues as well.

10. Mahanta, D., National Policy on Education, Bulletin of W.B. Headmasters Assocation, Calcutta-73, March 1981, pp. 3-9.

9

THE PRESENT SCENE IN INDIAN SOCIETY

Sociologically speaking India is in the grip of transition. It seems that everything is at the cross-road at this crucial hour when experiments are being made in different fields. In fact, the old tradition is crumbling down while some of the new values are emerging. It is also interesting that some old fashions and styles are taking new forms and dimensions, but basically they are not changing.

Historically, we have come to the end of British Raj system when the left out values have almost disappeared. The needs and interests are changing but still there is a fad for some British cults and culture. Speaking good English, wearing good suits are still regarded as signs of aristocracy. It is quite usual to have and interplay between the various values and cults in the shrinking world today.

It would be helpful if we take up the following perspectives for discussion with a view to doing justice to this topic.

(a) Family structure in transition;

(b) The community life of today;

(c) Individualism and group-life;

(d) Our changing education;

(e) The present mass media for dissemination of culture as contrasted to that of the past;

(f) The present trends in Indian economy and its impact on our day-to-day life; and

(g) Our changing values and lifestyle.

(a) Family Structure in Transition

As mentioned earlier, our family is a very important unit of our society. For obvious reasons it is the breeding ground of values, culture and education. A good personality develops in a good family and so a good education. It is thus important to discuss the role of family in the present social context of India.

As family is not merely a conglomeration of different numbers. It is an effective environment, a common forum and a shelter for sharing joys and sorrows, ideas and sentiments. India has built up a very effective family unit where it absorbs both young and old, present and past generations. It is a joint family system which has been easily introduced to cope with the challenges of Indian economy and values. There are certain deeprooted values of tradition in Indian culture, which not only includes utilitarian modalities of life but also few permanent modes based on faith, creed and experiences. For example, respect for the old people, compassion for the poor and hospitality are all projections of Indian values. It is a fact that most of them belong to some attitude towards life which has been accepted after long practice.

As a result of the drifting of values our family structure is changing fast. The unit is becoming smaller where only husband and wife with their children prefer to live together. Unlike in the past there is not much place for other relatives and even the old parents within the family at the moment. This kind of situation has been the outcome of the changing attitude and values in addition to other factors economic and social. There is a shrinking self-centred outlook which we find today influencing our social interaction. For some reasons the heart to heart dialogue between the old and the new members of the family is becoming difficult. Very often we call this 'generation gap.' In fact, the affinity and cohesion among the family members are gradually eroding and often we find conflicts and confrontations in the field of interaction between father and son, brother and other family members. In the community life we find the same picture. There is hardly any respect and love, nor is there any tolerance and understanding at any level in the society at large.

It is thus extremely disappointing to find disharmony and disintegration within the family and community, states and the nation. One may wonder around this picture of the present society so dismal and frustrating. The answer is not that easy to be put in a few words. It seems that the entire world is at unrest and on the way to a drastic change. It looks that man today is becoming desperate to find a new way of life without knowing what he wants. This terrible passion just for a change in his values and lifestyle is bursting out in various forms with various expressions. It appears that he has never become so unhappy as he is today. Maybe, he is unhappy with himself, with his own performance. When he looks back it is not difficult for him to realise the mistakes he has committed in ignoring the human values and putting priorities to the superficial and materialistic pursuits. Truly speaking he is in a trap at this time of confusion and crisis. Neither he can turn back as it is too far from the traditional goal, nor is it easy for him to have a smooth journey towards what he wants. This is a sort of confusion in his conduct and attitude projected in every walk of life.

(b) The Community of Life Today

An analytic study of the community life and events today reveals some significant behaviour pattern of the community people today.

The members of the family and community are seeking some satisfaction from outside and are on the lookout for external stimulation. Somehow, they are not getting satisfaction within the family as they used to do in previous days. The economic status of a family is held in esteem and the culture and tradition are secondary. At the time of matrimonial connection the cultural and social status was once regarded very important. But now-a-days family status is judged more by the wealth and possessions the family has got. The values attached to the quality of a marriage were also different. The daughter looked for the beauty of the bridegroom, the mother looks for the wealth, the father for the status and the rest for the sweetmeats. Unfortunately, our present community could not escape the irrational trend of accepting dowry in some form or other. The situation has not changed much as it tells upon the nerve of the daughter's father to meet the expectation of the bridegroom. This is one of the maladies of our society which theoretically denounces the dowry system. There are so many other examples of social injustice and disharmony and inequality. Marriage at an early age of minority groups, sati-daha system in certain communities, caste barriers, religious prejudices are few of the numerous examples of our social disequilibrium.

(c) Individualism and Group-life

No doubt, individuals form the society and community, yet, the social norms and the community constraints are hard to ignore. For a healthy society, the conformity to social roles is essential. Individuals have obligations to comply with the dictations of social ethics and jurisprudence, no matter what their preference is. Obviously, there are instances of various conflicts, arising out of strong individualities and attitude of community members. They tend to defy the social norms and stand out ignoring their obligations to the community. As a result, anti-social groups are forming almost within each community today. There is not much control to regulate their conduct and set them in order. The present age of transition is an age of experimentation when the chaos and confusion are allowed to prevail.

Recently people are becoming more conscious of their individual needs and comforts without much regard for the group and community in which they live. Somehow, they prefer individualism to altruism. Maybe, our present culture and education encourage this self-centred outlook and prompt the people to seek personal gratification. Priorities have been set without much reason, to individualistic goals. Examples of narrow outlook and self-gratification are everywhere.

While this tendency is prevalent in the modern society we feel handicapped and isolated for want of co-operation and unified strength. When there was a joint family system every member used to feel self-confident to combat any external threat or aggression, in spite of their limited economic resources. It is hard denying the fact that money is not the only strength, it is man-power which is also very important. In a joint family one could feel secure in the group-life they used to live, where brothers, parents and even cousins used to have a common life under the same roof. Besides, there was a fellow feeling among the neighbours and community members, particularly in the villages. They used to spend their days and hours together with mutual feeling of trust, tolerance and co-operation. Each village was a cultural unit, a centre of community activities and group interaction.

Individuals and groups are supplementary and there is a need for compromise for a healthy adjustment to one another. It is imperative that any compromise needs sacrifice and tolerance which we are lacking today. Of course there is a tendency to form different groups like clubs and associations in towns and villages today. People tend to share their ideas and experience through these associations. In addition, there are big organisations like Lions Club, Rotary Club, almost in every big town. Both adults and youngsters participate in activities organised by the clubs and interact quite freely in various ways. In villages as well, the students organise games and sports, through their clubs. There are different samitis (committees), like Puja Samiti for observing the various religious festivals. Thus we find that the group-life of individuals is enriched through such organisations and their activities. Cultural programmes including drama, music, recitation are also arranged by the literary clubs or libraries in towns and villages. The number of such organisations is gradually increasing today with a view to sharing the emotions and sentiments around ideals and beliefs of people. The individuality is, therefore, retained and projected through suitable channels and forms, although a group-life demands adjustments and sacrifices.

As mentioned earlier, we find our villages changing their character and their tendency towards urbanisation. The number of educated people is every village is increasing and superstitions and prejudices are giving way. Besides there is a growing awareness of party politics in every village and in many cases the minor conflicts among the villagers are handled by the parties themselves and not by the courts of law. Unfortunately, our villages are still neglected and there is not much improvement in transportation. This is a definite hindrance to mobility of the rural population.

(d) Our Changing Education

Education is the backbone of a nation and the national progress takes place through education. It is observed that since independence, India has made several attempts to bring changes in educational system as well as policy. Various commissions have been set up by the government with a view to reviewing the educational system, but with no tangible success. Experiments are going on emphasising the curricula or the examination system. Unfortunately, the human factors are yet to be given prominence for real improvement of our educational system. The teacher-pupil relationship, the ideology of the teachers, the team spirit within the school, the teacher-parent liaison and the school community interaction have yet to improve a lot for building up an effective system of education. The pupils have been treated like guineapigs in the experimental set up. The load of syllabus is increasing by leaps and bounds, ignoring the limited capacity of the young learners. Certain bias is projected in the name of new experiments of education. Moreover, there have been attempts to exploit the sentiments of the people around certain basic issues like vacational education and employment opportunities through education. If there is a mix-up between the two, it is doubtful if we could reach a real satisfactory end. It is, of course, the responsibility of education to help the learners to be self-sufficient in life but we cannot put the cart before the horse. We should never forget that education has to look after the personality development first and then the vocational adjustment. There should be certain basic education which is imperative for building up healthy citizens in all respect. Very recently, we hear of Navodaya school where we find some new ideas injected through education. It may be a good idea to relate education to life theoretically but there should be a continuity of the educational programme to lead to vocational ends. Moreover, one should not forget that India is a land of democracy where we have got to ensure equality of opportunity as a principle. In the Navodaya system, however, we find certain tendencies towards encouraging class system. In other words, those who would get opportunities in the Navodaya system would be eventually privileged to rule over the rest.

(e) The Present Mass Media for Dissemination of Culture as Contrasted to that in the Past

In all ages various media of expression have been used. Even the scripts on the marble or on the barks of the trees have served the purpose in the past. Gradually writing has been introduced to indicate a giant leap in the history of civilisation. Since then, books and journals have been able to serve as an effective mass medium of education. But the books were beyond the reach of the illiterate people. It was, therefore, felt that there is a need for mass media through which the people in general could gather knowledge and information. Pictures, models and music used to serve the purpose. There is obviously an appeal of sound of music as well as projected picture. The audio-visual stimulations generate interests to a great extent. This is why audio-visual aids are indispensable in the classroom today. Films and cassettes are used more than ever for making lessons interesting for creating interest in a lesson. Unfortunately, many schools of rural India are not even equipped with good blackboards, charts, maps and globes, not to speak of films and cassettes. Yet, we can hardly deny the effectiveness of these media particularly at the age of knowledge explosion. When competition is ever on its increase, a young learner is expected to cope with that challenge without much choice. At home and in school we have now a scope for availing of the radio, television and videos in the affluent societies. But there is a disparity between the two worlds, namely, the rich and the poor, the privileged and the deprived. Democracy in education has got to do something to bring some parity and uniformity. Beyond the Atlantic we find a tremendous conquest of computer science in every field of life, including commerce and education. Life without computer is incomplete in the countries like U.S.A. It is no wonder that computer has been much in use even in the classrooms of the United States. It is a sophisticated aid no doubt but it is very unique and helpful in learning.

(f) The Present Trend in Indian Economy and its Impact on our day-to-day Life

Indian economy has taken its turn from its conservative to aggressive direction. The old concept of economics has completely changed as it no longer believes in self-sufficiency on individual basis. The world today believes in interdependence and mutual exchanges of trade and commerce. For facilitating the exchange of trade and business export and import rules have drastically changed and there have been much relaxations in foreign trade and commerce. The Commonwealth countries have established a trade organisation for exchange of expertise. In this perspective we can easily conclude by saying that free flow of money and ideas is the main objective of the international trade today.

Indian economics has also been influenced by the modern concept of international trade. The World Bank has been set up for granting loan and advance for trade expansion in different countries. India has improved her economic position by expanding her export market and restricting the scope for import, by means of self-sufficiency in those areas. For example, she has brought green revolution by improving her farming operations and the programme of production of small tools, gadgets and equipments. Even India is earning a lot from the foreign tourists as it has been trying to set up strategies as on industry.

So far as our village economics is concerned, we find some changes as well. There has been a steady flow of capital from outside since the cottage industries including the handlooms, special handicrafts, and clay modelling have created interest and found some market, even in foreign countries.

With the introduction of small industries in towns and suburbs, we find some mobility among the villagers, particularly the women-folk. The cost of labour has gone up considerably and sometimes it is hard to get their services when we need them. With this changing economy we find our increasing wants in our day-to-day life. Our needs are multiplied with the growing complexity of our life.

(g) Our Changing Values and Lifestyles

Modern amenities have increased and people are no longer satisfied with their plain living and high thinking. The cost of living is much higher, with the change of our lifestyle. People have started side business for supplementing their income.

SCHOOL AND COMMUNITY

The development of school idea has been continuous since long. During ancient time the Gurugriha was the most effective school and the guru was the friend philosopher and guide of the young learners. He was concerned with the total development of the young disciple who was sent to him in good faith by the community. The guru enjoyed the highest esteem as he had no mercenary motive. The disciple was a full-time student under the total care and guidance of the guru. He was asked to do various things, viz., planting, gardening, tending cows, tilling soil, cutting of woods, etc. Besides every disciple used to gain knowledge and wisdom sitting under his feet. So unlike the modern schools, Gurugriha was meant for creating personalities and creative people, leaders and academicians. With the growing demand of mass education formal schooling was introduced. There were chatuspathis set up by Sanskrit scholars and pathshalas by village teachers before the sophisticated schooling started. No matter what form of schooling emerged from time to time, the need for community participation was felt more and for a meaningful education. After all, the aim of education was mainly to socialise the individual if not to humanize him. Both the individual and social aspirations were expected to merge at a point for making individual life and living geared to social needs and expectations. The pupils were expected not only to learn various subjects and subject-matter but also to grow as a social being. With a view to meeting these objectives social studies and social work have been incorporated in the syllabus at different levels of education. Credits have been given to extra-curricular activities and socio-cultural participation within the school. N.S.S. programmes, boys scout participation and such other adjunct programmes for socializing individuals have been included in the total framework of education. Nevertheless, education has been considered as a tool or medium for helping individuals to grow in every direction.

We live in a society, in a community and in a family, we cross our individual boundaries and extend ourselves in the context of the community and the society. We learn to behave to comply with the social norms, to fulfil the ambition of becoming a healthy citizen of the world. So the school today is regarded as a miniature society where there are lots of interaction, interests and events. The teachers including the head teacher are just like the guardians of the school community responsible for regulating the conduct of the growing pupils. There are also certain goals set up in the individual schools and attempts are made to reach these goals in a number of ways. The pupils grow through social and group interactions. It takes various forms like cooperation, competition and conflicts, within the classroom, in the sportsground and even outside campus. They interact and learn from one another, sharing experiences through participation in group-life in games, sports, dramatic activities and cultural functions. School thus becomes a replica of a community within its limited infrastructure. The different types of members who come in contact with the school authorities and management, teachers and pupils are guardians, public and visitors from different walks of life. The school administration should wisely give a wide scope for such exchanges of visit, views and experiences. A good school is one which tries to maximize this interaction between people at all levels from different corners of the community. It should organise regular socio-cultural functions, ceremonies and celebrations, inviting community members to actively participate, in every way. There should be a scope for community participation in school life by means of active involvement of the members in school programmes. Cultural functions, exhibitions, sports, birthday celebration, New years's days are the occasions for encouraging the social interaction in the school life.

Teaching is a part of teacher's function but not his entire role. He has the responsibility to create different learning situations to encourage the pupils to participate in various forms of interaction. Instead of lecturing, the teacher could encourage group discussions for free flow of ideas between one group and the other. In this way the classroom situation should be more stimulating. The pupils should come up with new ideas and feel free to express themselves even in a non-traditional manner. Thus the classroom should represent a community where members are allowed to interact freely and share experiences before taking a decision or reaching a goal. Thus a community life should be projected within the classroom and school life for making the school community relation really conducive to education.

Regarding evaluation and examination we find that there is still a traditional approach which needs to be changed for improving the system. Instead of focussing upon the individual assessment, attempt is being made to encourage group assessment by setting various groups and taking the total performance of each group into consideration.

This approach will help the individual members of the class to build up a team spirit and a cooperative attitude. They will learn and live together. The idea of bringing a cooperative spirit in place of individual self-centred outlook is the most befitting one during this age of transition. As observed by a professer of Sociology, there is one aspect of the development of the societies which disturbs observers of history, that is the persistence of evil. It is interesting to observe that economic crisis and famine have been faithful companions of human race. Evil is a historical necessity and the creation of a social order without evil has so far proved impossible. It goes without saying that the individuality and society are often at conflict and that leads to some changes in social order. Individuality is also free of all things which arise in the sphere of what is common and similar. Within the providence of individuality man transcends what is common and similar. He is, therefore, alone. Every group creates a system of mores, customs and opinions, penalties and rewards which are also set as behaviour control.

From the above observations one can conclude that the individuals merge into groups as individuality fuses the society. School provides the platform for such a fusion through planned programmes of curricular and co-curricular activities.

Today a school can hardly exist without a close and effective interaction with the community. Each contributes to the total growth of the individuals living in social context. It is the task of the school and community to come closer for more effective operation in the interest of the society at large. In fact, the well-being of a society depends upon a happy and harmonious relationship between the school and the community. It is thus very clear that home has a major role in strengthening the tie and affinity between the school and community. The parents and the teachers have to take positive roles for making this dream a reality. School is thus a community centre, a centre which echoes the spirit and aspiration of the greater society. The pupils are our future hope and it is through their functions and cooperative enterprise a community life will be enriched.

10

AN ANALYSIS OF SOME OF THE PROBLEMS IN INDIA IN EDUCATIONAL PERSPECTIVES

"The world is today passing through one of the greatest crises in its history. Shaken to its foundation by the great war, it has not yet been able to pick up the thread of normal progress. The political, social and economic doctrines on which the progress of the nineteenth century appeared to be founded have given way in some countries to complete uncertainty as to the next step ...", says I. L. Kandel in his "Studies in Comparative Education.

It is, therefore, wise to take into account socio-economic structure of the present society of India with implications.

Again the socio-economic problems rest on several factors of which population with its manifold aspects deserves special attention. This factor of population has particular reference to the sex ratio, the influx of population due to heavy immigration in India, the typical problems due to marriage, infant mortality and want of suitable occupations.

On the other hand, the problems which are more economic in nature have a special reference to maldistribution of wealth owing to the several factors, viz., wrong approach to the policy of production, procurement, consumption and control. Particular reference is also necessary to the factors like non-equitable division of labour, concentration of wealth in the hands of the few, problem of unemployment and wastage of energy of the young folk due to want of proper guidance, etc.

Next come a number of problems which are pivotal and which have got a close connection with the defects of the social structure of the day. These may be described as social disintegration and social stratification with their ramifications such as the caste system, racial prejudices, narrow provincialism, blind faith in social customs and traditions.

Thus the socio-economic problems are mostly due to several inherent defects in the present social structure. Besides these, another factor appears to play a predominant part in society. That is the psychological mal-adjustment which is deepening the crisis all the more and extending the dimension of the problems. Particular reference should, therefore, be made to the manifold aspects of these crucial problems, such as lack of mutual trust and emotional stability. Russell believes in the propaganda and the possibility of solution of problems through education. Thus he says, "One of the most important parts of education, and one of the most neglected, is that which teaches how to reach true conclusions on insufficient data"

Problem of Population

It is a fact that the proportion of the population of India living on agriculture is very large and it has been steadily on the increase. It will be seen that the percentage of real agricultural class is on its decrease. Most people who have got no other alternative but to take up agriculture as vocation of life. They are compelled to be directly or indirectly dependent on land or cultivation. As a result, the landless cultivators, increasing at a rapid rate are inviting poverty and financial deadlock.

The Royal Commission on Agriculture has pointed the same melancholy tale which is still true. "The overcrowding of the people on the land, the lack of alternative means of securing a living, the difficulty of finding any avenue of escape and the early age with which a man is burdened with dependents, force the cultivators to grow food wherever they can and on whatever terms are available"

This is the observation on the agricultural position of the whole of India, but so far as West Bengal is concerned the situation is more precarious. The influx of population in West Bengal due to heavy immigration after the partition, as well as the irreparable loss of the most suitable lands for cultivation because of the same reason have made the food situation more complex and alarming. When Bengal had an area of 77,442 sq. miles with fertile soil mostly in East Bengal districts, it was even then very difficult for the province to carry a burden of few crores of population.

It is, therefore, not difficult to imagine the present position of West Bengal when almost 60 per cent of her best productive land has been included in Bangladesh, whereas the number of displaced persons is on its increase. Dr. Radha Kamal Mukherji observes the position of Bengal before partition with reference to cultivable land and says that the area cultivated by a cultivator comes to. 47 acres as compared to 0.63 in U.P. and 0.74 in Madras. Dr. R.K. Das in his "Industrial Efficiency of India" has shown that the problem of population has become more acute not only due to rapid increase of population but largely because of wastage of our resources. It is a fact that the percentage of total land cultivated is very small in comparison with the area which West Bengal contains. This is partly because of the gradual deterioration of soil particularly in West Bengal due to the stagnant condition of the rivers after the British invasion of this land.

According to the observation made by Dr. Radha Kamal Mukherji, "Nearly half of cultivable land in tne District of Burdwan and Hooghly have been almost surrendered during last 30 years owing to the deterioration of river system due to embankments and Railway Bridges". Besides these, there are other States as well. These factors may be described as follows:

1. The over pressure of the population on agriculture, through the blocking of other economic channels.
2. The effects of land-monopoly and of the burdens of the peasantry.
3. Poor technique due to ignorance and prejudice of the cultivator class.
4. The sub-division and fragmentation of holdings, the individualistic petty farming due to the socio-political influence.
5. Negligence of soil due to want of proper manuring, irrigation system and supervision in the light of modern science.

This neglect is not only from the cultivators but form the state also. This has been observed by many who have ascribed the alarming features of this deterioration of soil partly due to negligence in various forms. Very recently, there has been some change in the Government policy for improvement.

R. Palme Dutta in his "India To day", observes the following typical features and problems so far as agriculture is concerned. He says, "The agricultural population of India still works on very meagre resources which, if we consider the well-being of the peasant themselves, are very poorly distributed. He also considers malaria malnutrition and such other diseases as another cause of this deterioration in agriculture. It is worthwhile to quote a report of the Bengal Irrigation Department Committee in 1930. This report throws some light on the agricultural position of the states, "Central Bengal is at present a decadent tract: it is malarious, the population is steadily decreasing, and the land is going out of cultivation. It may, of course, be the case that the deterioration has already proceeded so far that it cannot now be checked, and that the tract in question is doomed to revert gradually into swamp and jungle." But this is not all. The overcrowded cultivators within this limited cultivated area, the social condition, the paralysing burdens placed on them their extreme poverty and primitive technique mean that while the demands on the land are heavier, the level of production is lower than in any country. Many questions arise in connection with labour and capital as regards the crisis in agriculture of India. J.H. Hutton, C.I.E, has raised a very significant point in connection with the improvement of agriculture which also may be applied in connection with the study of agriculture position of Bengal.

The total mechanisation of agriculture, he points out, will redue the need for labour and will do little for solving labour problems though there is no scope for doubt about its suitability in the present crisis. It is, therefore, really controversial whether mechanisation will help to solve all the economic problems, and whether this will be rendered feasible under the present conditions of India.

In this connection Tarlok Singh in his "Poverty and Social Change" has made a very valuable discussion on the practical side of the problem. He says, "Any system of co-operation in agriculture has, therefore, to answer two basic questions: First, what are we to do with ownership in land? Second, how is the work to be allotted and evaluated? He further observes that the present owners and hereditary tenants form the backbone of India's agriculture. They are the heart and the substance of the civilization and of the social values which the village community represents today. In re-organising our rural economy, we must have the peasants with us and not against us. But it is equally essential in the ultimate interest of the peasants themselves that ownership should be dissociated from control over the use of separate bits of land within the village. It is, therefore, suggested by him to take up unit of the village as a whole for cultivation and to distribute the return on the basis of the ownership of the capital and the land which they have contributed to the village farm. Thus joint village management is perhaps the most concrete and immediately practical form which can replace the traditional system of individual ownership. This will solve not only the economic problem but also help to bring about social integration and harmony. When the village will begin to function effectively as an economic unit in agriculture and in relation to industry, the present division into groups will tend to be modified and all sections of the community including the depressed classes may hope to achieve equal opportunity and equal freedom.

Though different problems might crop up for the time being on the way to transforming the present economy by rapid change, they may still be tackled and controlled by suitable organisations and managements. But major group of problems which arises from the rationalisation of agriculture is really complicated. Even at the present moment "there is a great deal of underemployment or disguised unemployment in agriculture." Tarlok Singh also observes that "the increase in population deepened the poverty of rural artisans, field labourers and village servants and not many among them have full and regular employment in their own occupation." The question naturally arises as to how surplus thrown up as a result of the rationalisation of agriculture will be absorbed and how their financial position can be improved. This requires the establishment of a social instrument which will explore and create avenues of employment by a simultaneous development of industry throughout the land. Instead of large scale industrialisation, if small industry can be grown in rural areas on the basis of local products in order to meet the local demands, the problem of urbanisation and unemployment can, it is hoped, be solved to a great extent. In other words, jointly managed villages can act as sub-producers working in liaison with organised industry. For this the village artisans, the skilled labourers should be better organised, equipped and trained and the great deal of processing of local products can be done in the villages by the villagers themselves.

It is thus seen that considerable integration between rural and industrial economy must be ensured and a social control should come up to facilitate this integration. As discussed before, education can help a lot to improve the social and economic position of people particularly the cultivator class, handicapped by all means. It is, therefore, suggested that effective plannings of education should be put into practice for effective solution.

The Royal Commission on Agriculture in India suggests various ways and methods of improving agriculture, the most important of which is the opening of agricultural research centres in different areas whose function will be not only to discover the causes of deterioration but to carry experiments on manual problems, on fertilisation of soil, on hybridisation and acclimatisation.

In the circumstances, it is imperative that the lot of problems around soil, irrigation, the finance of agriculture such as poultry, fishery, etc., should attract the notice of the educational engineers as well. Education should take up certain responsibilities in improving the socio-economic position of people involved and as such definite well planned methods and programmes should be adopted while constructing the curriculum and system of training.

The defects of the educational system so long in vogue, have been realised by many and the objectives of education should be more embracing and suitable to meet the socio-economic needs of people than in the past. But all these pious wishes have not so far been able to bring about any thorough reform in this field. Needs of rural population have rather been neglected and the community needs ignored in the school curriculum and educational programme.

Special schools whether part-time or full-time are also to be started for training up the actual cultivators. Classes should be held in the evening or other suitable time so as to allow them to go on as usual with their daily routine of work. Practical classes, in actual field should be held for training them to use up-to-date means of cultivation, fertilisation of soil and production. Vacations of these schools should ordinarily cover the period of monsoons when they are required to toil in fields from morning till night. Besides practical education to the agricultural population, should be imparted for imparting social education which will help them to be socially conscious, medically fit and economically more equipped. These social and civic education are essential for enlightening them in every sphere of life

In short, the education for the rural population mostly consisting of cultivator and artisans classes should cope with the various problems in respective fields including economic development, education and public health. The essence of effective cultivation consists in combining four separate factors, viz., area, capital, technique and organisation, but each of the factors is dependent on education and training for the utilisation of these by people. It is, therefore, the task of education to reorganise peasant villages so that the chief factors, capital and organisation can fully play their parts. Many suggest co-operative farming as one of the solutions to the problem of fragmentation of holdings by individual owners. Co-operative farming is one of the means to solution for rationalisation of agriculture, but it can hardly be denied that under the present system and social condition there are many difficulties and barriers on the way to this formidable task.

The peasants who form the backbone of the society, are not unfortunately conscious of their own good and national welfare, and there is every chance that they will not easily submit to State control which is primarily required for through mechanisation. It is the task of education to remove from their minds all prejudices and narrowness of outlook as well as to foster in them a healthy co-operative spirit. Really speaking, due to ignorance and want of sufficient care, vast areas suitable for gardening or poultry remain neglected. As a result malaria spreads. The same may be said about the low lands which ordinarily yield one crop annually and then remain mostly un-cultivated throughout the rest of the year. But modern methods has helped the cultivators in getting many returns of crop out of the same soil in a year. The successive returns of crop throughout the year due to the scientific treatment of the soil many improve the food position considerably.

Various recreational centres are essential for the successful operation of the scheme as these will help not only to break the monotony of their life by catering joy and amusements but also to spread literacy and develop good sense among them. Films, television, radio and such other educational media should be utilised to supplement the programme of social and vocational education for the peasants. Social consciousness and co-operative spirit, proper encouragement and inspiration should also be fostered. In this connection, it is perhaps wise to impress on them the necessity of birth control and neat decent living. Periodic exhibitions, and other media will be of great help in creating a healthy climate for mutual understanding, exchange of ideas and experience.

Education for leisure is one of the crying needs of the hour not only among the peasants but also among the educated mass. In the present economic crisis, any one finds it extremely difficult to subsist on a particular occupation. A subsidiary income may be derived by utilising the idle hours in gardening, pottery, weaving, carpentry and such other sundry works. These are profitable and at the same time recreational is a necessity.

Similar measures are to be adopted so far as other vocations such as pottery, woodwork and such other pursuits are concerned. Schools for theoretical and practical training should also be started so as to suit the actual needs and demands of the locality and also to utilise the natural resources of the locality to the greatest possible extent. Thus in the area suitable for paddygrowing, agricultural schools should be supplemented with rice-mills, similarly the areas suitable for cotton and jute production require the development of small scale textile and jute industries. The same thing may be said of the area where mustard or linseeds are sufficiently grown. Not only this, the soiled and the mineral resources should attract the attention of the Planning Department so that suitable industry can utilise these resources for increasing the national wealth. People or state should start a network of small scale industries in rural area of India, as feeder industries, mostly to meet the local demands and solve local unemployment problems. The production of raw materials and the further utilisation of these products through industry should go hand in hand for their most successful operation. This co-ordination will help, it is hoped, the real solution of varied problems of over population to a great extent.

Moreover, education of many-sided character and the demonstration of an effective educational programme are essential for meeting the economic distress of the common mass of people. Scheme of agricultural and industrial education must both precede and follow the scientific development of India's agriculture and industries. Until such widely planned industrial and agricultural education becomes possible, the necessity of vocational bias in general education cannot be questioned on the following grounds, (i) it trains the practical intelligence of the pupils and (ii) it further fits them to divert their capacity for earning a livelihood into diversified channels.

It is really controversial whether general education should be left aside and industrial education should only be encouraged. In the circumstances, it is wise to introduce a co-ordinated system of general, agricultural and industrial education so that no single aspect of life should be totally ignored. It is beyond any doubt that the primary task of education today is to prepare the vast illiterate mass of population, to find out avenues of employment. For the educated middle class plan to foster a national and social consciousness may be taken up.

If we try to visualise the position of different classes of population, it will be evident that much harm is due to lack of proper soul education amongst them. Infant mortality, early marriage, dowry system, social disintegration, overbirth of children and premature death of majority of population are partly due to human follies and want of adequate education and planning. It will, therefore, be the function of education to remove all the evils by infusing knowledge and developing proper attitude and skills as well as to place higher ideals and noble missions before them.

So far we have discussed mostly about the various problems of rural community particularly about agricultural population, and suggestion has also been made for their best possible solution. It will, therefore, be proper to discuss the other factors of population problem. Beveridge in his book "Full Employment in a Free Society (1945)" observes, "Adequate and healthy housing presents the largest single objective for desirable outlay after the war and affords the largest scope for raising the standard of life, health and happiness". This urbanising tendency has not only affected the health and happiness of people of the city but also the education and culture to a great extent. City life has become most unsuitable for the real learners and particularly the beginners owing to the fact that the poise and tranquillity, the calmness and concentration which are essential for good education are badly lacking in cities. Besides the various corruptions which are so common in the cities and towns attract the attention of the tender aged pupils and exercise ominous influence on their life. The plenty of sun-shine and air, the restful life, the natural beauty which are in abundance in village life are beyond expectation in town life.

Moreover, the types of education which they receive in schools are quite inadequate for the development of their mind and body. Most of the town-schools are situated in busy centres of the city, housed in wretched buildings without any extra space for the movement of the students. More or less, with meagre equipments these institutions run on a commercial line and very little care is taken by the school authorities to pay individual attention. Many schools can hardly provide suitable accommodation for the students who sometimes huddle together in dark unventilated rooms and begin to count the unpleasant hours of the school. It is really unfortunate that the number of such schools in the cities is large where neither their body nor mind are stimulated. It may be mentioned here that members of the teaching staff appointed in the institutions are not enough in proportion to roll strength. They are uninspired and can hardly impress anything good on the minds of the student. Nor can they inspire and give proper guidance.

On the other hand the villages have been depopulated as a result of which the village schools cannot get sufficient number of students for running the establishment, nor can they arrange better equipments for teaching for a very thin population due to obvious sociological reasons. The contrast of pictures in town and rural areas is thus very prominent. In towns, the student population cannot properly be accommodated, whereas in village schools there is a very poor roll-strength some time inadequate for running an institution. The question arises, therefore, as to what should be the real solution. The problem of urbanisation, though complicated, may to a certain extent, be solved by redistribution of population over the country. The villages should again be made centres of learning and the seats of higher education may be established in suitable rural areas.

The next fundamental problem which is of no less significance in the field of education is of sex-ratio in a growing population. Though a lot of confusion prevails at present regarding the problems of population and sex-ratio still many believe that in the absence of a gradual increase of population of both the male and female in equal proportion, much social evils are bound to come up. It is really unfortunate on the part of India, that parents with numerous offsprings were once the objects of venerations. The proud mother is now forced to hang her head down in shame. This is all the more when a mother gives birth to a female child particularly in the middle class family. She thinks it to be a guilt on her part to give birth to a female child and takes her to be a family burden from the very day she first sees the light. But one of the striking phenomena which are of considerable concerns to a sociologist is that even in the 1951 census there has been a definite although a small decline in the number of females per thousand males in almost every district of West Bengal except Hooghly and Calcutta. This has given rise to fresh problems in society. This gradual decline of female population in Bengal entails a number of factors of which marriage is of great significance. On a critical analysis, it will be seen that marriage is not encouraged by the present circumstances, though it is a natural condition for men and women. As a result of the economic stringency, the marriageable age is being gradually shifted and the health of the young population is gradually deteriorating. Besides, there are several other social evils which are faced today. The consequences of these are not far to seek. The children born are mostly constitutionally weak, intellectually, over-burdened, and in particular cases handicapped due to various reasons. Moreover, the female population married at a very late stage are often victimised by premature death during the time of delivery resulting in a complete maladjustment in the domestic environment. On the other hand, if we look at the male population of this category, it will be noticed that they often die prematurely leaving, their dependents completely helpless and deserted. As a result, the young children lose every hope of life, and are deprived of educational opportunities and often take up undesirable courses of life. Of course, the present economic situation is mainly responsible for these evils, but at the same time it cannot also be totally denied that the present education has changed the outlook of people who hesitate in taking the responsibility of family before they can reach their ideal standard of living. But unfortunately in most cases they are engaged in wild goose chase and when they exhaust their energy and youth, they reluctantly enter into family life. Education has thus proved a hindrance in many cases to timely marriage by creating high ambition, in their minds.

So far as sex-ratio is concerned biological factors can be traced at the root of any disproportion between male and female population. This particular phenomenon of sex-ratio has a considerable bearing on society and education. If the number of male members is greater, then women become rare and various corruptions reveal; on the other hand, if the number of male members is less, marriage problem becomes acute on the part of the bride's party and the above problem of industrial units is faced by the country due to shortage of young men. Male members persist in demanding wealth and dowry from the party of the bride.

Fortunately or unfortunately, West Bengal has a higher ratio of males leading to many far-reaching consequences in society and education. Many biologists are of opinion that children of young healthy parents are the best physically endowed and, therefore, the most desirable from the racial point of view.

Some also assume that most male children are born of parents of strong vitality. In the case where there is definite weakness on one side, then there is possibility of the birth of female child. On a close observation it will be seen that like other States West Bengal consists of majority of agricultural and rural population which mostly depends on physical labour and maintains comparatively good health. It is perhaps one of the reasons that the agricultural and labourer class produce more male children. More females are born of parents who are naturally weak and lacking in vigour and vitality due to more exercise of brain than that of body. As a result, the gradual decline of female population as a whole is being observed, though there is definite increase of female population among the middle class families.

For a healthy society, there must not exist a wide divergence between the numbers of male and female population as major disharmonies are mostly created by disproportionate sex-ratio. Even the domestic environment, which is of very high significance to the education of a child, is determined to a great extent by this important factor. Sexual promiscuity is regarded in many circles as a social norm since the ideal of virginity is often endangered when this decline of female of population takes an extreme form. Divorces which increase in number due to the above maladjustments also mar the integrity of family life. Thus with the moral degeneration of the society, education loses its significance and the social harmony which is the soul of Indian culture begins to shiver. The young learners will then have a tendency to undermine the importance of moral scruple because the ideal of real education and moral training cannot be shown in domestic environment. The narrowness of outlook and undue conservative tendency of people, the racial prejudice and blind faith in customs present some serious problem as well. Like the colour prejudice in America or class distinction in other Western countries, caste system in India with all its false rigidity and narrowness have proved as a definite hindrance to the creation of a progressive society as desired by Raja Ram Mohan Roy, Maharshi Devendranath Tagore, Ram Krishna Paramhansa, Swami Vivekananda and others.

Though modern society has been partly able to propagate the communistic outlook and the principle of equality of right and opportunity through a group of people, still this caste distinction has not yet disappeared from the society particularly of the lower class people. At the same time, a fresh problem has cropped up due to a peculiar class distinction based upon the measure of wealth. The I.A.S. people and those in administrative service form a group whereas the engineers, the doctors have chosen a different group. On the other hand, the middle class mostly comprising petty service holders, viz., clerks, teachers, etc., has a different congregation. In short, the rank consciousness has unfortunately become so prominent now-a-days that the fundamental rights of human beings are even denied and neglected at times.

Therefore, the struggle between the aristocrats and the common run of people, the conflict between the employers and the employees are often found to give rise to different problems mainly due to self-centred outlook. It is the defect in the present system of education and human frailties which presents many other typical problems almost of the same nature, viz., provincialism, religious fanaticism, and communalism. What to speak of the man-made distinctions between people of different religions, different races and creeds or colours, the unfortunate maladjustment and misunderstanding even between the people of the same race and nation have made the problem more intricate. Much of the trouble, therefore, is the result of man's incapability of overcoming the prejudices, and narrowness. Prejudice may be compared to a fertile weed, since it grows from the seed of a person's experience and is watered by the imagination of many. These prejudices are often directed against social groups or classes, against nations or against particular religions. Strong nationalism has also been regarded by many philosophers and leaders as a sort of barrier standing on the way to universal love. In this connection, it is worthwhile to remember Rabindra Nath's observations on nationalism where he says that "she has made grave errors in setting up the boundary walls too rigidly between races, in perpetuating in her classifications the results of inferiority. Often she has crippled here children's minds and narrowed their lives in order to fit them into her social forms". This is the problem before us which is the outcome of the creation of imaginary boundary lines between man and man, race and race. Even the discrimination which has been increasing around is proving more harmful in modern times. The male and the female members find it difficult to move smoothly in the life's journey. Series of conflicts often arising between them affect the domestic environment to a great extent. The sacred tie of marriage, the relation between the husband and the wife as instituted in the Hindu society is being challenged. "The chief feature of female life in India is the cultivation of the domestic virtues. All the mental training imparted to them consists of the education received from their mothers which embrace a variety of subjects including religion as well. The principles of propriety and decorum are often instilled into their youthful minds with the greatest care and glimpses of their future destiny communicated to them. The information though given orally, is repeated so often that no part of it fails to make a lasting impression on the mind, and thus the girl learns everything that the mother knows", says some observer. At the same time, it also appears that want of adequate female education is responsible for many problems which have often proved disastrous in social life. Though the conflicts and complexes between the two sexes today are mostly due to misunderstanding, still it can hardly be denied that late marriage and artificial education are partly responsible for these maladjustments.

Thus it appears that most of the problems, which are mainly due to misunderstanding and conflict, defects in the social structure and human nature, require solution mainly through education. The caste system, the provincialism the racial prejudices, the regional outlook and even the conflict between the sexes have their origin in the mind of the human beings. "A complete freedom from bad habits in individuals, also the freedom from all unclean entanglements may help in holding the banner of civilisation of the future," observes Rabindra Nath in his "Nationalism"

Each individual has his self love and therefore the instinct of self-preservation leads him to fight with others in the pursuit of his self-interest. It is so natural in human blood that only preaching of abstract ideologies will not help much in the radical cure of these complicated problems. The solution, therefore, should be sought from all sides, economic, social and psychological.

The social structure as it stands today is also seen to exercise enormous influence on the economic life of this land, giving rise to varied problems. For example, we may mention joint family system which in spite of its certain merits has proved unservable in the present economic contest. It is generally seen that in a joint family the problem of unemployment, makes its headway and much wastage of energy is caused by callousness and indifferent attitude of most of the young men who hardly care to earn their own bread. Generally it is seen that in a joint family one or two members earn whereas many others idle away times in unprofitable pursuits, because they are not forced by circumstances to seek suitable employments. Thus a few sow the seeds while many others reap the harvest. Often this system gives rise to other types of disputes and undersirable situation in a family as a result of which the relationship between brothers, sisters, uncle and nephew and other relation is unduly strained. This disharmony and strenuous relation, damages the social integrity and affects the healthy family environment. On the other hand extreme individuality causes many problems as well in family life.

Economic Problems

Problems centre a round defects in respect of production, procurement, distribution, consumption, control as well as non-equitable labour.

"Under any economic system there will be a certain amount of stupidity and a certain amount of love of power, each of which will stand in the way of the creation of a perfect educational system," says Bertrand Russell. The influence of economic factors on education is undoubtedly profound and not always superficially obvious. And this influence of economic causes upon education may be dealt with mainly under the following heads:

First is the amount of production which determines to a certain extent the possibility of expenditure for education by the State. It is, therefore, almost certain that in order to improve the system of education and provide opportunities for education to all classes, the State is to depend on the economic resources as well as the amount of production which can be derived from the soil. But as discussed before, it has been seen that the economic position of India particularly in regard to production is far from satisfactory. Therefore special measures should be taken by the authorities concerned firstly to increase the amount of production by utilising the natural resources man-power as well as the technical aspects of education.

Secondly, the procurement policy is also of vital importance in the field of economics as a satisfactory production does not always ensure a successful procurement and distribution which are most important in the solution of economic problems of a country. It is, therefore, essential that a definite planning should be followed in respect of production, procurement and distribution. In this connection it is worth mentioning that though the State has adopted certain policies in regard to these, still it is of no use denying the fact that the honest intention and the policies of the government have not been fully successful owning to certain apparent defects in their approach to these problems. The food drive, the river projects, the procurement policies a thorough network of civil supplies departments, the rationing system as well as the price-controlling methods are, no doubt, commendable attempts of the State to reach a solution of the varied problems which the country is facing today. But unfortunately enough, most of the measures are not adequate to cope with the intensity and dimension of problems which are making their appearance in bewildering ways. It is not the contention of the present thesis to deal elaborately with economics as well as the laws of production and consumption, and as such, discussion will be directed mainly towards education and psychology. One of the most important developments in the sphere of economic planning has, doubt, been effected by the emergent situation of this land in war-time and particularly in the post-war period. The Second World War was bound to create a series of perplexing problems. The proper solution on the future economic welfare of the country had largely depended on each other. Some of these problems are international and others internal. The most important of these is the sharp rise of the Indian price level and the substantial rise in the cost structure. On the other hand, the internal value of a rupee has undergone a sudden fall followed by the inflation of currency. If we critically look at the very root of the problems it will be observed that war and subsequent conflits with the neighbouring countries have created evils.

It has inflicted definite injury to mental health of the people, giving rise to most of the evils of the day. Until this can be done away with, no policy of the State in any affair will be crowned with success. Thus we see, that every move of the government to solve the economic problems of the country is being faced with crisis due to the dishonest tendency of the people and corruption so strong amongst the mass. It is also surprising that even many government officials have now the least hesitation in taking bribes and other unfair means to fulfil their own interest or selfish motives. These are so common that the attempt of a few to elevate the standard of living as well as to solve the food problems and such other crisis is not coming to any fruition. Besides, difficulties in effecting the policies of procurement and distribution through appointment of procurement officers or rationing system have arisen mainly due to want of co-operative spirit of the public and even their distrust and hostile attitude to these departments. On a close analysis, it will be clear that failure of the government in the task of control. There are certain blunders at its root. Control measures are generally adopted right from the start of the war. In India unfortunately these measures had been adopted only when disruption in the economic structure had already gone too far and the country was engulfed in a vicious circles of conflicts. The social evils and maladjustments, the bad social habits cannot be removed overnight. They can be checked and gradually reduced through an evolutionary process by the application of all the social controls, in an effective manner. Amongst the social controls, two types of control will be noticed to render much help. One is more effective such as State, Government or Law implying command, and threats and the other is more spontaneous implying internal force such as public opinion, social evaluation, morality and religion. There are certain evils which have come as a result of reaction against certain undue controls and restrictions such as black-marketing, etc., whereas there are other types of evils which have revealed as natural consequence of heavy economic pressure of life. A different group of crimes and social evils, the seeds of which were sown long ago is also noticed to play very important part in the present society. They are mostly, due to undue oppressions, neglect and contempt of the stronger towards those who were once regarded as weaker and depressed. But the picture has changed today as a result of which much tension and repercussions are making their appearances in very unhealthy manners. The threatening of strike, the riots and such other unorganised revolutions will be seen to have their roots at too deep a level. It is thus seen that unless serious attempts for solution are made primarily through the development of good sense and real education among the people only external controls will do little for permanent check of the evils as well as an effective solution. In short, the problems which are more economic in nature should be solved more by bringing about the desired condition of society through economic uplift and suitable education for the purpose. The problems which are more due to the man-made stratifications and maladjustment should be tackled with the joint help of external controls like Law and Government as well as proper education of the mind through ideals and morals.

In India, the competition has so increased, and the social unrest is so strong today that people have lost faith in themselves. They are so much involved for their basic survival that they hardly look after their mental health and moral standards of life. As a result, a neighbour does not hesitate to thrive at the cost of his fellow neighbour, the brother hardly feels any delicacy to encroach upon the legitimate shares of his brother. Thus the present society of India has almost turned to be a hot bed of chaos and anarchy. All sorts of corruptions which were once not approved by the society have become so common now, that honesty is considered by many as foolishness in the midst of present disruptions. On a critical analysis it will also be observed that with the advent of the new set of problems specially due to displacement of a large group of people, the social structure, the economic position and the cultural heritage of this race have been completely shattered. Majority of the displaced persons are still living in camps completely at the mercy of the government, though a few opportunists are snatching away the lions's share of the government help and thus depriving the real sufferers of their bare necessities. This abnormal situation has unduly exercised its enormous influence not only on society and economic life of the race but also on culture. The most unfortunate thing which has been noticed during this period is that people equally affected have no unity and mutual understanding amongst themselves. It is really surprising that people coming from a particular locality cannot stand his brother sufferers perhaps coming from a different troubled area. It is really painful to observe this disharmony even at the time of a national calamity.

Thus our society is confronted with the variety of problems having their close bearing on education. One of the major problems in Indian education today is wastage and stagnation at various levels. It is rather depressing that there is a huge wastage of human resources in India partly because we are unable to plan effectively our educational programmes. Very few of those who take their admission at pre-primary and the primary levels reach the university stage and the number of dropouts at every level of education can hardly be overlooked. In most cases, the sociological reasons dominate over psychological factors. Yet out task is to see how we could bring a social change and promote social welfare through education. The problems of education emerge out of the present social set-up full of unrest and depression. Lack of security among the young generation is one of the outstanding factors contributing to the unrest throughout the country. Similarly democracy in our country has been recently challenged in manifold ways. Even the behaviour of the responsible persons does not befit his position in many cases and thus we very often hear of crossing the floor in the parliament or violent agitation here and there for trifling causes. It appears that education has to take a very firm step to bring about a stable atmosphere in this chaotic set-up.

Another common cry of today is that our educational standard is going down. It is rather a delicate task to evaluate educational standard when the base-lines are different but one can easily come to certain generalization. When we try to find an answer to the question, "Is education today meeting the various needs and problems of our changing society?" The answer would be disappointing.

Thus it seems that the objective we have set-up in our Commission reports are too many and perhaps ambitious. We are, no doubt, aware of the knowledge explosion and imperative need for wider outlook. Yet it becomes very much frustrating if it is experienced that none of the objectives is reached for some reasons or other. Is it the fault of our policy or planning? The question remains to be answered elsewhere.

11

NEW PERSPECTIVES IN EDUCATION

A Challenge for Education

The role of education for social reconstruction has undoubtedly been demonstrated in various countries at different ages, since time immemorial. Even recently China has brought a social revolution by using education as the main tool. It is, therefore, reasonable to be optimistic about the possibility of using education as a tool for establishing peace and harmony all over the world. Peace is thus a new perspective of education.

Unfortunately, the world today is in the grip of transition. Man of the twentieth century is terribly confused. In spite of that there is a hope that man can modify his nature and adapt himself to the growing demands of time and changing society. Toynbee expresses his optimism and says. "I believe that the human race is going to choose life and good, not death and evil. I therefore, believe in the imminence of one world, and I believe that in the twenty-first century human life is going to be a unity again in all its aspects and activities."

Much depends upon how we shape up in the context of the nuclear age. It seems obvious that we in India are passing through a critical period. It is not only economy which is dwindling our national life, our values and morality, our cultural heritage are also on the point of fading away. India is a country where peace and harmony have been propagated by a number of illustrious sons of India including Chaitanya and Gandhi. It is the land of Buddha who was an emblem of peace. Yet, we are involved in a heartless struggle and conflict. In society today, human beings no longer meet as friends or companions but solely in the field of struggle for power. Moreover, we as Indians are forgetting our national identity by segregating the entire population into segments and fragments. If harmony is not followed, this small world becomes uncomfortable and modern man becomes miserable. We find that recent years have witnessed much unrest and conflict within nations and races. On the one hand, we are planning space programmes on different planets, while on the other, our motherland is facing violence and disintegration.

Is it then a failure of our modern education to help us in living together with peace and harmony even within the same country and nation?

Thus we find ourselves at a disadvantage to justify our system of education introduced in free India. It is disheartening to see unrest, confusion and confrontation at all levels of our day-to-day life. We as individuals are emotionally disturbed for reasons not far to seek. Somehow, we are off the balance like boats without anchors. We have lost the tranquillity in our individual life and are subjected to emotional turmoils. Self knowledge is almost a myth and knowledge of the matter is gaining prominence. As a consequence, matter and not mind is ruling our day-to-day life. In short, our quest for peace and harmony is being replaced by our passion for power and greed for wealth. Needless to mention that there has been a shift of emphasis in our educational system today from self knowledge to subject knowledge. The values have changed and our focus has moved to the surface from the centre. One, therefore, wonders as to whether we should revive the old values in our educational system for saving the nation from a total disaster.

Concept of Peace and Harmony

Before planning a comprehensive programme for peace education it is perhaps, logical to analyse the concept of peace. What is peace after all? Thus peace as a concept needs to be analysed with reference to the purpose. An operational definition of peace may be attempted for working out the procedure for establishing peace. To some, peace is something which is positive, it is not merely avoidance of war. Peace is based on love and caring for others, according to Mother Teresa. Peace is thus a complex and multidimensional concept. It has many components and correlates. It involves love and loving. In a sense, peace is a transcendental state of mind, a balanced mental frame with quiteness and tranquillity. It also entails a feeling of togetherness and co-existence, affinity and compassion.

There exists a relationship between peace, love, harmony and tranquillity. As mentioned earlier, peace is co-related to progress and advancement toward perfection. In spite of the apparent difference, an operational definition would be helpful for practical purpose. On an analysis of the dimensions of peace, we come to a comprehensive view of peace as an operational concept as follows:

(a) Peace as an internal and inherent mental frame or state.

(b) Peace as a dynamic concept involving interaction.

(c) Peace as a social and political concept implying cessation of hostilities.

(d) Peace as a passive state of non-violence and inaction.

(e) Peace as a concept opposed to war, aggressiveness and hatred.

Peace is, therefore, a complex concept implying love, tranquillity harmony, mutual understanding, respect and tolerance. It is something more than that. It is equivalent to love, harmony, a positive feeling of oneness with the spirit underlying creation.

Now the question arises as to how peace can be generated among people, if it is possible to transmit awareness of, and love for peace. It is, however, felt that man is by nature a lover of peace and harmony. At the same time, he is very easily subjected to emotion of hatred leading to violence. The dual forces of love and hatred, of peace and unrest, work within an individual as well as outside at the national and international levels. It is the task of education to conquer hatred by love, and unrest by peace. It has also been seen that much of the conflict emerges because of difference in perception. Deeper insight into human nature is possible as a result of love and respect for each individual. Understanding and tolerance are the conditions for creating a climate for peace. Thus the cognitive processes involved in peace needs to be recognised as well approach to peace education made. Stagner says, ''Peace is compatible with human nature and that is why very few people prefer war to peace. Behaviour is a difficult subject-matter not because it is accessible but because it is extremely complex. On the other hand, some ideo-affective factor which is clearly a matter, of human values colours our personal feelings, belief and attitude.

On an analysis of the various factors contributing to peace awareness we find that information processing approach to cognition proves effective towards behaviour modification. Much depends upon what kind of experience and information we provide to a child through curricular and co-curricular activities in a school setting. It may be helpful if we organize and re-organize the contents of history, geography, literature and even science in the direction of peace and harmony. The role of a teacher in interpreting facts and contents in the perspective of peace is very significant. Moreover, group discussions, seminars and debates can be significant. Moreover, group discussions, seminars and debates can be organised with a view to reinforcing the concept of peace in the mind of the youngsters. The teacher has a definite role and technique to follow in upholding the value of peace and harmony in the context of culture and humanity. The entire school environment should be conducive to the generation of peace and harmony.

The relationship between the staff-members and pupils should be exemplary and ideal so than it can stimulate desire for peace and love in every mind. Both at the beginning and close of every day school session a prayer and assembly for peace education may be introduced. There should also be regular assemblies for observing special days like human rights days, Buddha Jayanti, etc., to encourage the child to grow in the direction of peace and harmony. Similarly, both the staff members and students may be encouraged to organize exhibitions of paintings and sketches on peace. Moreover, special days may be allotted to community and social work to be done by students. Love, friendship, understanding and mutual respect should characterize the behaviour of both the students as well as the teachers. As mentioned earlier, a comprehensive programme of peace education should be drawn for the entire session so as to incorporate the various dimensions of peace and harmony.

It is thus possible to experiment with the techniques of generating peace among young pupils from the early stages of development. In spite of the importance of cognitive approach to peace education it is felt that the affective domain should also be tapped to reinforce love for peace and harmony in the young mind. Music has a special role in the task of arousing emotions conducive to the generation of peace. Moreover, the behavioural approach may also be attempted, although behaviour is a difficult subject-matter. In other words, behaviour modification has a tremendous scope in the various experiments which may be conducted for the purpose. Suitable environment, social, educational and cultural, may be created to foster the spirit of love and harmony among pupils. Happiness within is a must for social and emotional enrichment. Thus school as well as home should provide freedom, joy and stimulation for making a child happy. Many studies have demonstrated that substantial differences may occur in the behaviour of the same individual when they are in different situations.

For example, children in a democratic system of education grow more socially and emotionally than in an autocratic system. They should be encouraged to share and show concern for others in everyday life in school and outside school. Behavioural science has recently shown increased interest in shaping the environment and it is possible to make an elaborate experiment on behaviour modification. Perception is the process of becoming aware of an environment. Much depends upon how perception and thinking determine our attitude and action. Our perception of reality and environment is influenced by what and how we perceive. According to Skinner, behaviour is shaped and maintained by its consequences. The second result is that the environment can be manipulated in a number of ways.

Concept of National Integration

As discussed earlier, "National Integration" is the beginning of harmony and unity within people. It is essential to have a sense of identity pride and belongingness around the nation one is identified with. National integration demands one-ness a common aspiration and affinity. Motherland should be regarded as no less than mother. All the people belonging to the nation should live and love the country and culture and follow the ethics and principles, the philosophy and goals laid down.

Concluding Observations

A time has come when we should think anew of our educational policy. Although the world today is divided into so many nation states, defined more or less by geographical boundaries and historical traditions, yet people all over the world and human societies have by and large become internationally minded. Science and technology have reduced the distance between one part of the world and the other. An event at any place of the world has its impact on other parts of the world as well. The world has become an organic whole.

Mankind today is moving fast towards its formation of one world family and the people of one part of the world cannot remain indifferent to what is happening elsewhere.

We had previously a more or less settled society and a settled outlook. We formulated our educational policy with reference to our needs and the situation of our society. Our goal was to make our children good citizens who would be physically and mentally fit to move in the world and serve our society and our country well. It is not that these needs have been out of place now. But new responsibilities have been vested in us today and the world situation has changed to such an enormous extent that we are now required to revise the whole perspective.

We have experienced the devastations of two great world wars, and a third one is knocking at the door. It is sure that if a war is fought with the scientific knowledge in our possession, that will lead to an annihilation not only of human race, but of the whole civilisation built by the efforts of man for thousands of years. The national rulers of the world are totally indifferent to and oblivious of the great disaster of human race. Hence the great minds of the world are today crying for a halt to all conflicts and confrontations between nations and nations. We no longer want conflict, but co-operation, not war but peace, not discord, hatred and domination of one nation by another but complete harmony.

But all this requires a complete and total change in the outlook of man, a transformation of character and a sincere real respect for the values of universal brotherhood and unity of man irrespective of caste, creed, religion and geographical and ethnic division. Our children must be taught to be universal men who will break the walls of their social or national ego-centric existence and look upon humanity as tied together by the bonds of unity, justice and brotherhood. We are not educated in that manner, although we have been from time to time confessed about the goal of education. Let us then proceed in a different way. We have thought too much of our society, our state, our nation and, last but not the least, of our personal ends. We have been hardly worldlywise and practical to be fit for the future world. Let us teach our child that the welfare of his own person is not all, but the well-being of all man, is the goal of his life. Let us remove from his vision all considerations of caste, creed, society, nation and all that divide men geographically, historically, racially and ethnically into fragments. Let us teach our child not to look upon him as Asiatic or European or African and so on. Let him see the world, think for the world and work for the world. The rest will automatically follow. In other words, let there be an education for world peace and not for world war, for harmony and not for discord, for unity and not for division. It is thus that we shall be able to lay the foundation for a new world order and a new world culture, and this is Education for Peace.

12

EDUCATION FOR EMANCIPATION OF CREATIVE CONSCIOUSNESS AND INNER HARMONY

The Modern Orpheus

The modern man is nowhere. His identity — is lost in the doldrums of abstractions and routinised ambiguities, not because he is whipped within but because he is, to coin Rabindranath, 'a torn outline of verse' seeking frantically the strings of harmony within and seeking in vain. A look towards the self is a look towards the self-cemetery. A dead or a cactus land in the desert of desolation: What a modernity? With education continually receding from the worthwhile and invaluable objectives of finding out the man within man and paying for a continual harmony within oneself, the human habitation shamelessly shakes hands with horror and hypocrisy. And the consequence can very well be ascertained. The finer sensibilities and softer emotions of life continually bid farewell from humanity. The unending striving for making the world a very beautiful place to live in and let live others with mutual sympathy, fellow-feeling peace and harmony get a severe jolt only to be mimicried and infatuated with flatteries and affluences born out of the sham exhibitionism in the names of so-called scientific and technological excellences. Who denies that the marvels of civilisation are the endless endeavours for the inner harmony of mankind? The creative consciousness of each and every individual is the creative urge of the human soul. Can this urge be stifled in abstractions for ever? But then, the eternal cry within each and every individual to find out the best within him/her wither in the absence of askances in a self-styled prison of passivities. A modern orpheus, today's individual neither looks at askance for today, nor looks at the past with promises to keep for tomorrow, nor even does he, again, ponder over the possibilities of a better future to forge ahead in fervent hopes and aspirations. The wails within are tears to move nobody, not even himself. The wrinkles on the forehead are so fashioned and fabricated hats off to scientists and technological gadgets that they are no longer the indicators of an unhappy soul. Tears fall only to be soaked in the duststorms of cruelties of passivities that ignite the fellowmen to recede far and far away till he himself asks: Am I alive?

Objectives

At the outset it should be categorically asserted that at the backdrop of the aforesaid maladies of modernity where creative consciousness and inner harmony of individuality suffer from acute abstractions and passivities, the following objectives necessitate immediate attention:

(i) to cater in the diverse needs of the individual for enabling him to be equipped with the alertness for his own unique reactions to each and every item contributing to betterment of humanity and strengthening of inner harmony.

(ii) to enable every individual to foster the spirit of self-consciousness and self-creativity leading to enrichment of the human soul.

(iii) to identify and analyse the vulnerable areas of human activities that promote self-growth and self-analysis leading to emancipation of creative consciousness and inner harmony.

(iv) to foster the spirit of looking within and looking askance at one's own self so that it might be possible for one to find out the favourable or unfavourable areas of development of creative awareness and chalk out programmes of activities in accordance with the findings and observations however insignificant those might appear.

(v) to identify and manipulate the catchment areas of creative awareness that more often than not are not given any importance in the diffusion of a generalised stream of thoughts and activities affecting freedom to grow and freedom to be as one should be.

(vi) to look into an individual's peculiar avenues of creative consciousness so that identification, analysis and synthesis of the positive points of individual potentiality might be worthily and most satisfactorily geared to promotion of inner harmony.

(vii) to enkindle the spirit of inner worth of every individual in accordance with the felt needs and priorities to be given weightage.

(viii) to identify and analyse the abstractions and anomalies that stand in the way of efflorescence of an individual's creative sensibilities.

(ix) to enable an individual to suggest by himself the probable avenues of his own inner harmony however little it might be felt.

(x) to identify and analyse the operational avenues of an individual's creative consciousness and inner harmony.

The Perfume of Promise

The education that is of utmost importance for an individual is to grow within and to enrich the finer sensibilities and softer visions of life. The world as it is necessitates for him to develop deep into the wonderland of feelings and trends of thoughts that react most thrillingly with variations of imagery patterns. For this he requires self-training through a maintenance of balance and harmony of his reactions for different and diverse antecedents awaiting new and wider veils of efflorescence and emancipation. Perhaps herein lies the difference between man and man a difference that is the consequence of uniqueness that must, at all cost, be maintained and must be allowed to be nurtured and thrived as and when an individual desires according to his own whim and temperaments. The world of free discipline thus gets a wider perspective of emancipation.

And when, from the above viewpoint, education beckons a promise of self development and self activity, it also ensures the fact that all education is, in the end, an education for self consciousness self creativity and ceaseless pursuit for inner harmony. The awakening of creative consciousness is the green signal that an individual receives along with the operation of educational orientations taking place intrinsically or extrinsically. The only caution to be taken against anomalies in educational operations is to see whether the successive steps for self development and self-activity are really leading to a synchronized outcome of creative consciousness — a fact, also, sandwitched in and throttled up in a mess of multiplicites of scientific and technological bangs.

Admittedly, the man within man is lost in the melee of dittos and proxies. But who denies the boundless sky of the mind of an individual?

Who can step aside from the unparalleled awe and agonies of the human soul? The search for synchronization even in apparent balance and harmony is again, not the last world of human excellences to be so cheaply lost in happy-go statistical acrobatics of evaluation. The evaluation of man is directed towards eternal flight of birds of the perfumes of promise so characteristically remarked by Rabindranath. Agonies arrived at and experienced are agonies for betterment of 'I' — the ceaseless breaker of all norms of human potentiality and creative consciousness.

> This is my delight, thus to wait and watch
> at the wayside where shadow chases light
> and the rain comes in the wake of the summer.
>
> Messengers, with tidings from unknown
> skies, greet me and speed along the road,
> My heart is glad within, and the breath
> of the passing breeze is sweet.
>
> From dawn till dusk I sit here before
> my door, and I know that of a sudden the
> happy moment will arrive when I shall see.
>
> In the meanwhile I smile and I sing all
> along. In the meanwhile the air is filling
> with the perfume of promise.
>
> — Gitanjali [XLIV]

The sense of delight seeking deliverance from the routine-oriented craze of dutifulness awaits the beckonings of moments of newer ecstasies, the consciousness in creative thinking being thus ready for a newer journey to seek delight in the harmony within refreshed and re-enkindled for a better promise of performance. The aroma of excellence comes out of the blooming mind — the joy of the mind sailing through the sea of imaginations sweeping over the web of ideas.

The Education of 'Being'

The highest education awaiting emergence and inculcation of autology presupposes the heightening and endless re-orienting of creative consciousness and inner harmony. The cetasa must broaden and enlighten cidakas, the sky of the mind. For this the education of being, of self-identification, is yet to usher forth in brilliance and lustre. Perhaps education misinterprets science or vice versa but that is entirely an outcome of our camouflaged vision of life lost in living.

Meanwhile, the modern orpheus is frantically expectant of the notes of optimism. Why not allow him to look back within with the words of a great creative genius?

> The song that I am to sing remains unsung
> to this day.
> I have spent my days in stringing and in
> unstringing my instrument.
> The time has not come true, the words have
> not been rightly set: only there is the
> agony of wishing in my heart.
> The blossom has not opened: only the
> wind is sighing by.
>
> (Rabindranath Tagore: Gitanjali, xiii)

The following are the correletes of creative consciousness :

1. an attitude of 'live and let live';
2. respect for others' views and tolerance;
3. a conviction that 'all human being are equal'

   in addition to

   (a) general knowledge;

   (b) proficiency in the application of knowledge; and

   (c) critical thinking.

and other personality qualities. Now this is again the question of values which would determine the issue. The question will remain unanswered until the criterion in terms of value is fixed up. This will remain a controversy as will be evident from few observations. Sardar Panikar, formerly Vice-Chancellor of the University of Mysore, observed that the standard of education in the country had not fallen as alleged by some people, but had gone up, while Sri Prem Kripal has indirectly supported the hypothesis that our educational standards are falling at certain levels in certain respects. So far as standards at university level are concerned, the same controversy would persist. The problems may vary in dimensions, but fundamentally most of them are alike.

There are various dimensions of educational standard. The continuous change in the composition of various factors of education stands on the way of any sound comparison. Curriculum, teachers, methodology, evaluation, etc., are changing in a dynamic set-up. In spite of the fact that all the changes are affected for the sake of betterment of standards, there is a growing dissatisfaction with the present educational standard. It may be that this feeling is partly due to emotional attachment with the impression 'when we were young'. But is it the only reason?

There may be another possibility that the modern age has the highest demands on our education with the expanding frontiers of knowledge. In that case we will have to survey our various needs and evaluate the educational standard with reference to each of the needs forming the criteria.

This seems to be a better proposition. Instead of trying to compare standards at two different periods, it would be perhaps more worthwhile to investigate into our present emerging needs as well as outstanding values in life, and plan our educational programme to meet those adequately. It would be a wild goose chase, if we fail to control the variables of background before comparing on an objective basis. Whether our educational standards are falling or not, would thus remain a subjective and debatable question, unless adequate data could be collected and interpreted with scientific precision. There is, of course, a general consensus that we are gaining more and more in range and less and less in depth.

There is a strong feeling that students today are more informed and less thorough, more sensitive but less critical, more distracted and less concentrating or persistent.

So far as the values of life are concerned, the picture appears to be blurred by so many images. It appears that the present student population tends to be less introspective with varied interests, more pragmatic and confused and less interested in knowledge for the sake of knowledge. These are, however, some of the general impressions formed by a particular group of thinkers.

It is indeed a gratifying phenomenon that 'old order change the yielding place to new', but it reflects a fluctuating tendency. When one sits to examine the oft-quoted statement beginning with 'old is gold' on the one hand, and 'new is noble', on the other extreme, it leads us nowhere, if we merely continue to relish the past glory and condemn the new change. Similarly, it is equally stagnating if we close our eyes to the past and fail to evaluate the change with reference to the emerging values of life. The values of life are unfortunately at cross-roads. It is thus essential to determine the values in order of priority before undertaking any other exploration of this nature.

*Acknowledgement : Contributed by Sri Mohit Kumar Chakrabarty in the journal New Purfectives edited by the author.

13

EDUCATION FOR PEACE

"Wars start in the minds of men", declares the U.N. Charter. Therefore, peace is a state of mind. It is this state of mind which is claimed to be moulded by education. It is theoretically possible to have a state of mind full of peace even amidst the heat of war. This applies equally to individuals, communities, and nations. Conceptually peace is anti-war, anti-destruction. It is also a positive attitude without reference to war. Peace is anti-competition and pro-cooperation. This is the societal aspect of life. However, it is possible to retain a state of positive competition while pursuing excellence as is the case of the wrestler in a ring. They have nothing against each other. They are supposed to be fighting to prove the superiority of a particular style or approach to fighting. If this is extrapolated to all healthy competitions, any competition can be peaceful. However, a lot can be said of human mind conducive to peace for inculcating this attitude. What are the factors associated with peace? Who are the persons responsible for generating peace? These are some of the questions that bother the educationists today.

Peace has become a crucial issue in the present state of the world where the entire humanity is threatened with a total annihilation. It is said that at present there is so much stockpile of nuclear weapons that the world can be finished within minutes. The entire control of these weapons is also under the power of some individual nations. There is presently no indication of solution to this problem. Human efforts to bring down the mental state of aggression among those powers building up lethal weapons have not succeeded in such a manner that the planet can feel secure for even another hundred years.

The lesson for education for peace will have to be drawn from different sources. One of the most powerful source will certainly be the texts of different religions. Apart from their differences in details and approaches to life we can be sure that all religions were meant to help man's survival, to help inculcate the habit of loving other human beings rather than hating them and to strive for a better harmony and better spiritual contentment. If we forget that part of religions which indulged in conflicts by initiating competition with other religions and generating hatred and look at the basic messages of the religions, perhaps the scriptures and texts will tell us a different story. It should also be remembered that the texts written centuries earlier will have to be interpreted in the context of the present and immediate future. These interpretations will also have to be unbiased and devoid of selfishness or propagation of one ideology or the other. The validity of those portions of the texts which referred to the narrow concept of communities, taboos and customs at the time of their writing will have to be ignored. Admittedly this is going to be a difficult task and may require sophisticated team-work and conceptual philosophical exercises of the highest order. Fortunately, persons like Vivekananda, Rabindranath Tagore and Mahatma Gandhi had attempted to bring about integration of different religious thoughts in this country in the modern century. Earlier we find works of Guru Nanak, the Sufi saints and others which may be of great help.

The next part of the lesson will have to be drawn from the history of human cultures and civilizations. If one studies the causes of human conflicts and their consequences, it is likely that the significance and relevance of peace will be revealed. Obviously this cannot be done all at once. Neither is a human child capable of absorbing these messages of complex nature at an early stage. On the other hand, if the message is given through pedagogical principles gradually building up as the child grows, it will lead to greater maturity and real attitudinal development. The messages, of course, will have to be drawn from authentic sources and interpreted in an unbiased way, without any adverse remarks against any human community. This also requires a sophisticated conceptual exercise. This has also been fortunately interpreted by great thinkers like Toyenbee and Nehru. These interpretations can be easily built into the standard curriculum of history. It can also be discussed separately in the context of literature, philosophy and social studies.

Auxiliary sources like human geography, economics, anthropology and linguistics can be helpful in re-interpreting the causes and consequences of various fluctuating tendencies among different human societies. The insight into such past conflicts may help in preventing similar instances for similar issues. It is also likely that the learner would see the shallowness, of such conflicts. It requires the same unbiased objectivity as in the case of religion or history. Unfortunately such exercises have not been attempted directly. There may be many other sources from different social sciences which can be brought into consideration for studying such conflicts. At the same time stories of communities which have learnt to live in peace and have learnt to resolve conflicts nicely within themselves will have to be focussed.

Whenever one thinks of education one thinks of the teacher. The role of the teacher in education for peace will have to be delineated some what independent of the context of subject, matter and methods. When it is a question of bringing out attitudinal and emotional changes and not merely academic attainments, the teacher must learn to handle the emotions of his pupils, to adjudicate the conflicts among them. In the attitudinal plane, the human mind can be extremely sensitive. One careless statement or a slip may cause havoc in the pupil's mind. It is here that the significance of moral education reveals itself in the context for peace and harmony. Moral education aims at self disciplined orderliness in thought and restrain in emotions. The teacher should not only impart the above lessons from the religious texts, history and other auxiliary sources but also must be capable of showing both by examples and precepts the significance of such lessons.

The parents and members of the communities around the school are also equally responsible for shaping education for peace. One cannot have a peaceful educational institution admidst a non-peaceful society. One cannot imagine full success of education for peace without reinforcement from the community. Ideally this will call for a total social change. At the same time, we cannot wait for such a revolution before beginning our attempt for education for peace. The community is even slower than the child learning the lessons for peace. If the teacher changes his role as an organiser, as a perceiver and preceptor, then perhaps the community will start responding. Such ideal things have happened in this country when saints started teaching about life in their monasteries. While it is too much to expect saintliness from each teacher, a modest beginning among teachers will be quite rewarding. Apart from the role of the teacher, the environmental changes required for an atmosphere of peace within the school will have to be properly thought of. This may include changes in the cocurricular activities, portraying of great champions of peace, reading and discussion of their life and philosophies, etc. Education for peace will be a product of many processes and multi-dimensional endeavours.

In view of the factors discussed above a tentative model for education for peace may be presented. It is being proposed to add a few more factors into the model which have obvious significance for peace in education. The position of the person is central to the model because education purports to address only individuals and the effects on the community, society, nation and the world are supposed to be consequential. Peace, which is the consequence, is interlinked in the process. This simply means that it can be interpreted both as a process and a product.

A TENTATIVE MODEL FOR PEACE

Lessons from the Past

Education..........................

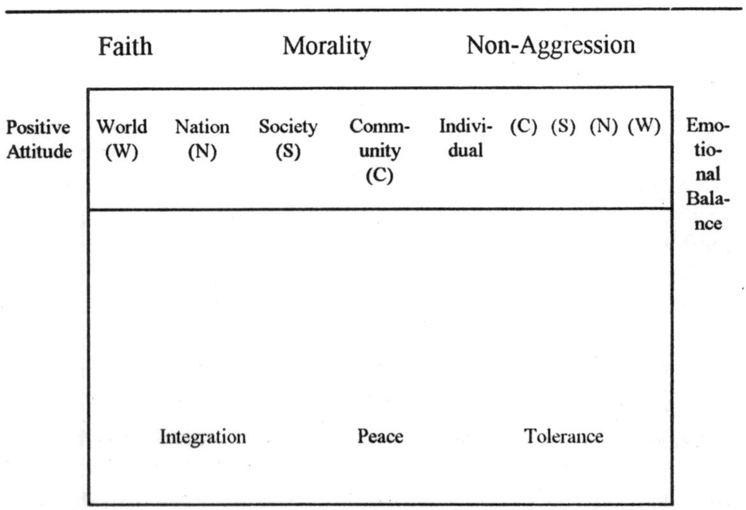

Education............................... Present awareness
Threats from Future

14

EDUCATION FOR HARMONY

Harmony is a coordinated and integrated progress towards the same goal. When the progress obeys a system helpful to the generation of relations and evolution of a higher order of integration it becomes harmony. In each aspect of life and life-function there are obviously many elements each of which changes. Where the change and rate of change of different elements obey the same rhythm they contribute towards the progress of the whole. They evolve a harmony.

Life in itself is an organismic function. It is a growth towards a higher order of relations with the different environments. Progress or growth is a change in two different ways. While one way of change is horizontal expansion of relations the other way is a change from a lower order to a higher order. Expansion in relations of the same order at any level is also diverse. It is a common observation that when a person becomes inclined to a set of specific relations he neglects the other aspects of relations. The balance in life-relations is lost. He gradually develops a maladjustment and progress comes to almost a stop. Life becomes a monotone, dull, mechanical existence. The cause is a loss of harmony. On the other hand if relations are multiplied at any level without an integration a disorder leading to a chaotic condition sets in and progress slows down.

When an attempt is made in evolving a higher order of integration without growth in all the aspects of life, integration fails. Progress in any one or more aspects of growth is possible but it does not lead to a stabler and more integrated life. Life becomes a void. The cause is again a loss of harmony.

Like the individual life social life is also a growth in two ways. One is the expansion of interpersonal and inter-group relations and the other is the progress of human civilization and culture from a lower order of integrated organisation to a higher order of integrated organisation of world society.

Interpersonal relations may take three different forms — a relation bringing the two together, a relation where the two move almost parallel to each other, each without any concern about the other and the third one moving away from the other. Symbolically if the first one is positive, the second one is zero or null and the third one is negative. The first set of interpersonal relations generates a cooperative society leading to social integration, while the third set generates a competitive society leading to social exploitation and disintegration, a sign of lack of harmony.

Without the evolution of a higher order of integrated organisation a gathering of persons functions without a specific goal. This again is the syndrome of a loss of social harmony.

Like all essential variables of life, harmony is also universal in distribution. No entity is found without the least harmony whether internal or external and no entity is possible in the fullest harmony with this word of substance. The second important characteristic is that lesser harmony can generate harmony through purposeful endeavour.

It is clear that greater harmony is manifested in two aspects of life both internal and external. Harmony in the external relations is manifested in organisation and harmony in internal relations is manifested in integration.

Harmony in external relations is evolved through the committed acceptance of a specific value-system or of value-systems similar to one another. Harmony in internal relations is evolved through a growth of the mind through its different phases.

A continuum of variation may be realised from disharmony to harmony through compromise. It is told that life is a set of compromises. Through compromise one can gradually move towards full harmony. It is also realised by intuitive realisers that Nature is moving through compromises towards harmony.

Education is claimed to be a process of purposeful interaction pointing to an immediate target and a remote goal. Even if the ultimate product of all interactions be realised to be harmony, a set of interactions may bring out a set of immediate products which retard the growth towards the ultimate.

Educational systems have been evolved in some cases with the immediate targets or objectives in view, in other cases keeping the ultimate in view. It has been found that even though these systems have proved to be effective in many respects, these have often failed to evolve a greater harmony.

Assuming harmony as a mental attribute or psychological organisation, manifested in behaviours the reverse has been postulated to be valid, viz., practice of a set of physical-physiological and mental-emotional behaviours lead to the development of a conceptual frame of behaviours and ultimately, generates a value-system in the individual. This system being stably established determines the motives underlying all behaviours internal and external, individual and social.

Thus it becomes imperative that a set of behavioural practices be determined which evolve from a value system which is in concordance with harmony. A programme may be set within a controlled environment to provide a sequential practice of behaviour synchronised with the natural growth.

Through the empirical reflective researches in psychology and education it has been found that cognition, concept, formation, evaluation, appreciation and creation are the hierarchical phases of growth functions. However hierarchical, they evolving in nature and as such in some form or other operate simultaneously. So in the education process, the scope for their functioning is to be provided. A two-way consideration with the accepted value-system of impersonal relations, growth and expansion both in time and space is useful for the development of the educational programme.

Age-grouping		Years			
Ed. function	0-3	3-6	6-10	10-14	14-12
Life needs behavioural					
Social Interaction					
Cognitive Development					
Appreciation Development					
Psychical Development					
Creative Development					

ENVIRONMENT — RESPONSIVE AND CO-OPERATIVE

A responsive environment is a constructed controlled environment where sufficient stimulus can be provided for the child to interact and respond. Where attention and scope is provided to respond to free and divergent stimuli from the child, where scope is provided for the child to share external stimulation, interaction, actions and responsibilities with co-operating adults. The adults are to seek co-operation from the child, utilize it and co-operate in their functions.

The programme is to be constructed in such a way that from the very beginning a harmonious growth is fostered through living a life based on harmony. The child is to be so habituated to a harmonious life that he can sense the lack of harmony, be dissatisfied, locate the causes of dissatisfaction and try to remove it.

The programme may be organised with the local resources available and so a stereotyped curriculum is not appropriate.

A system of evaluation may be inbuilt within the programme to assess the growth of each individual in each aspect. The evaluation is to be criterion-based instead of a norm-based one. The criteria are growth manifestations.

Teachers dedicated to the cause may gradually develop their competency. As a well-beaten path is not available, adequate and persisting research is to be carried on for evolving the alternate programmes on education as well as teacher-preparation.

15

EDUCATION FOR SURVIVAL

Man today is terribly confused and confronted with a number of problems. It is surprising that in modern society human beings no longer meet as friends or companions but solely in a field of struggle for power. As Margaret Mead remarks, "We have segregated the entire population into segments, into fragments so that no body has a whole experience. If this is reality, then indeed modern man is the poorest creature in the entire universe". In fact, very little is being accomplished with regard to the greatest problem of our day, the threat of nuclear war. Our survival is at stake and the possibility of annihilation of mankind is not very remote.

On a critical study of human conflicts it appears that war is in our blood as conflict lies in human nature. In spite of the bitter experiences of the past, we may not have learnt much from the history of mankind. Is it not strange that man has not yet been able to win over his inner nature, his frailties and frivolities although he has made remarkable progress in technology and science. The psychological forces still remain unconquered. Our education is causing knowledge explosion but not the integration of the propensities in human nature. An effective planning for avoiding the impending disaster demands education for survival, education for harmony and peace. It is obvious that the modern education is hardly balanced to contribute to the total growth of man. For reasons not far to seek, the cognitive area of human development is stressed. As a result, man is heading with a passion toward knowledge of facts and not the ultimate truth. Unfortunately, mere accumulation of information in various disciplines is receiving priority.

Even the knowledge of the method of science is not helping children much toward perception of absolute reality in human nature.

Indeed education has a great responsibility to provide the basic understanding of the world affairs as well as the reality we live in today. Advance in social sciences including education is yet to be made to strike at the very root of the problems around conflicts of all types. On the one hand, human aggression is to be accepted as a reality, while on the other, education has to be geared to the purpose of channelizing or sublimating our emotions. A study of the dynamics of hostility reveals that energy mobilization, if confined and unsuccessful to meet a challenge, tends to flow out into destructive channels. In this way the inner hostility affects and distorts perception through projection.

The purpose of this paper is to deliberate on the possibilities of engaging education and relevant techniques for developing every conceivable aspect related to the survival of mankind. No doubt, the problems facing mankind today are of varied dimensions which should be attacked in a number of ways both educationally as well as socially. Besides, the psychological approach to conflict resolution is relevant to the purpose.

Let us first concentrate on education as a tool for bringing the desired result, i.e., the survival of mankind from all kinds of disasters. As an agent of social change as well as a social control, education has tremendous potential to meet the challenges from physical, political, religious and socio-economic environment. Education, in all its perspectives, holds promise to cope with some of the vital issues concerning humanity today.

The various frontiers of knowledge have to be opened along with a vigorous attack on the inherent weakness of human nature. It would be, perhaps, relevant to mention here that a man's behaviour or even a group behaviour is determined not only by what he thinks but also what and how he feels. In other words, the affective domain has to be brought to bear upon the cognitive process underlying group behaviour. Moreover, the emotions which play vital roles behind human behaviour have to be handled properly for maximizing the role of perception and reasoning in the context of psychological reality.

It is possible to shape the attitude of human beings by reinforcing the perception, although it is difficult to handle the aggressive tendencies of human beings in an experimental way. It is experienced that an aggressive behaviour may be the outcome either of hatred or of expression of anger. Moreover, war has become a source of excitement, a liberating experience to many. In other words, the appeal of war is too profound to be neutralized by sensible arguments of rational men. Thus activities of war and international hostilities can be viewed as a series of inter-related paradoxes.

Education for harmony and peace depends upon the positive concept of peace. A desire for peace has to be generated in the minds of the people at large. In fact, various approaches may be made available not only for resolution of conflicts but also for creating a climate for peace and international understanding. Education in every sense of the term can be employed for promotion of human living and functioning.

Man has been intrigued by his own misdeeds and misjudgements resulting in the ecological imbalance and pollution of all kinds. It is rather strange that the technological and scientific education man is receiving to-day is at this stage of little help for his meaningful survival. It is tragic to go against the delicate balance in environment maintained by nature. Very little concern for harmony, happiness and humanity is shared by the nations and their leaders. Human nature is too complex to be manipulated in a planned direction. This is why the cognitive approach to survival of mankind is not proving very effective. In order to tap the functions and the unconscious domains guiding human behaviour, various methods and techniques are to be adopted. Of them the following deserves special mention:

1. Formulation of goals and objectives in terms of the well-being of mankind.

2. Developing educational programmes for betterment of world situation, self-fulfilment and social uplift.

The concept of survival of mankind is changing with the expanding horizon of human experience. It is not only the pollution of the environment or the ecological imbalance which is disturbing the present generation of man, the main threat of the catastrophe comes from the internal conflict within man, the basic contradictions in human nature. Thus we find conflicts and war at various levels over the globe at certain intervals. Besides, the natural resources are being over-exploited causing an imbalance in ecology. Similarly in the social context we find lots of unrest and tension, crimes and anti-social activities. These are the most outstanding menaces of man to-day. Survival of mankind is, therefore, dependent upon the remediation of the maladies described above.

The various dimensions of the survival problems are more conspicuous today than ever, mainly because of men's ignorance, indifferences and lack of concern. In addition, man has to learn from his mistakes about the drastic reaction of nature if over-exploited. It is thus imperative to educate people, specialists and readers to help them to ensure environmental protection and maintain ecological balance. With a view to promoting the understanding of environment in relation to man, a systematic programme should be developed. The approaches should be made in all directions including development of materials, tests and projects at all levels for generating the awareness of the need for protecting environment. Mass media of communication should be used for educating public in an informal way, so that steps are taken to prevent deforestation as well as air and water pollution. Some kind of attitude and outlook must be developed toward better living and harmonious functioning. As human mind is a frail instrument mere awareness and cognitive approach would be far from being effective. What is needed is the reinforcement of the balanced perception of reality and a zeal for meaningful life. In spite of the constant turmoils and havocs going on in the history of human race, Toynbee has expressed his optimism in the future of mankind when he says, "I believe that the human race is going to choose life and good, not death and evil". In spite of the inherent goodness within man the world today is being plundered and mishandled. It is the irrational man who is responsible for the present crisis.

In fact, problems will pile up until man will wake up to reality and start searching within him the reason for his failure to live together on earth with harmony and happiness. His quest will be primarily a moral quest seeking the foundation on which a morality for a new age can be established. It is not merely the lack of vision which is responsible for this crisis and confusion, it is the lack of determination and goodwill which is absolutely essential for a better world. One of the values of living in a transitional age i.e. an age of therapy, is that it forces the opportunity open for us to uncover new meaning in perennial man to see more deeply into his own nature.

As mentioned earlier, the approaches to all the problems enumerated before should be not only cognitive, they should be practical and experimental as well. Right from the very childhood, education should be oriented to the need for harmony and happiness for humanity at large. The educational programme should be drawn up to attack the various problems including confusion, intertia, prejudice and lack of proper attitude.

It is interesting to observe that people are not fully aware of the direction in which they are going and it is likely that they will awaken when it is too late and when the fate has been irrevocably sealed. Yet the history of man is, however, a history of growing awareness and, in spite of the tragic disproportion between intellect and emotion in our society today, man is perhaps at the beginning of the process of discovery of his limits and limitations.

It is indeed uncertain as to whether the destructive power which his present knowledge has given him will permit him to improve his life-style for peace and harmony or whether he will destroy himself before he can build up a fuller picture of reality on the present foundation. Man has not only his head, he has also the heart. The reason why he is mysterious is that in his nature lies a bundle of paradoxes. He is individual yet, social, unified yet diversified, complete yet incomplete. He finds meaning through cognition, yet he is often guided by his emotions. Margaret Mead asks a very pertinent question with deep concern for mankind, "Are we trapped, not by a set of innumerable instincts which determine that we will in all cases turn to aggression and exploitation of others when we are strong enough?" She suggests a very realistic and at the same time dispassionate solution by saying that one of the essential elements in escape from an infinitely greater threat is the willingness to acknowledge that our knowhow, is not enough.

On a critical study of the forces behind the problem of human survival, it would appear that the most outstanding problem is that of perception and perspective. They are important because without the right type of perception our knowledge of the entire perspective of man is failing to meet the challenge of his survival. His added knowledge of science and technology in isolation is not helping him much to live happily together on this beautiful planet.

It is, however, paradoxical to think that the civilized man of this scientific age is hopelessly dabbling into politics, pollution and prejudice.

Is it not a tragedy that man is standing at the place he was at the beginning, helpless and trapped by psychological barriers. On the one hand, he is trying to win over the challenges of nature, while on the other he is ruining the delicate balance prevailing in nature by his adamant spirit of exploitation. In fact, his knowledge of matter is not adequate as his ignorance of the art of harmonizing the matter with the spirit of nature is colossal.

As suggested in the *Unesco* publication (No. 22) on "Education for International Understanding'', in teacher-education the importance of adding a global perspective to various studies is emphasized. For example, science would deal with global concerns like disarmament, pollution and diminishing resources such as oil, farm-lands and water. Other subjects like the social studies would consider and evaluate national and international efforts to deal with such problems. Thus curriculum should be developed in an integrated manner to deal with the problem of human survival and teachers should learn to direct the subject knowledge to the relevant ends. In other words, catering information should not be the only goal of education. Both teachers and students be made aware of the need for processing and interpreting the information in the context of human survival. Besides instructional methods, creative teaching should be introduced at all levels to generate the sensitivity and awareness needed in each area as well as to challenge the creativity, imagination and resourcefulness of the learners. For example, children of various ages may be encouraged to make artistic presentation of their perception of peace, ecological balance and use or misuse of energy. Paintings and art-work, depicting the outcome of war or abuse of natural resources as well as pollution may have impact on the mass-consciousness. Films, slides, radio or television broadcast and other innovative materials may be effective for creating a suitable climate for reinforcing perception and attitude formation. Obviously simultaneous attacks should be made at both the cognitive and affective levels for directing appropriate behaviour for survival of mankind.

Particularly in teacher-education programme attempt should be made to create and strengthen programmes, designed to promote international education by creating favourable conditions with materials, organisation and support-measures; appropriate to the task. Besides the institutionalized programmes, the following may be organised for orientation to the basic issue for human survival:

(a) Regular courses for cross-cultural studies in different subject areas.

(b) Frequent exchange of visits, study-tours, etc.

(c) Organisation of seminars on different topics around human survival.

(d) Organizing regular radio and broadcasting programmes on different cultures and various issues including environmental protection, use and abuse of natural resources as well as various types of energy.

(e) Intensive research on the modalities of perception of physical, social and cultural environment in international context.

(f) Organising international exhibition for displaying the various art materials including painting, sketches, sculpture, music or poetry for creating impact on the affective domain.

(g) Manipulating human resources for focussing on the relevant issues even by using mass-media or audio-visual materials.

Regarding the problems of disarmament, it has been found that a feeling of insecurity and fear, stands on the way to the sincere effort for arms reduction. While one speaks of disarmament, nuclear weapons pile up. A lack of mutual trust and confidence always hinders any progress towards peace. It is extremely difficult to get rid of the distrust and apprehensions for generating a climate conductive to peace. Various types of experiments may be conducted for exploring the possibility of reduction of distrust and fear. Even therapeutic measures are recommended for the leaders to help them in coming out of the paranoid state of mind.

Experimental approaches have been made to explore the possibility of arousing typical emotions by means of specific stimuli or a combination of them. It has been observed that in most cases fear and a feeling of insecurity lead to aggressive designs, resulting in attrocities. With a view to generating the trust and confidence, the basic feeling of security should be instilled not by accumulation of destructive weapons but through psychological methods of interaction. It is very often observed that real war starts after the psychological warfare for a while. Either ego or pride and prejudice provoke warfare and hostilities at every level.

In conclusion, it can be said that human survival demands the potential to face the challenges of life as well as man's capacity for manipulation of environmental resources with a definite purpose in view. In every case there are problems both organisational as well as human. And the task of education is to offer the key to the solution of those problems. In the real sense of the term education has manifold functions including planning and programming in the right direction.

The fate of the world rests on two assumptions:

1. That carefully selected man will retain cool judgement during an intense conflict; and

2. That even if one man fails others will act as a 'fail-safe' device.

It is, however, doubtful if these assumptions are correct in all contexts. Many of our social problems today may not reach easy solutions. Nevertheless a science of peace has to be developed for solving our current social problems by way of scientific psychology and analysis.

Education for living in harmony with happiness for humanity is the top priority today.

REFERENCES

1. Angell, Norman, *The Great Illusion*, New York, G. P. Pitmans, 1813.
2. Berkowit, Leonard, *Roots of Aggression*, New York, Atherton Press, 1955.
3. Boulding, K. F., *Peace and the War Industry*, Chicago, Aldine Publishing Co., 1971.
4. Bhattacharya, S., *Dynamics of Human Emotions and World Peace*, Book Land, Calcutta, 1972.
5. Delhers, K. H., *Conflict Measurement by the Dynamic Calculus Model and its Application to Clinical Practice*, Multivariate Research, Special Issue, 1968.
6. Mead, Margaret, *Culture and Commitment*, New York, Doubleday and Co., 1970.
7. Nityaswarupanand, Swami, *School of World Civilization*, Calcutta R. K. Mission, 1967.
8. Rogers, C. R. and Steavens, Barry, *Person to Person*, California, Real Press, 1967.
9. Skinner, B. F., *Beyond Freedom and Dignity*, New York, Bantam Books, 1971.
10. Stangner, Ross, *Psychological Aspects of International Conflict*, California, Brooks/ Cole Publishing Co., 1969.
11. Bhattacharya S., *Long Road to Peace*, Vantage Press, 1977.
12. Bhattacharya S., *Peace and War*, Liberty Press, Michegon U.S.A.

16

EDUCATION FOR INTERNATIONAL UNDERSTANDING

Education has been considered as an effective means for bringing any change in the attitude, skill and behaviour of people. It has been regarded as a social control by Butrand Russel.

The world today is in the grip of transition. As it is shrinking every day, the entire human family has to learn to live in harmony and peace.

Education for international understanding has become for human survival.

Nothing can save mankind from total disaster unless a peace climate is created and the leaders can be influenced in formulating a policy of disarmament.

This is not an easy task and attempts are being made certain quarters to create a world opinion against war.

There are of course long term preventive measures and more constructive steps to ensure peace and harmony in the world. The most effective way is to generate a desire for peace and harmony at every level in the Society.

There are various approaches to peace education and more peace studies are needed to discover effective ways to handle human conflicts at all levels.

Promotion of International understanding is one of those describing special mention.

UNESCO's attempt to promote international understanding at schools through education may be mentioned in this connection.

There are even recommendations to start fostering the spirit of harmony and peace among children at the Primary and pre-primary level.

Children are our future hope. Montessori has rightly said, "Establishing peace is the work of education". The child in her view, is to be seen as a "Savior capable of regenerating the human race and society"

Besides, the rapid extension or the various forms of mass communication, seems to bring education a new dimension. Mass communication tends to reinforce common symbolic systems, to enrich, re-express and re-interpret them. The school must share its monopoly of education with the Institution responsible for communication.

The impact of educational action of the media on cognitive development or behaviour is obvious.

Much depends upon the psychological intellectual, social and cultural conditions of the individuals exposed to them. From this point of view, interpretation of the non-formal education of the media is undergoing the same change as thinking on education.

Emphasis is to be laid on the role of interpersonal relations and the influence of the values.

There has been discourse and discussion on the emergence of a new man whom this new environment could in varying degrees fashion from day to day. The emotional contexts and his habits of reasoning, his critical attitudes and imagination, his technical skills and behaviour are to be taken into account.

Up until the beginning of this century, the functions of the school and those of the family have been considered very important, although the growing presence of communication in most Societies raise the question of re-appraisal of the function of the School.

Some pragmatists hold that the communication media should purveys contemporary knowledge, while education should be responsible for passing on the heritage accumulated by tradition.

Thus the school and the communication as a system should supplement each other in carrying out their responsibilities for promotion of international understanding.

The schools at all levels should think in terms of education of children to help them to love and live in harmony and peace to understand and respect other cultures and to become a worthy citizen of the world.

The role of the schools is changing considerably with the changing time. Education for survival is the top most priority. The schools as well as other institutes of culture should develop the programmes, curricular and co-curricular according to the basic needs for human survival.

Need for Peace Education and Peace Studies in Indian Context:—

With a view to promoting peace education in India, a comprehensive Programme has to be set up for attacking the different demensions of peace education.

Accordingly, attempts are being made by the author of this paper to establish an Association or Society for Peace Education in India to set up Programme of activities as follows:

1. To promote Peace Studies in India.
2. To disseminate Peace Education in the Community.
3. To instill Peace and International understanding in the minds of School going Children.
4. To set up a model child development institute for experimentation and approaches to peace education.

Conclusion

The concept of Peace is multi-dimensional. It has implications and applications much wider than anticipated, that peace is within may be realized in any individuals life through harmony.

It may be cultivated and generated at various levels including individual and group, national and international.

In the present decade the entire humanity is threatened with the probability of a nuclear war. Behind this, lies, ignorance and prejudice, intolerance and hatred.

With a view to establishing peace at all levels both preventive and curative measures, have to be adopted. A strong faith in peace and harmony, an urge for international understanding should be instilled in the minds of the people including children, our future hope.

There is also a scope for research on the nature of materials to be used and techniques applied for peace-education.

The general aim of establishing this association is to generate and promote peace, harmony and international understanding at various levels.

With a view to formulating specific objectives of Peace Education for International Understanding an advisory committee has been set up.

Besides, an executive committee will be set up for suggesting ways and means for translating those specific objectives already formulated by the advisory committee.

The executive committee will include noted educationists in various State Organisations. Heads of the Institutions and experts in the area of peace education.

The specific objectives tentatively set would be to :

1. Encourage peace-studies in India by setting up a clearing house of information in specific areas and providing guide-lines for research on various issues.
2. Creating a forum for exchange of ideas in peace education by organising study circles seminars etc.
3. Setting up channels and mass media for dissemination of information on various cultures, lands and people.
4. Setting up a model child development institute for experimentation on the techniques of installing and generating peace and international understanding.
5. Publishing a News bulletin and quarterly dedicated to Peace Education.

The journal will be in the form of a quarterly with an editorial Board. Papers will be invited on different issues from people involved in peace research and relevant studies.

"At the time, when the world seems to have lost its reason, it seemed essential to give our *Children* the opportunity of considering *Peace*" as an issue which is relevant to them.

We can hardly afford the luxury of treating childhood as a time for play.

It is our aim to teach them to assume responsibility for their future, to preserve the natural beauty of their own surroundings and to establish values of friendship, tolerance compassion and harmony as a way of living. It is then the time to learn:

(a) To communicate with the rest of the world.

(b) To live side by side in a spirit of friendship and respect for others, regardless of colour, customs or language.

(c) To increase the Sensitivity to beauty truth and goodness from early childhood and understanding.

Thus, basic concept of peace and harmony has to be instilled in the mind of the children in their own way:

Example

* Peace is when we all love one another because we are all the same.
* Peace is friendship — when no body fights.
* Peace is light—peace is happiness.

UIESCO Circular No. 42 (1981) — International Understanding at School p-29.

It is one of goals to buildup a Peace movement, in the Young generation.

PART III

PSYCHOLOGICAL FOUNDATION OF EDUCATION

1

INTRODUCTION

The Psychological Foundation of Education is obviously a very significant section for studying the interaction between psychology and education. Child psychology deals with the mental structure and function of a child. Psychology provides the bricks and mortar for laying the foundation of education on a scientific basis. It has much to offer for raising the status of education as a social science.

As described in the following pages, Psychology deals with instincts and emotions, abilities and interest, individual differences and personality. There bearing on education is of vital importance to the parents, teachers and social workers.

One has to see what psychology contributes to education and education offers to psychology. The bearning of one on the other has to be considered for making the study of this foundation meaningful.

The present decade has focussed on experimentation in the field of learning and teaching in the perspective of behavioural sciences.

PSYCHOLOGY AND EDUCATION : AN INTRODUCTION

Psychology is a growing subject. It is a developing science extending its branches in different spheres.

One of the important functions of psychology today is to offer guidance of various types on the basis of individual differences. There are many approaches to the study of an individual and very recently emphasis has been shifted from ability testing to the study of personality as a whole. As a result, various techniques of personality measurement have been evolved.

It is obvious that any research in psychology today demands an objective analysis of data. With a view to arriving at certain dependable conclusions, statistics has become an indispensable tool.

In spite of the suggested techniques for analysis of data various problems often arise in the field of investigation.

The modern tendency is, therefore, to develop such statistical tools as to eliminate the element of subjective judgement entering so much into its operation. Wringley (1956) has focussed attention upon these limitations of factor analysis and has discussed the prospect of a further analysis named as quartimax analysis.

Another chapter has been opened by psychologists of the day and that is on social psychology. The importance of this branch of psychology is being increasingly felt.

The methods of modern psychology are essentially those of natural science. It is improper perhaps to advocate a divorce between psychology and natural science on the ground of differences in method. The question, therefore, arises, "Is there any method of formulating mind and consciousness so that their study may be brought more fully within the orbit of the natural sciences ?"

Challenge to experimental psychology has to be accepted and a middle course found. A psychologist should accept in principle the practical demands which the community makes upon him. But there is no assurance that every challenge will lead to a quick solution. Truth is not always found by those who seek it. Some time it emerges almost by accident. The new and vital challenges of study may bring with them a new spirit of urgency and reality. Every challenge comes with a risk, no doubt.

MODERN TRENDS IN PSYCHOLOGY AND EDUCATION

Psychology today has its challenges from the contemporary world of social sciences. The primary aim of psychological science is to understand human nature. The secondary aim is to serve society. It is probable that the psychologist, who works in the social field will be confronted with a number of challenges. Obviously psychology at present is yet incapable of solving a few human and social problems.

We see an increasing concern with the problems of mind and consciousness today. A marked development of research in the area of social psychology is observed in view of the new challenges. As a science of behaviour and experience psychology has a wider scope of application than before. The study of human behaviour in groups is a recent development and is, confronted with a number of problems.

There are certain typical issues involved in psychological study. In most cases psychology as a growing science has to depend mainly on observations. This is unsatisfactory because of the subjective nature of observation as a technique. Nevertheless, this technique cannot be done away with unless a relatively objective method is evolved. Psychology today has extended its scope and assumed a responsible task of discovering new laws and principles. It has also been extended to the classroom situation, in the field of industry and medicine.

EDUCATIONAL PSYCHOLOGY AS A SCIENCE

Educational psychology may be thought of a science with two main points of references human behaviour and education. It is concerned with behavioural questions that are related to the objectives and practices of education. The domain of psychology is rather broad, ranging from the study of the collective behaviour of human beings, to individual differences.

The methods of science are often employed in a systematic fashion and some techniques for applying the knowledge to practical ends in educational settings are used by educational psychology.

The following questions should be answered by an educational psychologist today :

1. How are children's abilities, knowledge and effective characteristics related to objectives of education ?
2. How does knowledge of learning process and theories contribute to more efficient learning and teaching ?
3. How do characteristics of the learner effect his readiness to learn and efficiency of learning ?
4. How do characteristics of the teacher affect pupil learning?
5. How do the behaviours of the teacher and the student affect efficiency of learning ?

New horizons in educational psychology are, thus inviting the attention of the educationists and psychologists.

The contribution of educational psychology may be broken down into two related categories :

(a) Educational psychology as a body of information and an avenue of research activity can help in the generation of educational hypothesis.

(b) It also helps to formulate hypotheses for particular purposes.

Educational psychology contributes a lot to the area of teacning and learning as well as a behavioural science applied in the class-room situation. Its main contribution lies in the understanding of the pupils as well as developing systematic programmes, according to the potentials and needs of the pupils and the community. As a growing science it has a lot more to offer in building hypothesis around the interaction between human factors involved in education. As a source of information it helps the teacher to come to right decision on the basis of what he knows about individual difference. Educational psychology has a definite role in providing insight into the processes of learning and teaching as well as the knowledge of group dynamics for underlying each learning situation. In essence, psychology as a science promotes action researches among teachers in classroom situation by way of helping them to form intelligent Hypothesis.

Thus Educational psychology is the application of psychological findings in the field of Education. It is obviously an applied discipline trying to combine the two different areas viz., psychology and Education. In a school situation the teacher has not only to know the subject, he has to know the pupils and their personality and problems as well. Besides, he has to know the developmental characteristics of the learner in addition to his individual differences. Moreover, as a teacher he needs to develop appropriate methods of teaching for meeting the individual differences. Psychology of Education helps the teacher to probe into and develop skills for effective functioning. In addition to the tasks mentioned before, the teacher has to function as an evaluator for measuring the outcome of his teaching. Thus, the various roles and functions of a teacher are facilitated by his knowledge and application of Educational psychology. In short, educational psychology provides a frame-work for looking at the learner, the learning process and the learning situation together. Teaching is thus based upon mastery of three areas :-

(a) Knowledge and concept,

(b) Teaching skills, and

(c) Decision-making skills.

The knowledge of Educational psychology helps a teacher to be more aware of class room behaviour, to interpret the significance of such behaviour and to plan purposeful strategy for bringing the desired changes in the pupils' behaviour. In other words. a major role of

Educational psychology is to make assumptions about the conditions that facilitate learning and to collect data for testing the hypothesis.

As mentioned earlier, a teacher has not only to teach, he has to make decision. Successful teachers hold realistic attitude towards students. They have to inspire and make decision in formulating effective methods for reaching the strategies. Psychology of Education orients a teacher to form the strategies as well as provides the skill to reach them.

To day we find most of the class rooms crowded and disorganised. He is perplexed with a number of challenges. It is not easy for him to solve the problems beyond his control. In most cases the syllabus is unwieldy and the students are not motivated. Moreover, there is a lot of unrest among the younger generation leading to anti-social activities. The knowledge of psychology of Education helps a teacher to meet some to these challenges.

NEW HORIZON IN EDUCATIONAL PSYCHOLOGY

The psychological foundation of education can hardly be ignored because of its relevance to teaching, learning as well as teacher's functioning. Recently the psychological approach to the class-room problems has been considered superior to other approaches. Particularly the behaviouristic model has been recognised and recommended today. The need for considering teaching as a behaviour involving communication and skill is acknowledged. Thus psychology of education is expected to provide insight into the area of pupil's behaviour and learning process. Books on educational psychology are opening new frontiers for dealing with intricate problems of motivation and group interactions. Today experiments are being conducted in the area of group dynamics for explaining certain complex behaviour patterns leading to indiscipline and unrest among students. Moreover, the social and emotional problems in the class-room are receiving attention of the psychologists. In fact, new areas of education and psychology are showing up with their varied dimensions. The teacher is not only a giver of information, he is an explorer and experimentor applying his knowledge of psychology in practical field of learning and teaching.

New experimentations are being carried on educational technology as well. This includes technology of teaching as well as programmed instruction. By educational technology the behaviourists put forward the following concept. It is a systematic application of scientific knowledge about teaching, learning and conditions of learning to improve the efficiency of teaching and training. Thus teaching has been considered as a science and attempt has been made to analyse the process of teaching with reference to various components. Various strategies have been developed for improving the approach to stimulate a learner at the memory, understanding and reflecting levels.

Another extension of the horizon of educational psychology is programmed instruction. Although skinner's operant conditioning is the basis of this new approach, various experimentations have been made for developing remedial programmes in the areas of learning.

It is interesting to note that a confusion still exists around what should be the scope of educational psychology. The traditional approach was to deal with the psychology of individual differences and theories of learning separately without discussing the educational implications and their relevance to or application in the educational setting. Only recently attempts are being made for an integrated approach so that the methods and principles of psychology are projected in the actual classroom situation. Emphasis is being laid on the role of teachers and analysis of teaching for making a realistic approach to education. Various new dimensions have been added to dynamics of student behaviour for facilitating the understanding of the needs and problems.

In the area of educational psychology an integrated approach is being attempted by synthesizing the teaching learning process in the perspective of teacher's function. This approach has gone a long way in making educational psychology more meaningful and relevant to a practising teacher. Behaviouristic and applied psychology is gaining more grounds, while simple pedagogy with its theories is losing ground.

2

SOME BASIC FACTORS

SENSATION AND PERCEPTION

Senses are the gateways to learning. We get our experience through sensation. Our sense organs are the windows of the soul. We derive our knowledge of the reality with the help of the five sense organs which respond typically to different stimuli. We become conscious of the various aspects of reality through our sensation. A sensation is a response when some sense organ is stimulated. Every sense organ has the capacity to be stimulated in response to a kind of stimulus. Our eyes respond at the sight of an object while our ears help us to hear a sound (stimulus)

There are branches or endings of sensory neurons within each sense organ which help to arouse the excitement and pass it on to the central nervous system. A sensation is a response or reaction aroused in us by the stimulus. This is an act of the sense organ which sends nerve currents to the sensory centres of the brain. It is the first response of the brain but the activity of the nerve cells at the sense organ does not by itself constitute the sensation. It involves an elementary mental process as well.

Each sense organ has its own set of neurons which are connected with a particular part of the brain or spinal chord. The type of stimulus to which every sense organ is adapted to respond is called the appropriate stimulus.

It is apparent that external objects impinge upon our sense organs and arouse sensation. We only receive the impressions without acting. Thus a sensation depends upon the brain response, the activity of sensory cells and nerves but less on the stimulus.

Many of our organic sensations are stimulated from within while a number of stimuli is external. For example hunger and thirst are our organic sensations stimulated from within.

Perception is sensation plus meaning. It involves sensation and an interpretation of the sensation. We sense qualities like colours sound, taste, smell etc. while perception interprets them as objects. The two processes involved in perception standout in our day to day experience.

The congnitive functioning of the mind makes perception complete. Our thought and interpretation, our experience and analysis contribute to the perceptual process.

Sensation and perception are both important for the purpose of education. The child gains experience and knowledge through the sense organs, no doubt, but his real knowledge of the reality and its perspectives is the outcome of perception. In short, sense perception makes a person conscious of the object and its meaning. The fusion of various sense qualities which are presented together in consciousness constitute the elements of meaning. Thus perception motivates more than a combination of sensations. According to the Gestalt view the total structure patterns of configuration come into play for forming perception. An experience of the totality or unalyzable whole is the keynote to perception. Mind works as a whole and responds to the whole situation. The awareness of the relation steps between the parts comprising the whole and brings the total perception. Each of our perceptions is a unique configuration pattern of relationships.

Perceptional Development in Children

Perception varies as the product of varied experiences. Children differ in forming impressions around the same stimulus because of different interpretation. The children's perceptions obviously differ from those of adults.

The child has experience and his sense organs can hardly perceive qualities and things of relationship. Childhood is described as a period of confusion. Every stimulus including colour, sound and shape remains vague and indefinite. The differentiation is slow and gradual. Children's perception are less analytical as they lack attention to details. Secondly the child needs to have a stronger stimulus to form a perception than an adult. Only bright things or sounds are perceived by him if repeated.

Perception is thus a process of "taking in". It is a mental assimilation of a new presentation. The stock of ideas and the stored experience form the perceptive mass which differs with different individuals. Sense training has been emphasized by Montessori as an effective method of child development. Sensory experience contributes to perceptual development which aims to cultivate observation. Observation implies thinking and ideas and depends on imagination, reasoning or sense perception.

Perception and Personality

Personality depends mainly on how one perceives himself and his environment. Self knowledge has been rightly emphasized in the upanishads as much depends upon ones relationship with the world around him. The relationship is congenial and conducive if ones perception about himself is happy and healthy.

Education helps to form perception in oneself in relation to reality. If the reality orientation is positive and strong there is every chance of happiness.

A healthy attitude is the outcome of positive perception of reality and relationship.

A balanced healthy educational programme is needed most in education to day.

INSTINCTS AND EMOTIONS

Instinct is a native behaviour. It is an innate disposition, a tendency to respond in a particular way to specific stimuli. McDongall defined instinct as an innate disposition which determines an organism to perceive or pay attention to any object of a certain class and to experience in its presence a certain emotional excitement which finds expression in a specific mode of behaviour in relation to that object.

There are certain characteristics of Instincts as follows :

(1) Instinctive behaviour is innate or native and not acquired or learnt.

(2) It is more a tendency to act or behave in a particular way.

(3) Instincts are universal.

(4) They do not imply any foresight of a useful end although they tend toward the well being of species.

(5) Instinctive responses are capable of modification, adaptation and development.

(6) Lastly, Instinct has its period of appearance, maturity and weakening.

Mr. Dongall believes that every instinct is connected with a specific emotion. He offers the following list :

Instinct	Emotion	Instinct	Emotion
Escape	Fear	Food seeking	Craving for food
Combat	Anger	Appeal	Distress
Repulsion	Disgust	Laughter	Amusement
Curiosity	Wonder		
Parental Instinct	Tender Emotion		
Construction	Feeling of creativeness.		
Acquisition	Feeling of ownership		
Gregariousness	Feeling of togetherness		
Reproduction	Lust		
Self assertain	Elation		
Self Abasenment	Subjection		

While the individual grows he shows various tendencies to satisfy his basic needs.

The children break and build, fear and escape, collect and construct, assert or gets depressed.

The instincts are called specific tendencies which are aroused in definite concrete situations. Besides, there are some specific innate tendencies like play, imitation, suggestion and sympathy. Tensley classifies instincts into three heads, the individual instincts, the social instincts and the sex instinct.

According to Mc Dongall instinct has cognitive affective and conative element. In an instinctive behaviours an individual knows, feels and acts with regard to a particular situation. While Jung suggested three primary instincts of nutrition, sex and heard, Thorndike defined instinct as unlearnt behaviour and left out its emotional aspect.

On a critical analysis one can find a close relation between needs, drive and motives. There are needs for food, protection and physical satisfaction. There are other needs which are less obvious but not less important.

The term 'drive' is also used in the same sense for energy or action which can be modified or affected by different factors or situations.

Instincts their Modification or Sublimation

Instincts can be modified adapted and developed in a variety of ways. Sublimation is the process involving the transformation of the basic instincts into socially approved channels.

For example, the instinct of combat or fighting may be redirected against poverty and ignorance. Similarly the instinct of curiosity may be used for motivating people toward research and experimentation. Similarly the sex instinct may be employed for creative and artistic purposes including poetry, sculpture etc.

All human behaviour arises from some urge or drive. Some of the drives are primitive but they may be modified. Besides, drives, there are social urges and motives. These motives are affected by factors like rewards and punishments.

In view of the complexity of the operation of human drives or motives behind behaviour, a controversy persists around the Theory of Instinct.

The present outlook is shifting from Instinct to needs and propensities. Yet one can not ignore the influence of some innate dispositions or human functioning.

Role of Education of Modifying Instinctive Behaviour

Man is known for his capacity to meet the challenge of the irrational tendencies in him. He has been able to get over some of his primitive tendencies for better adjustment of life and society. His education and experience, his will and determination help him to make the best of the Instincts or emotions he had been endowed with.

Cognition helps man to analyse his strength and weakness for practical purpose. The cognitive domain has thus gained prominence in human behaviour although the role of affective domain is hard to ignore.

Behind every behaviour thinking and feeling work together to determine the mode of operation. As man attains maturity he gains insight into his own nature and control over his impulses. Education helps man to refine his behaviour by modifying instincts.

It is strange that the modern age is encouraging primitive and Instinctive behaviour in spite of the technological advance. Man is learning to conquer nature. He has been making miraculous advance in medical science and space technology but yielding to the basic and primitive instincts of combat and sexuality.

The instincts of the children are not difficult to observe in their everyday life. They show their unending curiosity to know every thing in detail and test the patience of the parents and teachers. It is the duty of the teacher and parents to satisfy their curiosity as far as possible and encourage them to know more about things he comes across.

Similarly the instinct of collection is very dominant among most of the children who show their tendency to hoard things like pebbles, shells, seeds, or even tirifling objects. Trivial things have so dominant an appeal among some children that they irritate the adults by dumping rooms with things of no values to adults. The parents and teachers should respect the children's interest and instinct and treat them sympathetically. They should not offend the children by throwing them away or devaluate the objects they collect with care.

Another dominant instinct among children is the tendency to play. It goes without saying that childhood is the play age. The parents should on no account deprive them of this valuable opportunity to gain satisfaction through play and initiations. The children learn through their parents or adults they observe.

The school and its role in handling the instincts of the children helps children to grow. There must be enough scope for joy and freedom, creative activities and socialisation through schooling.

A rich variety of activity programmes should be introduced in day to day timetable of a Centre for child development. Children should learn through experience, exploration and experiment with joy and freedom.

Teachers should act as friends, philosophers and guides to every child. They should share their experience and joy with the children.

In conclusion, we may say the interest and emotions are the basic elements of personality. As teachers, parents and well wishers we have to be sensitive to the needs, instincts and problems of the children, Sublimation is the most satisfactory way of dealing with instinctive urges. It neither represses them nor gives them a free scope of expression. It is an effective and reconstructive method of utilizing the modes of behaviour. A good and progressive school organizes a variety of co-curricular activities and creates opportunities for recreation through games, dramatics, music and other healthy outlets.

An effective administrator should provide, leadership and guidance to his staff members in helping the children to grow spontaneously.

HABITS AND HABIT-FORMATION

We form habits for reducing stress and strain through practice. Any action which needs much effort and attention at the initial stage gradually becomes easier and less time consuming.

They become automatic and spontaneous through repetition.

Some of the characteristics of habits may be enumerated as follows :

(a) Habit is acquired through repetition in thinking and acting in the same way a number of times which makes the thought and action a part of the habit.

(b) Habit when acquired, does not require any effort and attention.

(c) It becomes automatic and almost mechanical.

(d) Habit facilitates any kind of action through frequent exercise.

Any habit once formed takes time to change. For example anyone who is used to eat rice and curry with finger and hand takes time to change.

Any men used to eating with hand and finger takes sometime to use knife and fork for eating. The modification of the habit takes place gradually as a result of repetition and frequent practices.

They Psychologists offer a different explanation of habit. They assume the role of nervous system when the current flows from one nerve centre to another. They refar to channel or path created or prepared between the two points as a result of the stimulation.

The habitual response, is made as regularly as the reflection or the instinctive tendency. Habitual and instinctive actions are psychical and conscious. They are mental phenomena.

One of the advantages of the formation of habits is the economy of physical energy. The performance of habitual action costs little or no effort. In short :

(a) Habit reduces fatigue. For example on the first day of typing one needs more effort than on subsequent days.

(b) Habit makes movements simpler

(c) Habits make our movements more accurate

(d) Habits ensure greater speed

In spite of the advantages of habit formation, habit is not without its limitations. It is mechanical stereotyped and is not adaptable to new situations. It is the mechanising tendency of habit which is hardly appreciated by many. As habit is considered to be opposed to intelligent behaviour, no fixed habit should be formed. It has been rightly said that the best habit is to have no habit.

It is difficult to escape the bondage of habits. Habits kill feeling, and make us insensitive to what may concern us most.

The Role of Habit in Life

Habit have definite role in life as they contribute to health, happiness and efficiency in course of experience. A man develops industriousness through habit, he may also become lazy as a result of his aversion to work. Similarly this honesty and sincerity, shyness or open mindidness depends upon his habit. Even the attitude and outlook depend upon how he spends his early days. Whatever we do, or think tends to become habitual.

In fact, every individual is a bundle of habits. Many believe that childhood is a formative period when good habits are to be formed.

Regularity, punctuality, industriousness, honesty are some of the good habits to be inculcated in early and late childhood.

Similarly social habits, good taste and positive attitudes to life may be developed during later years.

It has been seen that a nation prospers because of good work habits of the people or a community suffers because of bad habits, laziness, addiction and lack of cleanliness. Food habits also influence health and life style. The primitive life styles are examples which show lack of progress and prosperity of the community.

In short, the influence of habit can not be ignored and it is difficult to live without habit. Some how we tend to form habit as a result of practice and continuity of our routine activities.

Every home and school should, therefore, try to inculcate certain fundamental healthy habits during the formative period.

3

INDIVIDUAL DIFFERENCES

In spite of the controversies about learning and other aspects of behaviour, a number of important psychological principles may be widely used by a teacher with confidence. They are, on (a) nature-nurture, (b) learning process, (c) maturation and learning and (d) Individual differences and their implications. The personality of each individual is unique and knowledge of the differences in intelligence, skills, interest, attitude and personality is indeed helpful to a teacher.

The concept of differentiation has been widely used in psychology and the degree of differentiation appears to be an important characteristic of the structure of human abilities. Individual differences have been recognized in early days mainly because of the need for selection and guidance. Thus problem of differentiation remains still unexplored in spite of various attempts to analyse the structure of human abilities and personality. It is rather difficult to analyse the structure of human abilities. It is difficult to say whether the differences in the individual in respect of a particular behaviour or functioning, can be attributed to heredity or environment. As such Individuals vary in personality which is unique. Thus, the differences may be accounted for with reference to personality variables. There are cognitive and affective domains which determine one's perception and feeling and these differences are observed almost in every sphere of functioning. Apart from abilities or capacities, people vary to a bewildering extent in respect of their perception and judgment, attitudes and temperament. Emphasis has so far been laid on the differences in abilities and skills. It is of course, very difficult to represent a person by means of a single index, because all the integrated aspects of an individual's personality are the outcome of a complex process of interaction between the inner propensities and external forces. Scientific doctrines of human abilities and differences are also not in agreement with the popular opinion, that all persons fall into distinct types:

Biological Basis of Personality differences

Individuals develop the peculiarities that they show. The so-called laws of heredity, the extraordinary resemblances and difference between parents and offsprings, all these depend largely on the arrangement and behaviour of the genes, the knowledge of this biological factor is essential to an understanding of the physical aspects of personality. In the light of the present knowledge, it is difficult to predict the inheritance of men, including his physical characteristics. Yet some individuals speak of the transmission of such complicated and culturally influenced factors as mental ability, temperament and attitudes. No one has yet demonstrated the presence of 'genes', controlling intellectual ability or personality characteristics.

The mechanics of inheritance although mapped out are still regarded as too complex to be analysed in full. The general principle of inheritance is that, children resemble their parents and that like begets like. The individual differences of the children even in the same family can be explained to some extent by the principle of variation. As a matter of fact, the germ cells contain different genes which combine in different ways and the permutations and combinations can be varied to bring out the individual differences. Heredity as a source of a variation, may be a very important factor, but this is not all. Numberous studies into the pedigrees of eminent people have clearly indicated that eminence and mental deficiency tend to go hand in hand in families. But this is no clear guidance of the exclusive influences of heredity on individual differences. Systematic studies of correlation between blood-relationship and abilities bring out results which vary from investigation to investigation. It has been found out that in the case of identical twins the correlations come to .8 to .9. In the case of fraternal twins they come to .65 to .70. It is also interesting to note that the correlation between parents and children comes to .40 to .45 and that between grandparents and grand-children comes to .10 to .20. The above result be speaks the scope for variation between individuals even related through common ancestry. Besides, the variation within the people of same heredity, there is another source of variation which is known as environment.

Individual Difference—Their Implication

The hereditarians maintain that education can hardly increase capacity and they also point out that natural difference would find expression regardless of the amount of formal education. The environmentalist, on the other hand, reiterate that the greatest part of individual differences is attributable to discrepancies in cultural and educational opportunities. The present view-point is that of interaction which simply means that both nature and nurture interact in any individual's development. Heredity does not operate in a vacuum. This principle of interaction indicates that nature sets the limits of individual development in regard to various psychological functions but nurture is no less important in determining the extent to which the potentialities shall be developed and the direction in which they should be utilized. Several studies have been conducted on the impact of environment on individual differences. The following concluding observations have been submitted. In the case of fraternal twins, the median coefficient is approximately .70 indicating the influence of both heredity and environment, while in the case of indentical twins, the correlation is .85, showing the importance of heredity alone. Thus, the same kind of nature-nurture inter-relationships have been found in most of the investigations.

There are other sources of variation like race and nationality, sex and age. It is a fact that there are certain racial characteristics which explain to a limited extent the relationship between race and individual differences. Studies have been conducted on the relative positions of the various culture groups on intelligence scale and it has been seen that the difference is not too significant to be attributable to the race or nationality alone. There is hardly any evidence of any national superiority in mental abilities, although the differences can be better explained in terms of environment and environmental variation. In fact, the individual differences are so wide even in the same context that the difference due to race or nationality is nothing much significant.

As regards the other factors supposed to contribute to individual differences, sex, age and health deserve special mention. Studies have been carried out and very little evidence has been obtained in favour of the hypothesis of the woman's inferiority in general intelligence. There are of course, sex differences in specific traits and the females have been found to be superior to males in linguistic ability and in tests of memory. Males have been found to be superior to females in mechanical ability and manual performance. But such studies appear to be superficial because most of the disparities are attributable to cultural influences and motivational factors working in individuals.

Psychological basis of Individual Differences

The analytical approach to individual differences emphasises the concept of differentiation to a great extent. It is assumed that the structure of human abilities and personality can be explained in terms of specific characteristics and traits. Various attempts have been made to account for the individual differences with reference to human abilities. Thustone's concept of primary ability has put forward a challenging notion of differentiation.

Burt has of course, attempted to take a middle course by presenting the theory of hierarchical structure of abilities while the U.S.E.F. investigation has found out as many as ten specific factors underlying this structure of human abilities. A few have pointed out some broad categories of factors like sensory and perceptual for taking into account the multi-dimensional nature of intellectual functioning. It is however to be admitted that the whole system of human functioning is interwoven to such an extent that it is difficult to isolate them in a limited framework. Individual differences, may also be observed in the personality structure. In other words, besides that cognitive differences, there are differences at the temperamental level. It is thus necessary to account for these differences in the affective domain and discover the relationship if any, between the two sectors. With the growing complexity of the science of psychology differentiation is emphasised more and more for practical purposes of selection and allocation. Yet one has to judge with an open mind if this is realistic or purely theoretical as a concept.

Sociological basis

The sociological basis of individual differences has gained much prominence in recent years. Among sociological factors which are considered to be very much important, cultural environment and social heredity deserve mention. The role of the home and group life in the development of personality has also been recognized. Thus this is a great concern for the educationists today.

Structure of Human Abilities

Attempts have been made to unfold the mysteries around human abilities. Theories of intelligence have been put forward by Spearman, Thorndike, Kelly and others accordingly.

Spearman and his followers had to modify the "Two factor Theory" to incorporate at least a few "Group Factors" which were supposed to be broader than the specific factor but less broad than "g" Thorndike suggests that there are three different types of intelligence viz., (a) abstract, (b) social, and (c) mechanical. He also stated that there are three dimensions of our intellectual activities including (i) aptitude, (ii) speed, and (iii) range or width.

Kelly in 1927 claimed to have established the three types of intelligence, namely (i) verbal, (ii) quantitative, and (iii) spatial. These three types of intelligence were shown by him as being independent of each other. Thus, in terms of Spearman's Theory, individuals would be found to differ in respect of only one type of intelligence, i.e. general intelligence. Thus the assessment of general intelligence may lead to the prediction of one's future attainments at least in the normal sphere of work. But in terms of Thorndike's or Kelly's finding there are three different types of intelligence in respect of which individuals may be found to differ. In other words, we have to investigate on the distinction between types, as follows:-

Abstract, Social and Mechanical } According to Thorndike

Verbal, Quantitative and Spatial } According to Kelly

The work of Stephenson and Spearman's "Two Factor Theory" showed that over and above "g" there was at least one broad group factor of a verbal nature. His analysis, however, did not preclude the existence of another broad grouping related to tests of only non-verbal character. Cox suggested of a factor (mechanical aptitude) after his experimental study on mechanical and routine assembly operations.

Koussy established "k" factor (space perception) found present in certain non verbal tests

Burt stated that the practical factor (F) was probably of a composite nature differentiating later on, in the course of a child's development, into two sub-factors, visuo-spatial (K) and mechanical (M), the former again maturing earlier than the latter.

In short, according to the English School of thought, all the factors, in addition to the general factor "g" should be regarded as so many broad 'group factors.' Then came Thurstone with his test of seven primary mental abilities viz.

Spatial ability, perceptual speed, numerical ability, verbal ability, word fluency, memory and response.

These abilities are primary as they are basic to any functioning of an individual and independent in the sense that they can enter separately or jointly into any functioning of an individual.

Another group of psychometricians headed by Thompson would hesitate to approve any of the above theories as they encourage minimising the number of common factors. They advocated another theory, viz. 'The Sampling Theory of Ability', which would attempt to explain all individual functioning in terms of interactions between innumerable traits or factors. Fleming nearly describes the last view when she says, "Mind is a rich, comparatively undifferentiated complex of innumerable influences."

The recent developments in factor analysis have, no doubt, influenced the concept of intelligence. Spearman in his later life recognised existence of a few broad group factors in addition to the "g" or general mental ability, while Thurstone in his subsequent findings recognised the existence of a second order "g" factor over and above his primary mental abilities. Many recent factorial studies show specific factor loadings in multiple and group factors after they have been rotated. The real difference between these views lies in the mode of approach and in the attitude towards the solution. While Thurstone and his followers would maximise the importance of primary abilities and minimise that of the second order "g" factor, Spearman's followers would do almost the reverse. In the American field of psychometry the list of factors representing primary abilities or aptitudes has continually expanded.

A set of factors or groupings has been shown to be fairly well established in the frequently used tests of abilities, as follows:-

(a) Verbal Comprehension

(b) Numerical Ability

(c) Abstract Reasoning

(d) Perceptual Speed

(e) Word Fluency

(f) Rote Memory

(g) Spatial Ability

(h) Mechanical Ability

(i) Musical Ability

(j) Artistic Ability and a few psychomotor factors like finger-dexterity, psychomotor co-ordination, etc.

Burt, after a thorough survey of the experimental work, suggested a hierarchical structure of human abilities consisting of the following successive levels:—

(a) General Intelligence, (b) Relation, (c) Association, (d) Perception, and (e) Sensation.

Burt's picture would look perhaps like the one below:-

(a) "g", the comprehensive general factor covering all cognitive abilities.

(b) Broader groupings on the higher relation level, e.g. apprehension of relations, aesthetic processes, etc.

(c) Broad group factors on the intermediate associative level covering different activities classified according to their form or content, e.g. memory, productive association, etc.

(d) Narrower factors at the 'perception' level.

(e) Factors at the sensation level.

The whole series would thus appear to be arranged at successive levels, the factors at the lowest level being the most specific.

Vernon seems to follow the middle of the road. According to him, the following structure would perhaps represent the intellectual and practical factors in psychological tests:

(a) "g" (general mental abilities)

(b) V:ed group and k:m group factors

(c) V:ed group subdivided into rote memory, verbal ability, etc., and k:m group subdivided into mechanical information, physical, aesthetic ability, psychomotor co-ordination, spatial ability, etc.

(d) Sub-division of the broad factors of the above category into narrower sub-factors.

(e) Crosscutting the two main groups of v:ed and k:m there are in addition a few more factors which may be described as belonging to 'speed' group.

When we look at both the American and British sets of psychological factors, we find that quite a number of them are common. The difference lies in the mode of approach. In one, these factors are treated as being more or less independent of each other, while in the other they are shown to form certain broad groupings in a connected whole.

A general outline of the realm of human abilities cannot be drawn unless the elements out of which the mind in compounded are discovered. We cannot hope to make successful predictions about an individual child until we know every side of his make-up. As Ahmavaara has put it: "All the possibilities created by the new differential method cannot presumably be seen as yet; a theoretical all-round picture is only beginning to take shape and connections between its different parts are still to be found. The methods are still very much in a state of evolution.

Besides the highly complex and controversial issue of identifying and naming the factors, we should note that all these factors *should bc regarded primarily as categories for classifying mental and behavioural performances, rather than as entities in the mind or nervous system.

The findings of factorial research have, no doubt, important educational and vocational bearings. But opinions differ in regard to the usefulness of having test programmes of this or that type. It is being increasingly felt that educational and vocational guidance among adolescents is extremely difficult.

Individual Difference and attainment

The recent developments in psychology are more concerned with individual differences than with similarities. This is perhaps the outcome of a keen attempt at analysing human abilities and personality for the sake of selection and guidance. It is, however, strange that we are still confronted with the problem of mapping out the total personality of an individual in respect of its component parts. The psychometricians are optimistic on the future of such a thorough search for finding out all the individual differences. They have come to a general agreement in respect of structure of human abilities after a long pursuit. Intelligence has been regarded to occupy a pivotal place in the field. In spite of slight differences of opinion regarding the classification of intelligence, the nature and the function of this general ability has been accepted.

Three broad categories of intelligence have been identified in British school children at the time of entering secondary schools. Verbal, numerical and spatial abilities have been recognised as factors of intelligence, with their bearing on allocation of children. It is only recently that definite doubt has been expressed on the efficacy of the intelligence test in solving the allocation problem. This gesture leads to another controversial issue viz. what are the individual differences to be taken into account for the purpose of allocation? For a long time there was a tendency towards including personality qualities for a better prediction. But no systematic attempt has been made to enlist them on the basis of research evidence.

It appears that the British psychology clings to the traditional notion of accepting prima facie the human abilities more than dispositions for such purposes. Thus, aptitudes have been preferred to interest as a factor for determining one's course or vocation. The aptitude tests prepared for the purpose shows satisfactory results and they are being widely used at the moment for selection purposes. It is, however, accepted that the aptitudes involve some amount of ability and skill together with one inclination towards a specific area. Sporadic efforts reveal some amount of satisfaction as to the predictive value of aptitude tests particularly in science and technical courses. Mc Clelland's work supports the basis of selection by means of intelligence tests and at the same time hints at the possibility of including other tests for the purpose. Peel, Lambert and others confirmed that aptitude for technical drawing, etc., can be predicted by tests.

Peel points out that individuals differ widely in school attainments with respect both to quality and quantity. These attainments are the products of complex causes, viz. abilities, interests and opportunities. Feleming also observes, "neither the ability testing nor the aptitude testing have encouraged a belief in the possibility of exact prediction of the divisibility of human beings into discrete types."

In fact, there exists a large number of unknown variables influencing attainments. Vernon also assumes that personality factors like persistence, industriousness and interest contribute much towards one's success in almost all branches of learning.

The National Foundation of Educational Research, England in their first interim report of 1950 emphasised the need for identifying and assessing some of the non-examinable qualities of character and disposition. There are others like Himmelweit and Powell who stressed the importance of other characteristics such as ambition, speed and tendency to accuracy etc. Sanders also corroborates the previous result and refers to personality qualities and habits as important factors.

It would be thus clear that the individuals differ in various respects and a very few of them have till now received proper attention of the psychologists. Unfortunately, the problem of assessment of these qualities is so intricate that one would feel diffident in one's attempt to assess them accurately.

Very recently in his 'intelligence and attainment test,' Vernon has made a thorough survey of the present position of the intelligence test and pointed out the suitability of those tests for the purpose of any kind of selection. At the same time he has admitted with an open mind the limitation of these tests when he invites the attention to other factors like interest, relevant experience and opportunities, home background, physical strength and personality qualities.

Concluding Observation

No two persons are alike. If this be true, our interest would naturally be to find out the individual differences. In what respects do we differ from one another? In fact, human beings differ in many respects from one another. Abilities and aptitudes, vary from person to person apart from other factors.

What do we mean by abilities? Do they mean certain capacities or endowments with which people carry out their functions? Yes, human mind is made of a variety of potentialities and is too complex to be analysed. Also human mind functions at various levels of thinking, feeling (cognition, affection and conation).

The complex nature of human abilities has not been doubted. As a matter of fact, a wide range of capacities comprises the structure of human abilities. One may have a strong memory but a very poor reasoning. This indicates that our capacities are too diverse to be accounted for. For a systematic approach to this analysis psychologists have assumed that every individual has some fundamental power of adjustment to the outside environment. This power is known as the central ability or general ability. This is also known as intelligence in a broad sense of the term.

This term is, no doubt, very vague as it has various shades of meaning. Intelligence has been described in many ways. To a number of psychologists, intelligence is the capacity for abstraction. Here emphasis has been laid on the "Cognitive' aspect of mental ability, i.e. thinking and perceiving capacity. To some, intelligence is the power of problem solving while the capacity for reasoning has also been identified with intelligence by a few.

4

INTELLIGENCE AND ITS MEASUREMENTS —A Review

After a long search for a suitable definition of intelligence it has been established that it is the general ability which is manifest at various levels. It is like electricity which we find in every day use but which we can not determine.

It is really difficult to define intelligence. This is because of the complex nature of intelligence. The word intelligence goes back to Aristotle who tried to distinguish the emotional and moral functions from the cognitive and intellectual functions of our mind. Since then the structure of the mind has been questioned and the structural theories viewed and reviewed.

Various attempts to define intelligence have been made from different angles, viz. (a) the biological, (b) the psychological, and (c) the operational.

Charles Darwin and Herbert Spencer made the biological approach and pointed out the complexity of the higher brain centres and their bearing on the behaviour. According to this school of thought, intelligence has been regarded as an inherent capacity for profiting by experience, adaptation to environment and ability to learn.

Lloyd Morgan, Mc Dougall and Binet belong to this school. This approach to the definition of intelligence is not very acceptable for various reasons.

The biological conception in its original form refers to the modifiability of behaviour with increasing flexibility, which our intelligence test can hardly measure. Moreover, a follow-up study might give rise to a sceptical view of this approach because adaptation to the physical and social environment does not always indicate high intelligence or vice versa. Thus the term need be defined from various other angles, in order to explain the complexity of our behaviour in relation to environment. According to faculty psychology, our mind is composed of a number of major faculties, viz. knowing, feeling and willing. This faculty school went on extending their domain and included gradually various other powers of mind. Intelligence as a concept gradually developed and the question arose as to whether intelligence can be treated as a unitary faculty of the mind. As a corrolary, a second question arose: Is intelligence inborn or innate? Is it inherited from our ancestors or is it partly or wholly dependent on upbringing and education.

These questions have not been finally answered as yet, because intelligence is still an abstraction. It is only a mysterious, complex set of interpretations of "g". Rex Knight also supports Spearman by defining intelligence as the capacity for relational constructive thinking directed to the attainment of some end. Thorndike's attempt to reduce intelligence to the number of associations also deserves mention. It will be observed that psychological concepts of intelligence are being evolved out of confusion with a view to measuring intelligence in all its aspects. The most striking feature of these views is that all the functions overlap considerably and point to a general factor, difficult to be ignored. The different factors revealed by various mental tests constructed so far perhaps give out some partial aspects of intelligence. The theories of mental structure have been formulated by psychologists and various experimental approaches taken for identifying these factors.

Spearman's two factors theory recognised at last a dominant general ability accompanied by an amount of specific abilities, but the simple theory of hierarchy demonstrating generality did not explain the nature of the general factor of intelligence. Thomson pointed out this tendency towards over simplification expressed in Spearman's two factor theory. This is known as a sampling theory evolved by Thomson indicating the relativity of any general factor and any set of specific factors. These facts still await further exploration as neither the two factor theory helps to solve the problem of vocation or educational guidance calling for special aptitudes, nor the group factors of Thomson do account much of the variance of the test results. This controversy over general group and specific factors gave rise to Burt's concept of hierarchical organisation of mind based on the specific sensory-motor activities and tried to explain the mysteries underlying the concept of intelligence. In America a further development of the concept of intelligence was claimed by Thurstone. He challenged the overriding influence of a general factor of intelligence on all mental activities and discovered several primary group factors better known as "primary abilities."

It is thus clear that mere theoretical discussions about the nature of intelligence do not lead us anywhere. This is why Vernon has taken an operational approach to intelligence. He has dismissed the long-standing controversy by clarifying that intelligence is what intelligence tests measure. He supports his claim by an analogy. He says, "We can measure electricity without being able to define its precise nature and can put that to practical usage". He has gone further by saying that it is more consistent with the statistical evidence to think of intelligence as a fluid collection of abilities comprising the whole of mental life. It is a kind of average which cannot be pinned down to any single mental faculty, either by psychological or mental analysis. In his opinion the best definition we can give is rather simple, non-specific one such as all-round thinking capacities, or mental efficiency or general mental ability.

The Changing Concept of Intelligence

In recent years concepts of intelligence have undergone considerable changes. Hebb's neurological explanations are somewhat speculative, though he casts doubt on Gestalt psychologist's claim in explaining the intellectual behaviour of an infant through stages. An important feature of Hebb's view is that most perceptual schemata must be acquired at a suitable time, if further mental development is to be possible. Piaget also describes the stages and builds the sensory-motor schemata or patterns of response to external stimuli. He insists that intelligence is not one distinctive faculty nor can it be reduced to such. It is present in all adaptations of every living being. Behaviour in his opinion, becomes progressively more intelligent and the mental function more complex. It is thus a developmental concept of intelligences recently put forward by both Hebb and Piaget, influencing the modern views on intelligence.

Vernon classifies intelligence under three categories, viz, intelligence A, intelligence B, and intelligence C. Intelligence A is hypothetical only as we cannot directly observe or measure the genetic potentiality known as intelligence A. Intelligence B indicating the present mental efficiency represents the cognitive abilities developed in relation to suitable environmental stimulation. Intelligence C indicates the operational concepts of intelligence and is a later development.

Several significant points emerge from the discussion on these various concepts of intelligence. It has been clear that intelligence which can be observed in daily life or which is measured by tests should not be identified with the pure inborn natural capacity. If it were true that intelligence tests results depended almost wholly on innate ability, the I.Q. would be expected to remain constant throughout life. But unfortunately, a fluctuation has come to the notice of the psychologists in the I.Qs. under different circumstances. It has been seen that the effects of coaching and practice on intelligence tests brings out certain differences in I.Q. The effects of coaching, of course, seem to fade more rapidly than those of practice. Fortunately enough the fluctuation caused by either of the two is almost insignificant. It has also been observed that the home background has certain bearings on intelligence. It is really difficult to come to a definite conclusion as to the degree of the relative influence of heredity and environment on intelligence. It has been admitted, however, that the environment affects the child's intelligence to a certain extent. Burt's method of analysis yields a somewhat higher weight to heredity. In short, intelligence may be regarded as a product of both heredity and environment, though there may be some conflict regarding the relative weight of hereditary and environmental contribution.

Intelligence and Environment

Vernon in his book on Intelligence and cultural environment says. "It is the product of nature and nurture. In his opinion Intelligence test is no more than a sample of the kinds of skills we regard as intelligent. While intelligence A and Intelligence B refer to the genetic equipment and to the phenotype, there is another type of Intelligence which is non-genetic or rather acquire. Vernon adds Intelligence C to Hebb's dichotomy to indicate or refer to test-results as Intelligence. In 1951 the UNESCO consultants made the following concluding observation:-

"The Scientific evidence indicates that the range of mental capacities in all ethnic groups is so much the same. But Vernon does not entirely agree to this generalization. In this connection he comments "What they should have added is—there is no proof that innate mental differences do not exist."

Intelligence and its Measurement

What actually constitutes intelligence is a matter of controversy on which all psychologists do not seem to agree. In the beginning of this century, Stern defined it as the general ability by which a person can adjust his thinking to meet new requirements. Intelligence was thus a sort of master-key which is able to open, or atleast try to open the lock of all difficulties. Perhaps this fitted well with his theory of general factor of intelligence, for he held that a person's intelligence is able to work in every field. Patterson gave the corresponding behaviourists' definition, namely, a biological mechanism for integrating stimuli and producing adequate and unified response. It is really Stern's definition stated in other words. Terman who revised Binet's intelligence tests, thus working in verbal fields, defined intelligence as the capacity for abstract thinking. Wechsler, who worked with performance type of experiments, would define it as an ability to see through spatial (space) relationships. Perhaps, Colvin's definition as an ability to learn and adjust oneself to his environment seems a bit more impressive. We thus find intelligence being defined by some as general capacity to meet all situations as given by Stern, Patterson or Colvin, or as abilities in some specific areas, be it abstract as in the case of Terman or merely spatial as in the case of Wechsler. Thorndike would go to the other extreme denying its existence in any general field whatsoever and would admit only special abilities in specific fields. According to him, any comparison of general intelligence of a skilled computer, an expert mechanist, and a clever artist is impossible, for they have shown their abilities in various specific fields. Spearman would try to find a via media by admitting a general or common factor, which means an ability to meet difficulties of all sorts, whatever they may be, as well as a specific factor which means skills in several areas. Modern educators would, perhaps, improve upon this ideas by admitting that these specific skills again have two or more subdivisions. Abilities of a similar nature may be considered partly linked together and partly peculiar and isolated. They, would like to introduce group factors in intelligence and introduce what is known as the hierarchical theory of Parry, Vernon and Burt.

In the midst of so many conflicting definitions, it will perhaps be better if we try to find certain common qualities that are associated with the term intelligence. In the first place, it is a dynamic quality, namely a capacity to act. This action, of course, may not be visible in the shape of performance. It may be confined entirely in the realm of thinking, but is nevertheless directed to solve a difficulty, or to remove a certain obstruction. Secondly, it seems to be an innate capacity. Environment can develop it or make latent intelligence manifest, but environment can not produce intelligence within the person. Thirdly, though it helps us to accumulate knowledge, it should not be confused with knowledge itself. A person who has amassed a lot of knowledge may not necessarily be intelligent, he may not be able to adjust himself in a definite and novel situation, though perhaps the knowledge amassed may help him to find out a way some time. Fourthly, it should not be confused with such talents like memory or mechanical skill for both of these can be improved with practice, while intelligence is unaffected by practice. Lastly, though intelligence is one of the attributes of personality, yet there seems to be some distinction between what we call personality and what we call intelligence. Personality, has a distinct physical component. We can at the first sight pick out a person with a fine personality, and though with our later acquaintance we may not find him so attractive, yet our first favourable impression about him does not entirely die out. Personality, moreover, measures motivation, feelings, emotions, attitudes or interests, besides intelligence which merely measures efficiency or reactions.

The seat of intelligence is again a point of controversy. Psychologists of the last century held brain as the seat of intelligence and considered the size of the brain as a measure of intelligence. When it was found out that eminent writers like Anatole France, a Nobel Prize winner had a remarkably small size of brain, this theory was disproved. Modern psychologists have also failed to trace to what extent is quickness of reaction connected with intelligence. While skilled mechanists have generally a short reaction time, it has been seen that a clever artist or sometimes a novelist has a remarkable slow reaction time, and he takes more time to press the button in a Reaction Time Apparatus. Moreover, the rate of increase in the Reaction Time seems to be much more rapid than the so-called decline in intelligence, even when the intelligence is measured in the field of performance.

The modern theory of parry, Vernon and Brown would place intelligence at four distinct levels. At the base there is the strong undercurrent of General Intelligence which helps us to adjust ourselves into any new situation. Also are found major groups of abilities: Linguistic (Verbal), Quantitative (numerical), Ability to see space relationship (Spatial) and Ability to act (kinesthetic). Each of these abilities in turn may be subdivided into minor groups branching off into several specific capacities. While we have so far considered intelligence from a structural point of view, we may as well try to see it from a functional point of view. He has found three major components of intelligence namely:-

(a) An abstract capacity which helps us to deal with symbols, no matter whether these symbols refer to language or to quantities.

(b) Concrete capacity which helps us to deal with space relationships, as well as the ability to perform.

(c) Social capacity which helps us to deal with our social environment and gives us the ability to mix with other people. Shy and introvert persons if they are otherwise intelligent, will naturally give a good account of themselves in the first and in the second component, but will not perhaps do so well in the third. People who seem to impress us at the first sight and fail to impress us on closer acquaintance have probably the third capacity while their first two components may be sadly lacking.

Measurement of Intelligence : Binet's Test

Binet was faced with the task of grouping children who had the same acquired ability, but were endowed with different capacities. They were all illiterates but when a literacy campaign was started they proceeded at different rates, and it was an administrative necessity to group them so that each group would consist of persons having approximately the same abilities. He developed a test which did not require any linguistic ability beyond understanding and giving response. At first the test that was evolved in 1905, measured intelligence according to the number of correct answers, a person gave. This would perhaps solve the problem of granting persons admission to one class. Later as the scheme developed, persons came seeking admission to a higher class directly. The handicap of literacy alone should not debar a person to do so, for an intelligent person would be able to make up this deficiency in no time. It is so unfair to waste the time of a person of superior intelligence by putting him into a lower class. But how to find whether the claims put forward by an applicant for a higher class on the basis of superior intellect are justified. This can be done if we can devise tests suited to several stages of mental development. This was achieved by Binet when he developed his items according to grades or mental ages in 1908. Very soon a method was found to compare the intelligence of persons of different ages. The concept of I.Q. (Intelligence Quotient) was developed as revealed by his answers to intelligence test questions. The mental age thus found out by the test items was divided by his real or chronological age, and multiplied by hundred, to find out his I.Q. Stated symbolically,

$$\text{I. Q.} = \frac{\text{M.A}}{\text{C.A}} \times 100$$

Before applying a certain test to a group of persons and pronouncing the mental age of each individual, we must first ascertain its validity. With a degree of confidence the mental age groups have to be determined. Normally persons should reply according to their actual age norms (provided we work with a large number of children of each age group). For a subnormal person the response would be relatively poorer. It is, however, possible to put test questions to a large number of children of each group (which does not include exceptionally bright or dull children), and see whether their responses are according to expectations. Any question or item if not correctly replied by a large number of students in a certain age group should be treated as unsuitable for that group. This process is known as the validation and standardisation of the Test.

Although Binet's original test was meant for French students, its English counterpart was attempted both in England and in USA. In U.S.A. the work done was more outstanding. Terman went through an elaborate process of standardisation and modification, and ultimately developed two versions of the test. The advantage of the two versions is obvious. We may apply one version and get the results, then we may apply the second version for confirmation. We may thus find out the reliability of the test of intelligence. Each of the series, L and M contains 129 questions divided into mental age groups as follow:-

(a) Six questions for each half-yearly period from 2 to 4-1/2 years. This is done because the development at this period is more rapid than at a later age. A correct answer naturally adds to the mental age by a month at. this stage.

(b) Six questions each for early periods from 5—14, a correct answer at this stage gives a credit of two months.

(c) Eight questions suited to average adult, where credit for a correct answer is still two months.

(d) Six questions for each of three groups called by him as superior adults I, II and III, while the credit for a correct answer in superior adults III is five months. The longer period provided in higher age is backed by the theory that the growth of intelligence slows down as age advances.

The remaining 7 questions are given as alternatives in different age groups. When a person answers all the questions, his mental age will be 22 years and 10 months, at which age growth of intelligence (as measured by the test) stops.

A question may arise as to what will happen to a person, say 46 years old, answering all questions correctly. Evidently he can not do anything better than scoring a mental age upto 22 years and 10 months. If his achievement is divided by his chronological age and multiplied by 100, his I.Q. will not be above 50. Evidently, he is being penalised for his age. To avoid this, Terman proposed a modification of the real or chronological age.

For administration of the test, Terman would not ask the experimenter to put all the questions to every child. He would make a rough guess of what the mental age of the child is likely to be, (for mental age above eight, perhaps administration in vocabulary item of the test may be helpful, as answer in that test would indicate the rough mental age). He would then put to the child all the questions set for age. If the child is able to answer all the questions, he will be given the questions suited to the next higher age. Other-wise he will be given the questions suited to the next lower age. In this way, the basal age or the highest age upto which the child is able to answer all the questions will be determined. The credit in years and months suited to the basal age will be given to him to start with. Then he will begin answering questions from those mental age groups where his answers will be only in parts of each mental age group. For each answer he will be given the credit for the corresponding months (One, two, four or five as the case may be) till he comes to an age where he is unable to answer a single question. At this point, the administration of the test will stop. His total credit in mental age will be the basal age plus the sum of monthly credits he has earned. The mental age so obtained, when divided by the chronological age (actual age upto thirteen, corrected age between thirteen and sixteen, and multiplied by 100 will give the person's Intelligence Quotient.

Terman found with a very wide administration of his test that intelligence of different age groups is more or less normally distributed. Roughly about two thirds of the entire group was found to have an intelligence quotient somewhere between 85 and 119. For convenience, however, he took the demarcation lines at points 110, 120 and 140 on the right side of the normal line and at points, 90, 80, 70 and 60 on the left (normal line being 100, which represents the points where mental and chronological ages are equal). Terman found that about 60% of the people are distributed between 90 and 110. This is according to him, the score of persons of average intelligence. Between 110 and 120 on one side and between 80 and 90 on the other, there are about thirteen per cent on each. The former he will call high and the latter low. Between 120 and 143 are 6.75% cases whom Terman will call superior and beyond 140 are rare persons. About 25% of these he will call genius. On the other side, between 60 to 80 there are about 60% cases who may be called dull or morons, and below 60 are the remaining 1% who are idiots or imbeciles. Thus the test not only measures intelligence, but can be used for clinical diagnosis of morons and imbeciles. Mental abnormalities like neurosis and psychosis cause a regression. Such persons though physically mature, behave like children. They thus register an abnormally low mental age, and this fact added to other clinical observations would support the findings that they are of abnormal mind.

There have been various adaptations of this test in India notably by Sohan Lal and Bhatia at Allahabad, Kamath in Bombay and recently in Calcutta University. They are thus available in at least four Indian languages, Hindi, Gujarati, Marathi and Bengali. But these seem to have been standardised on a limited population, and perhaps are not yet complete for all age groups with two parallel forms as in the case of Terman. The application of Terman's Test in India, however, has its limitation, not only because of the language handicap, (which gives an additional advantage to a person whose command over the English language is better) but because of its cultural saturation. Sohan Lal's adaptation may be all right for U-P, but may not suit other parts of India.

Point Scale Group Tests

Binet Test or its Terman Revision, is an individual test in which each person is tested separately. Though it allows a certain amount of flexibility, yet it is very time-consuming and expensive. To prevent this, certain group tests like Army Alpha have been evolved. They may contain some true and false items and the subjects may find out which of them are true and which false. Another group may contain several plausible answers out of which the subjects may be asked the one best suited. A third group may need a rearrangement of items, a fourth group may need simple mathematical computation, and so on. For each correct answer a score may be given, and suitable corrections may be made to avoid guess work. The test resembles an objective test with the difference, that it has been verified as suitable, and it is again given to a number of persons belonging to several age groups. The score for each age-group is obtained. These scores are then distributed over a hundred point scale separately for each age group. This provides us with a suitable measuring stick with which we can assess any individual ability, according to the performance of the individual in terms of the accomplishment of the normal persons of his own age group. A person's score corresponding to sixty points in the scale of performance of his own group means that fifty-nine persons of his age group selected at random will get points lower than what he has scored in the test. His rating or percentile rank will then be sixty. This is known as the point scale and it is an average. A person gets a percentile rank of 50 instead of 100 in the age scale.

Semi-performance Scales : Wechsler Bellevue Test

Wechsler has evolved in the Bellevue University a combined test of eleven groups of items six of which (Nos. 1, 2, 3, 4, 5, and 11) are of the verbal type and may be applied to the literates and the other five of the performance type which are applicable both to the literates and illiterates. Both the categories have been standardised separately as well as together. In fact, Wechsler's aim at evolving the test seems to be two fold.

He wanted to find out objectively whether ability known as variable intelligence is interrelated to abilities in the performance type of activities. If the correlations are high, it will prove that it measures intelligence correctly, and the scores would be the most general measures of intelligence. It would thus justify Wechsler's definition of intelligence.

He wanted to develop further scale by which adult intelligence could be measured. Binet's Test or its Terman Revision can register mental age only upto 22 years and 10 months. What happens afterwards? Does the adult intelligence remain stationary or does it decline are the pertinent questions one may ask ? Wechsler has tried to answer this.

The Bellevue scale of intelligence is somewhat in between the Terman's or Binet's conception of intelligence quotient based on the consideration of mental ages and the point scale for finding a percentile rank of a person's achievement compared with his own age group. Wechsler would first get the score by administering the entire test to his subjects (ages between 10 and 50) and for the convenience of marking will allot points for a correct answer which will generally be one and rarely upto three (as in block tests). He will also allow time credit for quick and successful answers given before time and this will also be upto three in case of exceptionally quick and correct answers. Now some of the groups contain easier items and some harder, their weightages in predicting intelligence can not, therefore, be considered same. Wechsler would, therefore, give added value to certain items according to their importance in predicting intelligence, and reduce the values of others. Thus the weighted score for intelligence will be calculated.

The weighted scores of an individual are then compared with the achievements of the person's own age group to find out his position according to a method which resembles the point scale.

But Wechsler does not write his answers on a simple point scale. He takes up Binet's conception of intelligence and holds that median intelligence should be rated at 100. He, however, holds that normally fifty, out of every hundred persons should be showing the average intelligence (as opposed to Terman's 60%) and these should be between the scores 90 and 110. Wechsler thus takes 100 as the mean and 90 and 110 as plus and minus P.E. distances according to statistical concepts.

Wechsler has found a fair degree of interrelationship between the performance and verbal intelligence, and his scale is able to measure intelligence in terms of I.Q. (his own concept of it) for all age groups from 10 to 50 years. It has the disadvantage, like Binet's test in being individual and its administration is both expensive and time-consuming.

WAIS is an extension and modification of Wechsler Bellevue Intelligence scale. Important changes have been made in the directions for administering and scoring the tests. Some items have been dropped and some new items have been added. The WAIS norms were based on groups considered representative of U.S. adults.

Norms were developed for each of seven age groups ranging from 46 to 64 years.

When assessing the effectiveness of Intellectual ability in an adult, one is primarily interested in two kinds of comparisons: how the individual compares with his age peers and how he compares with those who are at the base of mental development.

The WAIS intelligence Quotient (IQ), whether based on Verbal. Performance or Full Scale is obtained from a direct comparison of the subjects test results with those of persons in his chronological age group.

The WAIS standardization sample was chosen with exceptional care to insure its representativeness. The verbal, performance and full scale scores can be expressed in terms of I.Qs. with a mean of 100 and an SD of 15.

Other Intelligence Tests

The tests of intelligence of a simpler type are those of Maze learning or Draw a Person Test. These measure spatial relationship or only one aspect of intelligence. Koh's block measures both spatial relationship and ability to perform. Pegboard judges only performance, but Seguin's formboard measures spatial relationships as exhibited by patterns and performance ability. These tests thus measure only one or at best two aspects of what we call intelligence.

More complicated types of performance tests have been evolved like Army Beta test which like Army Alpha is a group performance test in India. The psychological Bureau, Allahabad has evolved Bhatia's Battery which is an adaptation of several tests including, Alexander's

Pass along test and others. This has been standardised and can be used as a performance test suitable under Indian conditions.

One great objection that is often raised against these tests are that they are not entirely culture-free. They give some additional advantage to the groups whose socio-cultural background represents that of the test maker. Some critics have indeed asserted that the tests constructed provide a justification for the higher socio-economic groups to obtain more favourable treatment in the matter of educational opportunities for their children. This is perhaps a rather strong and uncharitable remark to make against the use of test. The cultural saturation is always a strong limitation which we may not always be conscious of and this sometimes handicaps one in constructing a test.

It must be noted, however, that to meet this objection some culture-fair tests have been evolved where the cultural saturation is at least perceptibly reduced. International group mental test of Dodd is a pictorial test prepared according to common culture of human beings and in co-operation with the anthropologists. It includes Code Substitution, Block Counting, Maze Tracing, Series of completion and arrangement of Items. International Performances Test is another which has been revised in 1948. It eliminates instruction altogether. Each test begins with a few easy tasks to be performed which are self-educative. Among the tasks included are matching of identical colours, Block design, Foot print recognition spatial relations, classification of animals etc. Tests are arranged in year level from 2 to 18. Cattell's culture fair tests are available at three age levels, Scale I for 4-8, II for 8-12 and III for higher ages (up to Terman's Superior Adults).

Raven's Progressive Matrices Tests have been designed to measure the 'g' factor of intelligence. It consists of sixty matrices or abstract designs from each of which a part has been omitted. The Subject chooses the missing part from six or eight given alternatives. The items are grouped into five series each of which consists of twelve matrices of increasing difficulty but similar in principle. The earlier series require chiefly accuracy of discrimination, the later includes analogies, permutation, alteration of pattern and other logical relations. The scoring is done on a point scale and Raven has worked out percentile norms for all ages 5-14 in half yearly intervals and then form 20 to 65 in five year intervals. Testing in Argentina has proved significant saturation with culture. But Green working in Ceylon has found that it is not entirely culture free though favouring certain professions rather than others Mat-weavers of Ceylon who work with patterns got better scores than college graduates. Recently, an easier and coloured version of Raven's test suitable for 5-11 years have been made both in book and in board. The subject is to choose the right piece rather than choose the correct completion. Its ceiling value seems to be low for even children of average ability score in India.

Although we seem to know what is intelligence, we can not like many other terms, define intelligence in a way that may be acceptable to all. Different psychologists have tried perhaps to measure the different aspects of intelligence and have emphasised one aspect or other. We can not deny that one shows the average in his performance or actions even when he is confronted with difficulties of a different nature. This points to a general ability factor in intelligence. But one cannot at the same time overlook that while some people are clever in verbal responses, others are good in number responses or performance ability.

Spatial relationships may not show themselves so well in verbal responses. This points to the intelligence being somewhat specific, running into some groups. We can not at the same time deny that in addition to group ability some persons show remarkable cleverness in some specific area of either verbal, spatial, number of performance aspect. Thus we have to consider intelligence to be consisting of several factors or levels, eg. general, group and specific.

Measurement of intelligence is necessary, for obvious reasons, to group children or adults of the same intelligence range so that they may be given guidance or instruction accordingly. This is possible, provided one can devise suitable tests. Such tests may be either individual with advantage of flexibility and scope for adjustment to fatigue or boredom of the subject. They may again be devised along on age scale where questions are divided according to different groups and the successful answer gives the subject a credit in years or in months. This finally settles the Mental age of the subject and when we divide this by the subject's real or chronological age we can get a measure by which we are able to compare the intelligence of other persons. We may have to adjust the real age so that the I.Q. may not be inflated. As the age scale provides not one but several tests, it is also called a 'battery type test'. Besides an age scale, there is a point scale in which the same test is given to all subjects. The test may contain several groups of items, but their administration is common to all groups. The test of this type is thus an 'Omnibus' pattern. Here the performances of normal persons of several age groups must be collected and spread over a hundred point scale. To fix up the position of a new person, all that we have to do is to compare his performance with others of his own age group and to find out where he stands on a hundred point scale. Evidently more intelligent persons would stand high in the list and the position of less intelligent ones will be low in the scale.

While Binet's test or its Terman and Merrill Revision, measures verbal intelligence along an age scale, the Army Alpha measures it on a point scale. The former is an individual and the latter a group test. Wechsler Bellevue Test is a semiperformance test, measuring both verbal and performance types but either part can be used separately or both together. The fact that two parts correlate well, proves some connection between verbal intelligence and an intelligence of the performance type. Wechsler has devised a scale in measuring intelligence according to the performance of a subject being compared to his own age group, but he makes adjustments by taking probable error value to bring it to a form similar to Intelligence Quotient of Binet.

There are many other tests of Intelligence which have been devised, some of which like the Form Board, Maze Learning, Draw a Preson Test, or Peg Board Test measure limited aspects of intelligence. Others have been so constructed as to give objective measurements of intelligence in any cultural context. Among the latter, may be mentioned the names of Dodd's International Group mental Tests, Leiter's international performance Test (Devised in Battery pattern), Cattell's culture-free Test and Raven's progressive matries. While reducing the influence of culture one can not, however, say with certainty that these tests are entirely culture-free.

5

PERCEIVING AND THINKING

What is perception ?

To a man in the street there is hardly any difference between perception and mere looking. To a scientist, however, perception has a special significance. It means receiving impressions through any of the senses including sight, hearing, smell, touch or taste. In a psychological sense it further involves two things namely to receive the sensation and to interpret them. Besides good senses and effective sensations there must be a proper span of attention and motivation for learning.

Thomas Reid distinguished between mere sensation and perception. In an ordinary sensation, the sense organs receive certain impressions and there the matter ends. In perception, there is not only a stimulus but also some meaning, which can be derived by a sense of awareness or knowledge of the subject. We may for instance see a red flower and its redness and roundness are apparently sensations though they too need previous experience or acquaintance and in that sense they are also perceptions. But to recognise that flower as a rose, a previous knowledge of the details of the property of the flower is needed. Brown holds that perception is really grasping of relationships. We perceive not merely similarities, but the differences from other objects to establish peculiarities. Before we have perceived the red flower as the rose we have not only noticed how it resembled our previous impressions of roses, but at the same time how the particular flower differed from other red flowers. Wundt and James hold that perception combines a number of sensory elements. When we perceive a rose, for instance, we consider not merely the colour and shape, but its smell as well. The sensation of pleasure that a cup of tea offers is a combined sensation of its warmth and its flavour which is a blending of two more sensations namely smell and taste. Thus touch, smell and taste are all involved in it.

Cattell working on attention span found that adults can apprehend six to eleven objects at a time, provided the objects are not too big. The average is generally eight. If, however, items are bundled into groups more can be perceived. An ordinary person can note as many as thirty letters provided these letters make a meaningful sentence.

Urban Schis and Necker found that our attention fluctuates. We can test this fact ourselves through many experiments. On looking at cube the surface ABCD appears in front for a while, and PQRS at the back. At other times PQRS may appear to be in front, ABCD at the back. What is true for sight is true for other senses also.

William James and Edward Titchener hold that when we pay attention to some thing, we bring it to a focus and other things go into the margin of our attention. Morgan studied the problem of distraction. Subjects in a certain experiment were made to learn a certain code on a kind of type writer by punching certain signs. While they worked bells were rung. For a short while in the earlier part, the work slowed down showing the effect of distraction. After a while, as the subjects got used to the sound, the distraction did not have much effect on their perception or attention, and they worked at their usual speed. Now the bell was suddenly stopped. Curiously enough work slowed down again. The explanation is quite simple, formerly the bell was causing distraction, but the persons got used to them. After a while it is the stoppage of the sound, that caused distraction. Titchener also found that the size, motion, colour or as a matter of fact any stimulus which can stand prominently against the background of experiences, serves as a factor to control attention.

Cattell, working on the reaction time apparatus, found that our attitude or expectation influences the speed of our reaction. Some subjects were asked to concentrate on the response they should make when they saw the light. After a while they were asked to concentrate on the stimulus itself. It was found that they worked faster in the former case.

Watt, working on controlled association, found that when a subject was told to give the opposite of each word, he usually adjusted himself to this unusual situation by practising a few cited before-hand. While he had thus practised, the perception of opposites became automatic.

These experiments threw much light on perception. They showed that factors like distraction are relative to the situation, we get used to. In case of opposites, we adapt ourselves to a situation to be ready to receive the stimulus and to perceive. Perception thus needs a preparation.

Gestalt Theory and Perception

Wertheirmer, Kohler and Koffka have held that our experience is a total process in which parts can not be easily differentiated or analysed. We perceive a rose as such, we can not isolate either the colour or the shape and say that this is rose. Even in case of its smell, we can not isolate the several items that blend together to give us the peculiar smell of a rose. A cup of tea of a peculiar blend is perceived as a whole and declared delicious. We can not break it into its elements of taste smell and other things that make its flavour.

Kohler trained a hen in such a way that when she picked up grains from a grey paper, she was permitted to eat them. When she picked up the grains from a white paper, she was driven away. By and by, she became so used to this situation, that the hen would pick up only from the grey paper. After a time the white paper was removed, and the grains were spread over two papers, one black and other grey. Now it was seen that the hen went straight for the black paper, thus showing that what the hen perceived was not the particular paper which was grey, but the entire situation, namely the comparatively darker part of the two bits of papers.

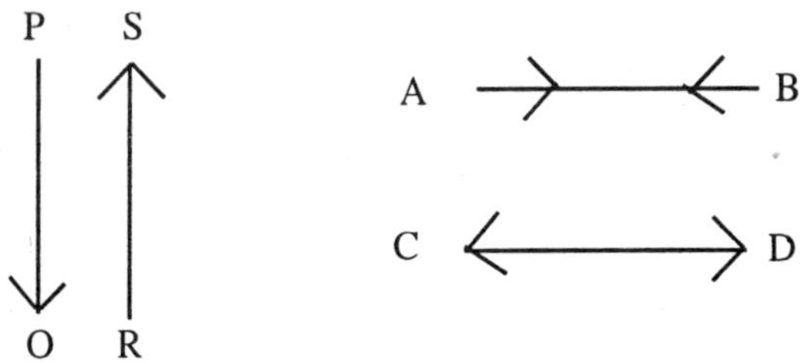

An illustration of the false deception, how our eyes can deceive us is shown in the above figures. The lines AB and CD are of equal length, and yet CD appears longer, because of the projection pointing outwards. The line PQ and RS are parallel and yet they appear approaching each other because of the trim transversal lines approaching each other.

In these two illustrations also, the total situation affects us. Perception of depth is caused by perspective lines converging at a vanishing point. This was found and used first by the clever artist De Vinci. Here too the total situation, the relation of a thing with regard to its background gives us the idea of the depth. Descarte's discovery that changes in the eye help us to gauge the distance, looks at this issue from an organic stand-point, but this kind of accommodation of the eye itself is an evidence that we perceive things together and that our eyes try to accommodate all.

It is on this basis that Whetstone constructed stereoscope in 1838. Two pictures that were presented to the right and to the left eyes were not exact carbon copies, but they had slight differences only. It is by accommodation to these differences, that the eyes get a vivid impression of the depth. This fact thus objectively shows not only the accommodation of the eyes but also a tendency of reaction towards the total situation of the Gestalt.

Thinking and thought process : Behaviourists' View

Upto the time of Wundt, it was believed that images are absolutely necessary before thinking can start, and that our thoughts go in terms of sensations, images, and feelings. Binet and Oswald Kulpe tried to disprove this but it was Buhler who succeeded in giving an experimental evidence. Buhler tried to analyse the thinking which evolved when a subject was confronted with a paradox. The apparently impossible things in a paradox should at once strike the subject had he used his past images, but he found that a subject was made to think and draw conclusions thus showing that an image is not necessary. Likewise, a subject may be made to think and draw conclusions when he hears a fable. Certainly, in this case there are no images, for no one has heard an animal talk; yet there is thinking.

Robert Woodworth's Publication : 'Imageless Thought' also gives evidence of sensations not affecting our thought process though evidence of such sensations received in the past may be provoked deliberately by introspection. Based on these and on his own experimental evidence, Wundt held that the core of thinking process was merely a conscious perception of relationship and not necessarily of past images.

Watson put forward the viewpoint of the behaviourists on this subject. According to him, thinking is nothing but talking to one's ownself in a manner that no sound is being produced. Sometimes, many of us, especially children, think aloud. We generally give up this process as we grow older, because we are afraid of being ridiculed. Watson believed that thinking can go in terms of any muscular experience. Certain deaf and dumb individuals, he found, try to think by moving their hands, thus showing that they are merely repeating the mode of expression that they otherwise use. Under normal circumstances, as we speak, these individuals express themselves, by show of hand. While thinking they are using the same method, or in one sense they are thus thinking aloud.

Experiments by other psychologists have, however, failed to reveal any significant relationship between thinking and movement of vocal muscles, perceptible or otherwise, which would have proved this theory.

Several hypothesis have been put forward. According to the motor theory, thinking is something like muscular action. The supporters of this viewpoint have not, however, been able to give sufficiently convincing experimental evidence.

In 1939, Berger reported that he had found the existence of an electric current with about ten oscillations (to and fro movement) per second when a person is made to think. This he called 'Brain Waves'. Berger found this by placing two metallic rods or electrodes on the surface of a person's skull. These were connected with a Galvanometer or an electrical measuring instrument while a person was thinking. Berger's followers have claimed that the intensity of waves increases as a person's mental age increases. Unfortunately, not many researches have been carried out in this direction. All that one can say at the present moment that when sufficiently convincing evidence is available, this may change our present trend of psychology and establish once more that thinking is a process in which brain alone is involved. At present, however, we are not in a position to assert this so convincingly.

Thinking Process in terms of Gestalt Theory

Gestalt psychologists have introduced 'insight' to describe the thought process. Persons, it is held, grasp relations unconsciously and the solution of the problem strikes one suddenly. Kohler found many examples of insight in apes. If food is hung from the ceiling of a box, the apes could pile up boxes to reach it and some time they would pull the food down by attaching one stick to another, if a single stick would prove a bit too small. This attachment would be conveniently done. These do not show a mere chance reaction as has been claimed in the solution of maze problems, when an animal was to run a maze to procure its food, more or less blindly. Kohler held that even in the maze problem entire relationship was surveyed before the problem was solved. Tolman and others built and elevated transparent maze wall so that a rat could see the type of maze they run through. Within the maze there were two paths, one shorter than the other. The fact that 90% of rats choose the shorter path was a clear evidence that their choice was not a matter of chance, but a result of deliberate insight into relationships. When however a hurdle was kept along the shorter path, the rats chose the longer path which did not have the hurdle. This is again the result of the perception of the total relationship.

Hunter kept three boxes. Only one of them did contain some food and this was momentarily lighted. Children were told to find their food from one of the boxes. Perhaps at the start, they made a few mistakes, but after a while, they could reach the right box without any mistake. That this perception of the right box associated with lighting, was proved by switching on the light to a wrong box. Then the children went to the wrong box invariably for they had grasped the relationship of the box to the light.

Reasoning

Reasoning is an orderly or logical sequence in which thinking follows. John Dewey has established five distinct steps involved in a reasoning process:-

1. There must be a problem, some perplexity or difficulty. If everything runs smoothly where is the need for an individual to exert ?
2. We must be able to locate or define the difficulty. If then the situation is so complex that we can not make head or tail out of it, we are likely to give up attempts of solving it, and get desperate. There will be no attempt at reasoning, for there will be no attempt of problem solving.
3. While reasoning, we try to put forward a hypothetical solution. This is only a tentative or a trial solution, and while putting forward, we are conscious that in the light of further investigation, we may be required to modify or alter it.

4. We examine and develop this hypothesis in the light of the given conditions and see whether the hypothesis meets all our requirements.
5. We finally verify our hypothesis or put it to actual test to see whether it actually fulfils all the conditions. If it does not, we may have to repeat the process involved in steps (3), (4) and (5) with a new hypothesis.

The five steps indicated in the above may not occur in the order given, though it generally does so, but it is essential that all the steps must be involved in the process which we call reasoning.

As an example we may take the case of a man observing a long pole projecting horizontally from the upper deck of a boat. For an observer it may be a problem as to find out why is it put at all ?

On attempting to locate the difficulty, the man notices that the pole is horizontal, which at once rules out the possibility of its being a flagpost. The observer is now confronted with two hypotheses, it may either be a wireless post or the pole erected to point out the direction to the steerman. On testing the first hypothesis, he concludes that had it been a wireless post it would have been pitched higher up on the top of the pilots cabin, for higher the pole the better will be its transmitting and receiving power. If on the other hand, the pole is meant for pointing out the direction to the steerman, it would not be pitched so high as to obstruct the pilot and would be just high enough to be visible from the steerman's place. The former hypothesis, therefore, not being able to withstand verification is rejected.

Two types of Reasoning:

Reasoning may be of two types. After we have already established a law we want to prove the conclusion for a particular case. This is known as deduction and is used in our geometrical theories. For example, we take the particular case of two triangles whose corresponding sides are equal. Applying the general fact that in such cases, the triangles become congruent, we prove the congruency of this particular case using the general law.

Yet all our reasonings are not of this type. At times we generalise and get a common underlying truth out of the study of a number of particular cases. This common truth in the concept and the process is known as induction. A child's concept of an animals is, for instance, formed out of a study of a number of concrete experiences of dogs, cats, goats, rabbits, rats from which he might have formed the common and essential feature which he called the concept of an animal. Having drawn this concept, the child may use it to compare new cases and thus applies this inductive knowledge to deduction. Induction and deduction are, therefore, complementary processes and are by no means exclusive. When a new problem confronts us, we certainly try to find its solution in terms of our past experiences, and to solve the novel and particular case with some similar past experience or concepts. But after all, these concepts or general ideas are built out of a study of a number of isolated experiences which are grouped together for facility of remembrance.

Summary

We find that perception is not mere seeing but is connected with experience with all the senses. It has several characteristics. It is no doubt, selective, for we react to one aspect of the total environment at a time, which we focus our attention for the moment. But at the same time we are not indifferent to the total situation which serves as the background for our observation. Perception is moreover, a meaningful process. Our past experiences and our present mental set up are both connected with it. Sometimes several sensations from several sense organs are blended together to give a meaning. How many separate items can be comprehended together, depends on the nature and difficulty of the items as well as on the mental age of the learner. Further, it depends also on the fact whether the items can be grouped together or not. Distraction prevents perception, but what we call distraction is really a chance in the situation one gets used to. If a person gets used to noise, it is quietness that will become distracting. When we expect a thing to happen in a certain way, our mind gets adjusted to this situation and our responses become automatic.

What constitutes thinking, has given rise to many conflicting theories. In many cases, thinking may be as the behaviourists claim it to be, mere talking to oneself, which may or may not be backed by past images. Perhaps under such circumstances, it may depend on conscious perception of relationships.

Yet it is not clear whether thinking takes place in the brain alone as Berger claims it to be. His experiments have been carried on a limited scale. We are not yet in a position to state whether it would give us a general truth applicable to all cases of thinking. It is undeniable that at least at times, thinking is based on the result of the perception of the total relationship. In such cases the final solution comes out as flash as if by insight, but it is really an outcome of the analysis of the total situation going on within the mind as the Gestalt psychologists claim.

In more complex cases, we have to reason out in a logical manner which involves not merely a perception of relationship, but also that of locating it. After locating the difficulty, the mind puts forward a trial solution or hypothesis, which is put to test and which needs verification. If the hypothesis does not stand verification, it is rejected and a new hypothesis is called for. If it stands verification, it is accepted.

The two processes of reasoning, deduction or applying general truths to a particular case, or induction or building up a general concept by studying a number of particular difficulties are really complementary and one can seldom be treated as exclusive of the other.

Concluding Observation

Perception is dependent upon the impressions made upon our senses by different objects or conditions around us. It involves a meaning or a recognition of these objects. Sensation is a step towards perception. It is a question of not only how things are, but how things appear which is important in perception. In other words, the character of the perception is more important than the character of objects that are perceived. It has been admitted that consciousness is one of the important conditions of perception. The phenomenological experience of an object is dependent on one's own organism, so the phenomenology has to depend upon the two sides of the same process. It does not cover the whole of experience.

Recent evidence supports the views that perceptual organisation is related to experience. The process of perception itself is susceptible to social influences. This is also evidenced from various research findings. Besides, the operation of rewards and punishment, personal needs and emotional states influence the way in which an individual perceived. The experiences help one to acquire meanings and thus they become more dominant in the perceptual field. In other words, the patterning of impressions gradually leads to organised percepts.

The organism and the environment offer an extremely crowded perceptual field and selection of certain stimuli is one of the basic questions involving perceptions. Clinical evidence indicates that much depends upon the nature of stimulation. If the stimulation is intense, perception is enriched. As mentioned before, the nature of experiences determines to a large extent the behaviour pattern of an individual in the formation of an attitude towards a particular object. Similarly, the culture context has got an important bearing on the formation of percepts. Communication, language, symbols and perception are inter-related to some extent. The complexity of perceptual process is significant particularly when we consider the process within the context of social situation and social interaction. Some of the experiments with chimpanzees go to prove that the response to a stimulus depends upon one's perception of the object. The relationship of the objects to the perceiver determines the perceptual process which depends upon past experience and action. A knowledge of the learning process is relevant for understanding the part played by culture in the specification of perception. Such knowledge includes an awareness of biological conditions basic to learning and understanding of the operation of repetition, generalisation, transfer and dominance.

There are few questions which are important in this connection:

1. What are the contents and properties of an individual's perception? What determines these properties? while we perceive, our perceptual world is dependent on the nature of the physical objects which surround us. It is also much dependent upon objects and events not immediately present. It is a complicated way in which we perceive the world and how we perceive the world is a product of memory, imagination, fantasy as well as our sense experiences. In other words, certain cognitive structures and substructures emerge out of this process. In the field of social psychology, various problems, emerge in connection with cognitive organisation. To get a good description of man's cognitive world is extremely difficult, and various errors creep in and create confusion.

On a review of the psychological aspects of perception it appears that here are two major determinants of perception. There are structural, as well as functional factors involved in perception. By structural factors are meant those which are derived solely from the nature of physical stimuli and the neural effects they evoke in the nervous system of the individual. The functional factors of the perceptual organisation are those derived primarily from the needs, moods, past experience and memory of the individual. The experiments performed by Bruner and Goodman show that differences in perception of the two groups of children asked to estimate the size of the coins are mainly due to the effect of need upon their perception. The greater the individual need for socially valued objects, the more marked will be the operation of behavioural determinants. Another experiment by Lewin, Chain, and Murphy illustrates the importance of functional factors operating in perception. The more important part in the perceptual process is played by the inter-relation between structural and functional factors. The piecemeal approach does not offer a complete picture of the various aspects of perception. It is, therefore, important that perception should be approached from the standpoints of both an experimental psychologist and a social psychologist. With a view to analysing the nature and process involving perception, it will be better if the following propositions are formulated:-

1. The perceptual and cognitive field in its natural state is organised and meaningful. Man is an organising animal and any fact we experience will be organised into some sort of meaningful whole. This tendency towards organisation is a universal characteristic of the cognitive process.

2. Perception is functionally selective. In every day life, the physical stimuli we are exposed to are various. It is, therefore, important that selection of certain stimuli will have to be made for integration and specific organisation of our cognitive field. It is true that objects that play the major role in the organised perception serve an immediate purpose of the perceiving individual.

3. The perceptual and cognitive properties are determined in large measure by the properties of structure of which it is a part, It is a fact that experience in the natural state is organised and meaningful, but our cognitive field does not consist of completely independent organised structure. In other words every perception is embedded in an organisation of other percepts. Thus, each of these cognitive structures can be broken down into several relative sub-structures. It is the interrelationship among the structures and substructures of the cognitive field which should be determined for the understanding of any perception.

Illustration from simple visual perception will indicate the importance of contrast and assimilation in understanding the substructure of a major structure as related parts and wholes. This general whole-part principle has so many extensions. As a result, the formulation of whole-part principles proves sounder in terms of constancy of the cognitive field. If there were no object constancy in our perceptual life, all objects of our world would look radically different every time. The whole-part principle can be better explained in terms of frames of reference.

The term frame of reference is simply used to denote the functionally related factors which operate at the moment to determine the particular properties of a psychological phenomenon such as perception. Sheriff has demonstrated the importance of major concepts in social psychology. Nelson and MeGravey had shown the importance of phenomenon of relativity in the perceptual field.

For every organised perception the individual is attuned or adapted to the central stimulus in the light of his needs and judgment.

4. Final proposition indicated that certain perceptions are organised together with other perceptions to make up a single cognitive structure. The common structure is influenced by the objects or events, by contiguity of space and time or resemblance. This is a very important proposition so far as its social implications are concerned.

Differences in social behaviour among men reflect differences in the cognitive structure which is dynamic. There is a constant organisation and re-organisation in the perceptual structure which takes place with reference to the needs and attainment of the goal. The cognitive process of re-organisation typically consists of hierarchically related series of organisation. As already mentioned, cognitive structures undergo progressive changes according to the principles of organisation determined by the function of the differentiation, isolation and rigidity.

Social factors in perception

Perception is a peculiar mental process influenced by a variety of feelings and emotions forming experience. In other words, the psychological factors of perception can hardly be brushed aside. In some experiments, it has been found that the accuracy of shape perception depends upon not only the shape but also the surrounding. For example, if some shapes are shown in a very dim light, they appear to be circular before the actual shape can be fully discriminated. Another experiment shows that there is a general tendency to perceive any shape with the maximum degree of simplicity, regularity and symmetry. The Gestalt psychology attached more importance to the forms of the object known as configuration. They also stressed the importance of meaningfulness in the field of perception. It appears that visual mechanism of the eyes and the brain do not readily offer a correct information of the stimulus present before our senses. Detail must be observed if they (complex shapes) are to be perceived. Greater intensity of illumination is required and at the same time more time is needed. As mentioned before, the surroundings have effect on perception. Judgment of shape tends to be subjective as the objects cannot be isolated from the context offering a scope for illusion. It also seems that normally we relate the size of any object to the sizes of all other objects in the total surrounding at that distance. The size is, therefore, perceived in relation to the size, and scale of the object and the distance. Thus there are factors like, shape, distance, illumination, context and previous experience which influence one's perception. These are more or less psychological because they have got a direct bearing on the conditioning of perception and the stimulus. On the other hand, there are factors which influence perception even without having any direct bearing on it. For example, motivation is related to perception. In other words, perception is affected by motives to a considerable extent. In one experiment observers were shown blurred pictures of articles related to food and of their household articles at varying periods after the last meal. There was an increase of value and brightness in the number of food-related objects perceived after about six hours after the last meal. But thereafter there are a decrease. In another experiment, the pictures of food and other objects are shown as first very dimly and then increasingly brightly. The brightness at which the food objects were perceived decreased up to about 3 to 4 hours after the observer's last meal and then increased again. It appeared, therefore, that there was at first, a tendency for food and related articles to be perceived more readily, but the observer became increasingly frustrated and ceased to take the trouble of responding as hunger increased. This again suggest that the observers become apathetic during their periods of deprivation. There are other experiments which show clearly that there is a complex interaction between need and expectation. The individual in a state of need is in a better position to perceive something which will satisfy his needs provided he can sure of the thing he wants, at the right moment. Another interesting observation justifies a positive correlation between the degree of aggressiveness and the speed of perception. From these experimental findings, it is obvious that perception is highly susceptible to the influence of various internal and external factors. The effect of values on perception has also been demonstrated by different experiments. A different type of interest and value effecting perception is related to people's relation to one another. This is a social factor that affects the manner in which they perceive those whom they like or dislike. Observers were asked to rate photographs of Negroes and Whites as to the degree they showed certain Negro characteristics. Those observers who were prejudiced against Negroes showed a definite tendency to exaggerate the degree to which these characteristics appeared in the Negro photographs.

There are various experiments which confirm this finding. Several other studies have been made·to prove that individuals judgement is influenced by of a group of the opinions expressed by other members of the group. Numerous experiments have been carried out to demonstrate the effect of various forms of valuation upon the perception of certain peculiar qualities of object.

The earliest experiment was one by Bruner and Goodman in which ten-year old children were required to adjust the size of a disc of a light to equal the sizes of coin and cardboard discs. It was found in general that they tended to overestimate the sizes of coins by comparison with the size of the cardboard disc. The more valuable the coins, the greater was the degree of overestimation.

Moreover, children from poor homes overestimated to a greater extent than did those from well-to-do homes. Unfortunately, the experiment repeated on various occasions has shown varying results. Other studies have been made to investigate on perception. Here also the results have been different and even contradictory.

Like other factors, success and failure, pleasure and pain are also influenced by perception. This has been shown by a number of experiments. In short, the complex process involved in perception is yet to be analysed. It has been clear that perception is influenced by various internal, and external factors no doubt, but the amount of interaction between these has not yet been explored. It is extremely difficult to isolate one variable from the other.

Gestalt Psychology and its Bearing on Perception

Research in the field of human behaviour has recently revealed a new world. The gradual dawn of psychological knowledge has flashed light on the mysteries of perception and thought processes. We still think of psychology as a young science growing and gradually extending its scope. Introspection as a psychological method has been accepted and there has been little scope for doubt about its importance. It is a fact that an attempt has been made to raise the status of psychology by considering it as a science of consciousness. As a result, functional psychology became more important that structural. While the former struggled for finding out the elements comprising mental life, the latter sought to discover the needs and expressions of inner organism. This new trend inspired Watson to discover the biological significance of the conscious processes and make an objective study by suitable means. A strong feeling of temptation to ignore the complexity of human mind expressed itself in the form of behaviourism.

The limitations of the behaviourism emerging in America did not escape the vigilance of a group of young psychologists in Germany. This group used the word "Gestalt" as its slogan and was known as the Gestalt school. The old idea of association was rejected and the new concept in terms of experience was brought to light.

Gestalt psychology emphasised the complex process of organisation of experiences. They tried to discover the relationship between the part and the whole in our perceptual fields. In other words, a pattern or form was recognised to play a part in the process of perception. There is no doubt that, the Gestalt psychologists have insisted most strongly on the organised wholeness of behaviour. The dynamics of brain activity presented another problem to the Gestalt school. It has been persistently held by the school that much of our experience which has been regarded as built upon sensation by higher mental process is really included in sensation. They urge that the sensory brain process is part and parcel of the total situation and also that the primary brain response does not depend simply on the visual stimulation, but also on other factors on total situations.

6

LEARNING AND ITS IMPLICATIONS

In the opinion of a school, any stimulation reaching the brain is taken up into a dynamic interacting system and its effects thereby depend on the total activity going on in the brain. In short, the Gestalt psychologists emphasised the total process controlling the brain response to the separate item of stimulation. Thus the influence of background and pattern has been pointed out and demonstrated by the Gestalt psychologists. The various demonstrations particularly in the visual field proved the limitation of our senses and the role of the inner brain dynamics in determining the shape or pattern emerging out of it.

From the day of Eblinghaus up to a subsequent date the psychological theory tended to build up a mechanical conception of learning. The Gestalt psychology tried to look at the field of learning and perception more closely, than others and stressed the importance of insight in learning. The instinctive responses indicated that trial and error behaviour have little value for effective learning which demands insight and direction. The organisation and reorganisation of experience in the light of changing circumstances is the key word used by the Gestalt psychologists. The perceptual factor in learning is emphasised by the school and true learning, according to this school, means doing something new to reach the goal. The gap is bridged up by meeting the situation.

The term insight, of courses, is relative because it may vary in respect of order and degree. Higher the order of insight, greater is the learning. As it stands today, the Gestalt school has still much possibility. The process of dynamic organisation in the field of perception has been analysed by the school, for further exploration into the perceptual process long neglected.

Nature and Scope of the Learning Process

Teaching has been defined as a process of continuous adjustment, leading to improvement of the behaviour of the learner. This adjustment takes place in course of learning which stimulates the experience and even the perception of the child. As the child learns, he gains more and more experience which helps him to understand the environment more closely than before. The relationships between the various factors in the environment are gradually discovered. With the enrichment of experience, an insight emerges and the situation proves more meaningful to the learner. Thus, a continuous development takes place in the learner's cognitive, affective and conative life.

Learning has been described mainly as a process, because it is a progressive function in human behaviour, a multipolar process. It involves the learner, the teacher as well as the environmental factors. It is a sort of process of interaction between the learner and the other factors around him. On the one·hand, the learner has his own needs, drives and propensities, while the environmental stimulation helps him to meet those needs in the learning situation.

While learning, one acquires some knowledge and experience and retains them for future guidance. Thus, learning involves both acquisition and retention. But all this acquisition and retention should have a reference to some goal. If there is a definite goal, learning becomes more effective as a result of motivation. Motivation is the essential condition for learning, and much depends upon how a learner can be motivated. It is a fact that, the need-satisfaction brings motivation in learning. The teacher is, therefore, required to know means of creating motivation in learning. Practice facilitates learning no doubt. But this is not all. There are certain types of learning which requires perceptual orientation and this is possible by means of effective stimulation of the learner's mental process. Their previous experience also helps better adjustment to new situation.

Learning involves a number of stages as every learning depends upon certain factors, internal and external. Among the internal factors, motivation and individual drives deserve mention. It is a fact that age and learning are also related, because maturation is a determining factor, for effective learning. It is a complex process involving acquisition and retention. At the same time, it is an active process.

It entails a journey from known to unknown beset with variety of experiences. Laboratory experiments have yielded valuable data on learning and forgetting. It has been found out that learning takes place in a rhythmic manner and, increase or decrease in learning may be due to several causes.

Learning curves have been introduced for graphic representations. Some phases of the progress made in successive attempts to learn a new skill, may be represented by Curves.

Curves vary from situation to situation. In some curves positive and negative acceleration takes place; while curves may also have plateaus, that is, periods when there is neither a rise nor a fall. The knowledge of the fluctuations in learning is helpful to a teacher. Learning curves of one individual for a short period of time are not so reliable as there may be rise and fall in the strength of motives or interest, or there may be other factors, like distractions or fatigue. Besides, learning curves help the learner to know his progress and the extent of progress of learning for better adjustment. Learning curves are also useful to the teachers for diagnostic purposes.

Some fundamental questions, still persist around learning. How permanent is learning, how much of what is learned or retained, and for how long, are some of the basic questions. Experiments have been conducted for objective finding. It has been found out that learning by itself, is not sufficient unless it is frequently assessed by active recalls. So, recall helps the learning process and frequent attempts of recall, reinforce learning. Recall requires more participation by the learner, than does reading or listening. It also ensures greater confidence in the learning. In addition to recall as a method of learning, recognition also plays a very prominent part. As a method, recognition stimulates learning although it is doubtful whether it is as effective as recall. There are various factors influencing learning. It is assumed that age is one of them and many believe that childhood is the best age for learning. But the findings of the experiments show that learning ability increases upto the age of 16 or 17. Learning ability varies not with age but with learning materials. Their value and the degree of interest they can arouse, are all important considerations. Motivation forms the pivotal factor in the dynamics of learning process. It is agreed that learning is much facilitated if the motivation and a need for learning are aroused. This brings an action and propels the learning to a considerable extent.

So far as the retention of learning is concerned, one has, no doubt, the need for preserving the experiences derived from learning.

Retention is also an individual capacity varying from person to person.

It is rather difficult to see how permanent will be learning in individual cases. Recall is a more active process which helps learning and also strengthens retention. During recall the learner gives much more attention than what he has done during learning. The confidence of the learner is also acquired during recall. As a method of testing what learning has been retained, recognition is also of much use. Through tests which demand recognition of the right response a learner reinforces his experience.

Educational Implications

The whole learning process is rather complex and one has to be careful at the time of application of this knowledge in the field of education. A teacher has to consider the individual differences in the capacity of learning and retention, while drawing up certain educational programme. At the same time the teacher must know how to create motivation among the students.

The methods of teaching, the use of the materials and aids of teaching and the interpersonal relationships between the teacher and the pupils are of much importance in the field of learning and teaching. As regards the method, it is obvious that the same technique doesn't apply universally, because much depends upon the materials to be learnt. In spite of the controversy on relative value of the whole and part methods, it has been found that the learning material should be studied as a unit although the difficult parts should be tackled separately. But this should not be regarded as a rule because a question of the learner's ability comes in. If the learner is less mature, the part method may be more useful. Thus, there is a scope for selection of methods according to the situation.

Learning is thus a process by which an activity is originated or changed. The characteristics of the change in activity cannot be explained on the basis of native response tendencies, or maturation of temporary states of the organism. The above operational definition of learning points out that learning is a deliberate process and not an instinctive activity or a product of certain maturation.

The time of maturation of behaviour sequence through regular stages is independent of intervening practice. A child does not learn to talk until it is old enough. The child behaves under the influence of maturation. Similarly, learning is different from reflex activities or instinctive behaviours which do not involve any cognitive process. It is thus difficult to formulate a comprehensive definition of learning because it is a complex process including a variety of activities. There are a few who believe that learning is related to problem solving and reasoning as well. Similarly, there are others who define learning as a change in the central nervous system, Learning takes place mysteriously and we can hardly know what happens inside the organism when learning occurs.

There are few typical problems around learning theories as follows:—

(a) What are the limits of learning ?

(b) What is the role of practice in learning?

(c) How important are drives and incentives, rewards and punishments ?

(d) What is the place of understanding and insight ?

(e) Does learning of one thing help to learn something else ?

There are the basic questions which very often confront a psychologist struggling for a full proof definition of learning. So far, learning theories have been classified under two major heads, viz. stimulus response theories and cognitive theories. In the former category the name of Thorndike, Skinner and Hull are specially mentioned, while in the later the names of Tolman, Lewin and other Gestalt psychologists deserve mention. The basis of learning has to be discovered before any further exploration will be attempted. It has been seen that Thorndike accepted as basis of learning the association between sense impressions and impulses to self expression. Such an association has also been known as a bond or connection which might be strengthened or weakened in the making and breaking of habits. Although Thorndike's theory has undergone remarkable modifications, the three postulates to explain the theories of learning are very fundamental. They are laws of readiness, exercise and effect.

The law of readiness states the circumstances under which a learner tends to be satisfied or annoyed. Readiness means preparation for action. Thus it is quite likely that interests and motives influence one's readiness to learn.

Another postulate of Thorndike, namely the law of exercise refers to the strengthening of the connections with practice and the weakening of connections or forgetting when practice is discontinued. The last but not the least important law formulated by Thorndike is the 'law of effect' which states: "when a modifiable connection is made and is accompanied by satisfying state of affairs, the strength of the connection is increased." If the connection is formed by an annoying state of affairs, its strength is decreased. Besides the above theories, one of the major developments of Thorndike's laws was the discovery of the spread of effect and belongingness. According to the principle of belongingness, the connection is more easily learnt if the response belongs to the connection it strengthens. Similarly, the discovery of the spread of effect has brought certain new concepts. It has shown that the influence of the rewarding state of affairs acts not only on the connection to which it belongs but also on adjacent connections both before and after the rewarded connection. The effect acts to strengthen, even punished, connections in the neighbourhood of the rewarded one. Thus it is interesting to note that the spread of effect is the most characteristic feature of most contemporary connectionism. Punishment has proved to be more effective than Thorndike believed. It has been found by Stiffen that symbolic rewards strengthen weak connections more than symbolic punishment.

Estimate of Thorndike's Position

Thorndike's position on typical problems of learning may be summarized with reference to capacity, practice, motivation, understanding, transfer, forgetting etc. Learning capacity depends upon the number of bonds under the capacity. As regards practice, it has been seen that repetition of connection leads to an eligible strength unless the connections are rewarded. Practice is important because it permits rewards to act upon connection. Similarly, reward acts directly on neighbouring connection to strengthen them, while punishment has no corresponding direct weakening effect. The best way to get understanding is to build up a body of connections appropriate to the level of understanding. Reaction to the new situations benefits by the identity of the new situations in part with the old situation and principle of analogy described as assimilation.

7

REMEMBERING AND FORGETTING

Early theories of Remembering

The object of learning is really remembering. When we learn any thing, the ultimate object of our doing so is to retain what we have learnt.

The oldest theory of remembering like that of learning is association, and this idea was first given out by Plato. Plato said that we remember things by nearness or contiguity of experiences. Aristotle said that recall takes place through suggestions. One item causes us to recall another, because they are either similar or opposite in form. In both the cases there are certain significant points that suggest the second when the first is present.

David Hartley in the eighteenth century differentiated between two types of associations. If impressions are made simultaneously, we get synchronous association, otherwise we get successive association. In 1820, Brown put forward certain modification to Hartley's theory. He said that we associate and remember according to four conditions:

1. *Relative duration of the impression* : longer the duration the greater will be the impression received.
2. *Vividness :* the clearer the impression, the longer will it be remembered.
3. *Frequency :* the larger the number of impression, the greater will be the effect of them on the memory.
4. *Recency* : more recent events are better remembered than more remote ones.

Nine years later, James Mill repeated the same theory which had been started by Plato centuries earlier. It is the contiguity of associations that helps us to remember things. Hamilton, however, disputed this and held that one impression does not always revoke a single idea, but really recalls the whole situation of which both the impression and the association were parts. The sight of a lyre for instance, does not recall simply the tune or a particular player but the whole conference in which the tune was previously played, in which both the tune and the player will perhaps stands in prominence.

In 1885 Ebbinghause carried out his famous nonsense syllable experiments to analyse the function of learning and remembering. He thus attempted to reduce the problem to its basic elements. His experiments on learning and memory from a connected series deserve special mention. In remembering, much that is learnt is forgotten soon, but what remains is retained for a longer time and the rate of forgetting becomes slower as we proceed. The two factors involved in spacing learning periods for effective remembering are:

1. The length of the learning period, and
2. The successive interval between two learning periods.

Warden studying maze learning found that if a rat was forced to run in a maze in order to get its food, it learnt better successive practice for shorter periods for several days. But learning is not that effective when the practice was continued for one long period on a single day. There is, however, no hard and fast rule about the length of a period or the interval suitable for all cases. This will clearly depend on the nature of the task set. When the material is easy and the motivation is high, a longer period or two long periods of learning may do. But when the task is different or when the interest slackens it is possible that boredom will set in if the practice period is long. Well distributed frequent short periods may be better.

Ebbinghause's Experiments on Learning and Memory

Though much criticised, the experiment on nonsense syllables by Ebbinghaus is a classical one being the first objective method to assess the relation of learning to retention. It also finds out to what extent do fatigue and boredom prevent both learning and retention. Ebbinghause selected nonsense syllables for examining the process of learning and remembering. He felt that when ordinary words are selected, they may convey different meanings for different individuals. Thus some persons have a better memory for certain words than others, and therefore, such words may be learnt better and remembered longer not for their basic qualities, but because they happen to have a greater stimulation. In selecting his syllable Ebbinghause, therefore, wanted them to be nonsense so that every learner may be placed at an equal disadvantage. He further made certain rules about their formation. The syllables should be so selected that the consecutive syllable should not together form a familiar word. Further all the syllables should be of the same length, if not, the longer or the shorter syllable may be remembered better because of its peculiarity. All syllables should be similarly constructed. He suggested that they should have two consonants and a vowel in between. The same vowel should not be repeated in two consecutive syllables nor should the initial and final consonants of two consecutive syllables be the same. Even the initial consonant of one syllable should not be same as the final consonant of its immediately proceeding syllable. All these, he held, would help in the retention of the pairs of syllables. All the syllables should be presented to the subject for exactly the same interval so that no one gets a prominence by a longer presentation. This can be ensured by presenting the syllables through a tachistoscope where the syllables are pasted on the roller and only one is visible through the opening. The movement of the roller is timed by a watch or a metronome. The number of trials or presentations necessary before a subject is able to recall, would demonstrate the rate of learning of a person. When the full list has been learnt, it has to be confirmed by a second presentation which should also be repeated in full. The number of words learnt on each presentation can be plotted on a graph and thus the learning curve may be drawn. This generally shows a steep rise at the start followed by a general flattening which is again followed by another steep rise. At the flat portion, evidently, learning has been slowed down and this Ebbinghause calls Plateau. There may be more than one plateau during learning in some cases. The existence of these plateaus signifies either fatigue or boredom.

Ebbinghause has also used his experiments to measure memory. This is measured by asking the subject to reproduce what he has learnt after an interval which may be from a few hours to a few days, Evidently, one does not remember the whole list fully and therefore needs another series of successive presentations before he can recall the whole list again. But it is also seen that in relearning he needs fewer presentations than before. The difference between the number of presentations on the first and on the second occasions would be an index of the person's memory. Presenting the list after successive intervals, sometime longer and sometimes shorter, may help us in finding out the rate of forgetting. Ebbinghause found that 44% of the original material in nonsense syllables are usually retained after an hour to two. After nine hours this falls to 30% and after two days it falls down to 28%. There is, however, a lot of individual differences. Some persons are found to remember the whole list even weeks after. In India it has been found, that on an average, the retention of nonsense syllables is higher. Over half is remembered after two hours, 37% after 8 hours and 31% after a week. The experiment thus serves several purposes. Subjectively, it can compare the memories of two persons. Objectively, it shows the important fact that much of what we learn is forgotten at the earlier stage.

Seashore repeated the experiment using nonsense geometrical figures where each figure consisted of three lines, two of equal length and one shorter (resembling Ebbinghause's distribution of vowels and consonants) so arranged that they neither resembled any letter or an alphabet known to the subject nor any known geometrical figure. With these results, wc can likewise draw learning curve for the initial set of presentation and memory curve for successive presentations. He also got result like Ebbinghause regarding forgetting.

Psychologists like Bartlett have criticised the technique of Ebbinghause. They hold that when remembered the syllables no longer remain nonsense. The subject by virtue of some association, if no logical association is available, creates a certain amount of sense. Perhaps certain sounds in nonsense syllables and certain configuration of space in geometrical figures create stimuli of meaning. Thus all that Ebbinghause and others have done is to drive out the natural stimulus of meaning and create room for accidental and totally uncontrolled factors. The bonds of accidental associations, will naturally be different with different persons.

Researches after Ebbinghause

Researches after Ebbinghause have established that mere passage of time does not cause a person to forget. Other factors like interest and tension come in for they cause better attention. Zeigarnik gave a number of pupils some twenty puzzles to solve and along with these puzzles he included a few problems which touched matters of their interest.

While the pupils were working for the first half of the period the pupils were interrupted, but for the other half they were free from interruptions. Normally one should expect that the second half which proceeded without interruption would be remembered better, and that they would forget most of what they had learnt during interruption. But contrary to expectations, it was found that they remembered and could recall more of the solutions that had been performed in the midst of interruption, than those which proceeded without interruptions. Zeigarnik explains this strange behaviour by asserting that since interruptions created a tension in the mind, attention was evoked better by the tension and hence the subjects could remember better.

Emotion affects both learning and memory. Freud explains forgetting in terms of his theory of repression. We tend to forget unpleasant memories and ideas because we repress them. In the same way we forget the names or faces of persons we dislike. Meltzer and Stagner have however tried to work out quantitatively the extent to which dislike aids in helping us to forget. It seems from their experiments that the amount is not very large, being only the 15%. Evidently, both Freud and the other experimenters show that when repression causes a certain amount of tension, forgetting would not be so easy.

Jenkins and Dallenbach have shown that if after learning a new thing, we fall asleep, we are likely to remember it better than when we keep awake after learning. The explanation of this is obvious. When we are awake we can not help new impressions entering into our minds and these would certainly overlap and reduce the intensity of the impressions. But when we fall asleep immediately, we prevent such possibility and this helps us to retain things.

Muller and Pilzckar have found that memory of a newly learnt poem may be interfered due to learning a second poem. Subjects were found to recall 56% or even more of the learnt material, if there had been no additional assignments imposed. But when engaged in more than one task, they can recall less than half, often 26% or less. This is also due to other impressions overlapping. Busy people are often found absent minded, because new images are being blurred by the appearance of overlapping images. This they called 'Retroactive Inhibition.'

Jost has found a principle of review which is commonly known as Jost law. Stated briefly, it holds that if two associations are of equal strength, but have been formed at different periods, it will be seen that with passage of time the older one will lose its intensity though rather slowly. In order to retain a learnt material, therefore; frequent relearning and review are essential. Thus, Jost really found the same for memory what Thorndike had stated for learning by two laws of Frequency and Recency.

A mysterious effect was noticed by Ballard in 1913. He found that sometimes after the passage of time, old and forgotten things become vivid once more, even if an attempt of review is not made. This he calls "Reminiscence" and should not be taken as opposing Jost law in any way. Ballard's findings are for single items that are learnt, while Jost's findings relate to a comparative retention of two items. Ballard's findings are also complementary to Ebbinghause's findings, for he assumes that after an initial learning, a lot of learned material seems to be forgotten. What Ebbinghause assumed as forgotten, Ballard holds that they merely sink to the bottom of the mind so to speak. Some of these sunk materials may suddenly rise up under certain conditions. Strictly speaking, reminiscences are not so well found in case of nonsense materials. It has generally to do with experiences which are more meaningful. Perhaps by getting fresh stimulus of association, conscious or unconscious, there is a sort of perception and therefore, the old things also come up. This kind of reminiscence is more common with childhood experience than with experiences of later times.

Remembering in terms of Gestalt Theory

Gestalt theory holds that all mental phenomena have a structure or pattern, and that ideas and events are never isolated. They always exist with some connection or association with each other. If these connections are just perceived or vaguely remembered, naturally they will not have so much effect as when they are intelligently perceived. When relations are duly understood, Gestalt theory proves why it is easier to remember the whole poem rather than stanza. Gestalt theory will explain "Retroactive Inhibition" or interference of one learnt material by another. It assumes that either they do not represent two different portions of the same pattern or two contrasting patterns, or else if they belong to the same pattern or configuration, they interfere because connections between them are not well understood. Reminiscence according to Gestalt is nothing but a rehearsal of the entire situation which comes up when the general pattern is recalled and all the portions including things that were apparently forgotten get recalled.

Summary

The gains of learning are really in the direction of retention and remembering. As in learning so in remembering, the associationists offer the explanation that by creating bonds of association experiences are retained and so are the bundles of thought. Hartley and Mill as well as Brown subscribed to this theory and made substantial personal contributions to it. The best and the most well known experiment on Association had been those by Ebbinghause in nonsense syllables. The conditions imposed on the selection of syllables and on their presentation prevented any type of bias from creeping in and the experiment was able to show the nature of learning and of forgetting. Learning and memory curves showed for instance, plateaus of boredom or fatigue during learning. The results indicated that much is forgotten at the initial stage. His experimental results have been corroborated by similar experiments in other fields, notably by Seashore. Psychologists like Bartlett, however, express some doubt whether Ebbinghause has after all succeeded in driving out the stimulus of meaning. They hold that perhaps accidental associations are able to give meanings to these nonsense syllables.

Recent researches like those of Freud, Meltar and Stagner have proved that our retention is not merely dependent on the article, but more on the attitude of the learner. The common assumption is that interruption causes distractions and makes us forget things quickly. But that is not the real fact. They may cause tensions and thereby things get better remembered causing the mind to strain calling forth better attention. Emotional changes and interest are also vital factors. When two things are learnt simultaneously one learning overlaps with the other. This perhaps explains Jenkin's findings why we seem to remember better when we fall asleep immediately after learning. Muller and Flizkar have given a special name to this interference of the second material namely Retroactive inhibition. Of the two associations the older one is forgotten unless reviewed. This is really a repetition of Thorndike's Laws of Frequency and Recency. Ballard found that very often forgotten things are brought back into the mind, proving that they remained sunk perhaps at a subconscious mind, proving that they remained perhaps at a subconscious level.

8

ATTENTION AND INTEREST

What is attention

Attention is the name of that condition within a person which enables him to be clearly aware of a certain object or activity. It is a condition of preparedness or alertness.

While sensation means merely receiving certain stimuli of which we are just conscious of, perception means the general awareness of these stimuli. In perception, therefore, the sensations which are received convey some meaning. Attention is focussing perception in a definite direction. In a way therefore, attention is a cause and an aspect of perception. In order that perception may acquire some meaning, it is necessary that certain features of perception have to be focussed. Yet it must not be supposed that we attend to only one thing at a time. About a hundred years ago Sir William Hamilton noted that as many as six or seven different objects can be perceived at a time. Cattell found that adults can apprehend six to eleven objects at a time, and if the items occur in meaningful groups many more can be comprehended. Thus if letters are grouped into words and the latter into meaningful short sentences, as many as thirty can be comprehended at a time. It is thus found that in such a situation, the sentence is comprehended as one single unit. Attention may also be described as a process of adjustment of the organism to the stimulus situation.

William Jones has divided attention into kinds, in various ways. It is either sensorial attention or objects connected with sense or intellectual attention, where the objects are represented either by ideas or written symbols.

Thus when we concentrate on a toy or a picture, the attention is sensorial. When we are reading a book, the meaningful words are expressed by mere symbols and hence the attention is intellectual.

When the book represents a story with complex characterisation, the intellectual element is still further raised to a higher level. In another system of classification, attention may be immediate, when the topic or stimulus is interesting by itself without relation to anything else. Thus as the sweets are presented to the child, the child pays attention to the movement and the attention is immediate. But attention may also be derived in which case the child's immediate interest may not be connected with the thing acting as the stimulus, but the source of interest springs from an object with which the particular stimulus is associated. Thus a student may pay attention to a verse not because the verse itself is interesting, but because the student has been promised a reward on successful recitation of the verse. The source of interest here lies in the promised reward. In the successful learning the attention may either be passive, involuntary and effortless or active and voluntary: Involuntary attention always accompanies an intense or voluminous or sudden impulse. It is always immediate and generally sensorial, though rarely intellectual. When we are posing to take photograph the sudden flare of the flash light may draw our immediate attention. While in a running bus, the sight of a magnificent building may likewise draw our attention and so would unexpected appearance of a person who has been reported as dead. But all our sources of attention are not involuntary. Some times we make an effort at attending to some thing. Voluntary attention is always for a derived object. If the stimulus is interesting by itself, attention will come spontaneously and involuntarily. But if it is not so, we consciously make associations of the source of our attention. The particular stimulus which is before us, directs our effort to the latter in order to reach the former. Though generally intellectual, voluntary attention may be sometimes directed to sensorial subjects as well.

Constancy of Attention

James has also found that the nature of stimuli for attention fluctuates with age. While children are more excited with immediately exciting and sensorial stimuli, the adults are generally trained to select those stimuli which are connected with permanent interests. It is, therefore, no wonder that the famous mathematician Archemedes could quietly work out mathematical problems amidst the din and noise of the Roman invasion. He was so engrossed in his work that he took no precaution to save his life and ultimately met a tragic death.

Cruze says that the teacher who requests 'whole and undivided' attention of the members of his class is guilty of a loose talk. Attention can not but be whole and undivided for the moment when one concentrates towards a particular stimuli. The stimulus may be a picture or a group of words, a statue which we see, or a musical note we hear, or an object with fragrance. It is of course possible that attention may fluctuate or the focus may move from one stimulus to another. The continual shifting of attention should not, however, worry a teacher unless the shifting takes place outside the general area. The person reading an exciting novel shifts his attention from line to line, from page to page and yet his attention to the novel is sustained for hours. The spectators of a match shift their attention from one side of the play ground to another along with the running ball and yet their attention to the game remains sustained till the match is over. The best way to maintain a sustained attention is thus by developing an intense interest in that area or activity. When other stimuli begin to draw attention from the object to which we want to focus our attention, we call the latter distractors. When we are distracted, we are attending to the situation, which we feel should not be receiving our attention. Distraction, like attention may be sensorial, viz. noise, want of light, bad smell or any attractive object, or it may be intellectual. It may either be immediate or derived. It may be external or internal. Hunger, nausea, tension, worry, anxiety and similar things act as internal distrauctors. Distractions are thus conflicts between stimuli and we try to avoid them. Thus we may avoid distraction of the noise in the hostel and go to study in a quiet park. We may also overcome distractions by spending an increased amount of energy.

Determinants of attention are the factors that produce the condition of attention in a person. They may be internal or external. The nature, size, duration and intensity of the stimulus comprise external determinants. The internal or subjective determinants are interest, needs, desires and purposes of the individual.

Interest : its importance

People vary greatly in their interest, which acts as the source of motivating attention. The same situation may produce different kinds of interest to different persons. Thus a farmer inspecting a plot of land would be interested in the nature of the soil and plants growing on it, while a geologist will be more attracted in the layers of rocks exposed. A contractor may look at the same plot and think of how it can be subdivided and used to make residential buildings, while an artist would walk round until he found the position from which the landscape looked as a balanced composition would be painted. Thus all the four persons are looking at the plot with different interests and each is focussing his attention from a particular angle and point of interest. The interests supply the necessary source of energy to focus attention or to sustain it and also to overcome distractions, if any. Thus it is found that we may spend the same time in reading a novel as we might in working a number of mathematical sums. Yet we shall probably feel a greater strain in the latter. It is because the latter act is of less interest. It has been seen that interest reduces the fatigue considerably and the work itself proceeds quite smoothly. What will constitute an interest? Are we interested in an act whose outcome brings us to a desirable end? This leads to a further question, who is to decide and what end is desirable? The answer to that is, it is the pupil who has ultimately to decide. A real interest can not be created, it has to be generated within the person. Interests are not totally inborn, they are acquired in course of interaction with the society in which we live. In most of the cultures men are more interested in adventure, in physical activity, in mechanics, in aggressive games, while the women are mostly interested in artistic work, in domestic activities and in social services. It is so because these are the roles that men and women play respectively in their later lives in cultures. Alexander Goldenwiser has found that in some of the cultures hunting is done by women and cooking and housekeeping by men.

It is thus clear that, if we want the child to be interested in any educational activity, we must generate interests in particular areas. In other words, education will be interesting, if it is connected with life.

How to make our lessons interesting

In order to make the lesson interesting, we must connect it with real life situations. Dewey has further stated that in order to sustain interest, the goal should be quite visible. Analysing the play activities, he states that the reason why a child is interested in the play activities is that, the outcome of the play is immediate. The child's action immediately leads to a result. In our so-called activities, the child is not so interested simply because the outcome is so far off. How can we expect a child to put in strenuous effort at the beginning of the session in his class work, if the outcome of his efforts will produce results at the end of the whole year? He thus advises us to devise our programme in such a general way that we may say that interests are created in socially useful activities. One may probe deeper and find out the particular region in which an individual is interested. For these we have individual interest tests. Most interests are measured by personal inventories. The subject indicates his likes and dislikes by appropriate markings of words and phrases, measures of interest, tests of information of objects and activities. There are special interest inventories and tests like Strong's Vocational Interest Blank. 400 items comprise the Blank and the subject marks them with his remarks 'like' indifferent' or `dislike'. Thrustone, analysing the Blank found that there are really four basic interests: Science, Language, people and business. Similar interest tests are available for recreational, literary and other fields of activities.

Summary

Attention is focussing perception in a definite direction. Though a person can direct his attention to several things almost simultaneously, it has been found that he really focuses his attention either to one single object or to a cluster of objects. Attention can be divided in various ways, it may be sensorial or directed to object of immediate perception. It may be intellectual or directed to objects represented by ideas or symbols. It may be immediate. Or it may be derived in which the thing may merely act as a stimulus to an outside object or idea. Attention may also be passive, involuntary or active. It has been seen that while immediate, interests are always involuntary, derived ones are voluntary or active. The latter distinction does in no way differentiate between sensorial or intellectual attention. Both of these can either be passive or active though in a majority of cases intellectual attention is active. While children are more excited with immediately exciting and sensorial stimuli, more mature persons are generally trained to select matters of more remote and permanent interest. Attention is seldom steady as it fluctuates. There is no harm if this fluctuation is kept within bounds. Any one reading an interesting novel shifts his attention from line to line, and yet retains his major interest in the outcome of the story he follows. Distractors like noise, bad illumination, act as impediments to attention. These may be immediate or derived, external as well as internal like hunger, worry or anxiety.

Relationship between attention and interest

Attention is closely related to interest as interest brings motivation. It is essentially a matter of enduring settings of our conative tendencies and impulses and is determined by our instincts and sentiments. Dewey affirms that genuine interest is the accompaniment of the identifications, through action, of the self with some object or ideas. According to Vernon, "an interest is just as complex as an amalgam of subjective feelings and objective behaviour tendencies." These feelings and tendencies propel human drives and reinforce attention.

INTEREST—ITS BEARING ON MEMORY AND ATTENTION

Interest is a word with different shades of meaning. Drever describes interest as both functional and structural.

The feeling of worthwhileness accompanying attention to an object or activity, may be ascribed to the functional sense of the term, while element in make up is structural. Although it is usual to regard interests as personality traits, together with attitudes, needs and aptitudes, the structure of personality has not yet secured agreement on its basic dimensions. While some progress has been made recently, the study of Interests awaits exploration.

The difficulty should not be under rated. As mentioned before, there are various aspects of interest involving the cognitive process, affective and the conative elements. On the other hand, there are other aspects which may be roughly described as dimensions.

Dimensions of Interest

Very few have doubted the complexity of interest. The expressions of interest are too diverse to be detected. In the first place, intensity may be termed as one of the dimensions. This dimension in question may include psychological energy or dynamic power with which the interest is charged. Nature of interest may be taken as another dimension of interest.

Duration of interest may be assumed to be the third dimension of interest. Nature of interest may be indicated by the type of organisation within the mind. Interest may thus be potential or acquired.

Memory traces of past experience conditioned by inherited propensities and by the physical and social environment may give some indication of the nature of interest.

The cognitive aspect of an interest is first noticeable involving attention, perception, discrimination and judgment. The selectivity of attention that accompanies interest is remarkable. It also involves the dispositions to attend to a particular object to select, discriminate and compare. It refers to the organisation of past experiences and to the immediate recall of selected elements to meet the interest situation.

The weighing of certain elements in the schemata might be determined by the senses or by drives, but with adults mostly through the operation of persistent interests.

It has also been recognised that in any interest situation there is present an affective element, that is, a feeling or emotion. This is implied in such terms as "self-identification" and "ego-involvement". In the "dynamic" psychology of recent years, this feeling is related to the state of tension existing in the subject's mind.

The feeling is accompanied by a discharge of psychological energy which has accumulated on the interest.

The conative element of striving towards a goal appears to be distinctive. It is, however, possible that there would exist certain relationships between the aspects or dimensions of interest. For example, the intensity of interest may be more related to the affective aspects. But the more perturbing question is to determine the nature of interest and discriminate between what is potential and acquired.

Emphasis is also being laid on the determinants of behaviour. According to Allport, personality represents an individual's style and mastery within his behavioural field.

In order to test the hypothesis that there exists a good deal of overlapping between various aspects and dimensions of interest one has to construct suitable instruments designed to measure each aspect and dimension already formulated. Centroid analysis of the inter-correlations may reveal the fact whether there are so many aspects or dimensions.

If various dimensions emerge out of factor analysis it would be evident that the existing approaches to the assessment of interest and other personality variable are far from being adequate.

The history of measurement of interest shows that both subjective and objective approaches have been made to assess interest in one or two dimensions. As a result, the earlier attempts have not been crowned with full success. Among the earlier classifications, most of the attempts are towards taking up one of the dimensions of interest and approaching the problem by means of one or two techniques. Inventory has been employed mainly for attacking the cognitive aspect of interests whereas information tests and other techniques have been employed for attacking the unconscious level of interest formation.

In the broadest terms there has been a constant shift of emphasis from one sense of the term to the other. It is a fact that the complexity of the nature of interest has been brought to the notice and considered while constructing the test.

The study of the structure of personality has not yet secured agreement on its basic dimensions, and so the approaches to the assessment have varied considerably. Another outstanding problem around interest is that of classification. Workers in this field were not particularly aware of this problem and they went on classifying interests in their own ways. This classification was really arbitrary and it is difficult to arrive at an agreed list of interests. If interests are interpreted as expressions of satisfaction of certain needs in the course of adjustment to environment, then it is likely that various kinds of interests would appear in various fields. On an analysis, however, it will be observed that interests are related to the various fields of activities as motivational factors. There have been attempts to find out the broad patterns of interests which can be roughly described as:-

1. Theoretical or intellectual.
2. Aesthetic or artistic.
3. Economic or utilitarian.
4. Mechanical or technical.
5. Scientific.
6. Social or humanitarian.
7. Religious or spiritual.
8. Political.

It is just obvious that these categories of interest may be superficial and the surface study of these might lead to nothing. According to Cattell, the reason behind the failure in a perfect classification may be attributed to the inability in constructing indirect measures of interests and attitudes. He also points out that the chief trend is in classifying general interests either under arbitrary, convenient logical categories or else by using factorial analysis and similar methods to find the groups in which interests cluster. It is, therefore, desirable that attempts should first be made to discover the basic patterns of interests.

Most of the classifications have been of a—priori nature and on the whole there is a tendency to use the five categories which may be called the "classical" ones.

(1) Aesthetic (2) Scientific (3) Social (4) Mechanical and (5) Business.

The writer was conscious of the difficulty of reconciling some of the results of previous study and an investigation was made to explore the field for improving the position. It has been found from a factorial study, carried out by the writer elsewhere that very few patterns of interests emerge out of factor analysis. The reasons were not far to seek. It was felt that the limited number of assumed variables may be one of the reasons for smaller numbers of factors emerging out of the analysis. He was not, therefore, convinced that the number of the basic patterns of interests is so limited.

9

MEANINGS, IMAGERY AND IMAGINATION

Importance of Meaning

Unfortunately much of what passes for learning in the classroom is really mechanically memorized statements which pupils cram without understanding. The inevitable dependence of learning upon meaning is thus being ignored. The language in which statements are given are really means of conveying thought and are the vehicles of ideas. They must, therefore, be understood, and not merely mechanically memorized. Confusion arises when words that are used are in areas remote from the perception or experience of the persons. Words, as such are used to symbolize experiences. Their capacity for conveying ideas depends not only on the extent they are able to convey experience. Meanings that these words stand for, are to be evolved out of perception. The perception of the child becomes more refined and generalized, as he becomes more and more aware of the detailed aspects of objects. Thus he recognized the difference between a round ball which has depth, and a round disc which is flat. Perception depends on the use and experience of an object. Dewey has given a good example of the circumstances under which the child learns the meaning of the word 'hat'. Probably his mother before taking the child out puts hat on the child's head. The child's primary interest lay in going out, for it meant seeing new things and going to new surroundings. But he at the same time noticed the inevitable connection between the putting on of the hat and going out. Thus the thing, hat, acquired a meaning for him because it was necessary to fulfil his interest. The child's interest in the hat was thus aroused and the hat became meaningful. Now, if the mother utters the word 'Hat' the child will notice the inevitable connection between the thing in which he was interested and the name. The word 'hat' now stands for the thing, and hence it becomes meaningful to the child. But if we ask a child the definition of 'hat', he will simply say, it is something to put on the head. Most of the children's definitions are similarly functional. A chair is something to sit on, a ball is something to kick. Perhaps these definitions may not seem to be quite logical or exhaustive but by this method of identifying objects by naming them without any mention of their specific characters, a child gets the primary basis of meanings. With experience, meanings are extended to other functions, than what the objects are supposed to stand for. This is more true when meanings are extended to actions besides objects. There is of course some connection between the fundamental or primary meanings and the secondary or derived meanings. The latter is more symbolic and convey something more than what is immediately perceived. But as words are used to convey certain experiences, a word becomes capable of conveying a primary and one or more derived meanings. It may give room for misunderstanding, for the experiences of the user and the listener may differ. As an example let us take the simple word 'lift' which is a word conveying an action namely 'to pick up'. This is the primary meaning of the word which everybody understands. But this word is capable of giving atleast four different types of meanings under four different situations:

1. Let us lift the book up from the shelf (Primary).
2. Give me a lift in your car from here to the Station.
3. He got a lift as he became the headmaster.
4. There is a lift, here in this building.

Misunderstandings are bound to crop up when the user speaks of the lift in one sense and the listener understandings in another. A village boy who has never seen a lift may feel that it literally picks up people or one who is not accustomed to giving or getting lifts in a car may feel that the driver literally picks up passengers and the like. Again one may think of a lift as a rise in the salary, while another may understand it as being given work at a place which is served by electric lifts.

From these derived meanings abstract concepts of a more generalised nature are developed. Of course not all the words are capable of this type of generalised meanings. But in those that are thus capable, there is perhaps a greater danger of misunderstanding. The user may utter a generalized word without realising its full implications. Such danger was responsible for the development of socratic method of counteracting the abstract definitions of the sophists. Such dangers are no less, evident today. Perhaps our restricted field of experience vitiates the meanings which these terms have in a wider context. But this word is capable of giving at least four different types of meanings under four different situations mentioned earlier.

1. Let us lift the book up from the shelf (Primary).
2. Give me a lift in your car from here to the Station.
3. He got a lift as he became the headmaster.
4. There is a lift, here in this building.

Misunderstandings are bound to crop up when the user speaks of the lift in one sense and the listener understands in another. A village boy who has never seen a lift may feel that it literally picks up people or one who is not accustomed to giving or getting lifts in a car may feel that the driver literally picks up passengers and the like. Again one may think of a lift as a rise in the salary, while another may understand it as being given work at a place which is served by electric lifts.

From these derived meanings abstract concepts of a more generalised nature are developed. Of course not all the words are capable of this type of generalised meanings. But in cases where one word has many meanings there is perhaps a greater danger of misunderstanding. The user may utter generalized word without realising its full implications. Such dangers are no less, evident today. Perhaps our restricted field of experience vitiates the meanings which these terms have in a wider context. To a labourer, Democracy perhaps means the rule of the mob on a strike day and social justice may convey the idea of an unruly meeting demanding a rise in wages. Their thoughtless use may produce such situations as may be embarrassing or dangerous. It is only after widening the field of experience so as to give a suitable opportunity for such generalisations that one should use them. Herein comes the role of the school. Since these abstract words are to be used in real life situations, it is the function of the school to provide an opportunity for imitating the life situations and to show the context in which such generalisations and abstract terms can be used. This is possible only when the school is connected with the life.

How can the meanings be clarified or enriched

One of the first steps that must be taken to clarify meanings should be to make the fullest use of the environment. Pupil's experience should be supplemented with a great variety of all types of visual aids available. These must as far as possible be the accurate representation of the reality. A toy motor should look like a real motor for instance, otherwise, they may convey hazy and incorrect impressions. In using these representations however, one should remember that aids are just aids and should not be confused with ends. They should not for instance be used in preference to real things when there are opportunities available for showing real things.

Since it is not always easy to communicate specific objects of experiences, as they are so many, we must classify such experiences and arrange them into groups so that they become more handy, useful and therefore, more meaningful. Here we are really borrowing the technique of the labour-saving device shown by associationists.

After generation, ideas have to be abstracted or the essential process must be taken out of the specific and concrete situations. This is possible by a careful survey of the specific or concrete situations and by extracting from them the essential element. The boy's idea of 'affection' for instance, is the result of the generalised concept of a number of concrete and specific situations of a mother fondling her child, a bird feeding its young, or a girl playing with her dolls. His concept of 'democracy' may likewise be built for him in the school by what he sees in orderly organisation of his literary societies, students' governments in his hostel or in the sports organisations.

We thus find that whatever be the type of the meaning, primary or secondary, generalised or abstract, we can get them only against the background of a concrete reality or specific cases and situations which clarify and enrich these meanings. Some of these concrete situations are of course provided by the home or other agencies that are giving informal education. It is the work of the school or any other institution where a teacher is to give a formal education to think of other situations and provide opportunities to the students to get as near as the concrete reality as possible. This, the schools can do provided they identify themselves with as many of the life situations as are practically possible for them to do.

Imagery and meaning

The meaning that is gained in any situation is stored in the mind in the form of images. These images are later recalled when the need for them arises. Images arise out of specific experiences, that an individual has. If a boy uses lift in the sense of a rise in the salary that his father might have got in the office, and another uses it in the sense of a free ride that a kind motorist gave him on a rainy day, it is because their experiences differ. Even abstract ideas are generalised experiences of a number of concrete situations.

We must, however, remember that the images are not merely conservative. They do not only retain whatever impressions are given, but sometimes they blend one or more images together and reconstruct something new, something that did not exist before. In such cases the images are the causes of imagination. One must have a stock of images gathered from the concrete reality as well as experience and a number of images built before they can be blended together.

Whether specific or, generalised, concrete or abstract, images help the children to form imagination.

A child of four or five by dramatising the situation, by playing the role of an engine driver, gets an opportunity for his diversion. He is really building up his images of the engine which he has once seen. Perhaps he is at the same time using the law of practice and repeats the process to get the images of the essential and perhaps symbolic forms of the functions of a railway engine. Perhaps this gives a clue to the schools about the methods they should follow in building up these images. They may likewise try to give opportunity to practice, with lifelike models or by dramatisation when real things are not available. This helps the learner to gain more impressions and to consolidate these in order that proper images may be formed.

Theories of Imagery

In the eighteenth and in early nineteenth centuries, psychologists used the term 'Image' in the same sense as they used 'Ideas', 'Associations', or 'Thought'. They assumed that memory and thinking involved a definite imagery.

Hume distinguished between impressions and images for the first time stating that whole impressions occur in presence of the objects; images are just faint copies of the original impressions. His views were shared by James Mill. Hartley tried to define images on a psychological basis.

He held that sensations cause nervous vibration and arouse miniature feeble vibrations within the brain. He believed that these vibrations build up images.

In 1860 Galton reported the astonishing results of his study on mental images by means of questionnaire which he had put to many persons. An ordinary man had after all a limited field of experience in which his images are formed. But wherever these images are formed they appear to be quite clear and well defined. In case of highly qualified and experienced scientist and literary men however, the case appeared to be quite reverse. They had no doubt images extended over many fields, but such images appeared to be quite blurred and diffused. Women and young boys had fewer but on the whole better defined images than men. Evidently, it seems there is something wrong with image formation in an educational surrounding. Galton ascribed the deficiency of imagery in the scientists to be due to the fact that they were called upon to do a lot of abstract thinking without a concrete background.

As the images are formed out of impressions, and the gateway for these impressions are the senses, it is necessary for us to find which sense in particular is more active in giving us the impression. Different persons it was found, used different senses. Perhaps, if we could ascertain which sense is predominating in which person, we may build up his imagery accordingly.

Kraplin and later Smith by using words and phrases conveying sense impressions with different sense areas have attempted to find out which sense department is more predominating. 'A cup' for instance gives the impression of a beautiful utensil to one and thus provides an opportunity to form a visual image To another with a more developed sense of smell or taste it may convey the flavour of delicious tea, a third with a specially developed taste for food, will probably smack his lips for some delicacy that can be served in the cup.

Kraplin used a number of phrases, from each of the five sense departments: visual (sight), gustatory (taste), olfactory (smell), tacticle (touch) and auditory (hearing). To these he added a sixth sense

Kinesthetic that implies motion. Kraplin's division of the original words or stimuli were such that they were equally divided. The classification of course being subjective, depends on the judgement of the experimenter. The subjects were asked to state the impressions, which these words seemed to convey. It was found that the experimenter's classification of the words convey the classification of the images the person experimented upon. Very often he gave more images in one or more sense departments and fewer impressions in others. Care should, however, be taken while performing this experiment that the actual objects are not present before the subject, for in that case it will be as case of perception rather than image formation. Smith repeated the experiment with phrases instead of words and found similar results. The educational implications of such experiments are important.

This can help to diagnose which happens to be more effective for the formation of impression of a particular student. This is the proper area in which he is apt to form his images, to suit his individual needs. We must so organise his impressions mostly through his more effective gateway of predominating sense perception. It is only then that his images will be meaningful.

Galton found that imagery of abstract things is some time peculiar. To some, different arithmetical numbers represent bars or lines of different lengths, while to others, these represent different colours and different shades of red, black or green. The images of different colours are some times blended with auditory tunes. When they see a red colour they are reminded of a peculiar tune and when they see a green colour they are reminded of another tune. Some people have hearing associated with colours. When they hear a particular tune they are reminded of one colour and for a different tune they have another colour. Such impressions are perhaps results of accidental or chance associations. They may often cause much embarrassment to the persons. The remedy lies in freeing them of these impressions quite early in their lines by producing the right type of impressions. They should have these abstract generalised concepts from many concrete impressions.

Stern tried to devise an objective measure of the amount and quality of imagery. He wanted to test how vivid an image a person can form, since all persons do not form equally vivid images. Stern would show a picture to a subject and ask him to recall as many details as he could possible do. In 1907, Urbantschits and later Jarnesch found that some persons have the remarkable capacity of recalling clear-cut images of things presented before them for a short time, say, half a minute. It is evident that the time is insufficient for a normal person to perceive so many details. Such persons are said to have idiotic Imagery. Often they would recall such details as might have escaped their conscious perception, thus proving that their perception has been at least, in part, somewhat subconscious. Allport however, finds nothing very wonderful in this idiotic imagery. It is the ordinary power of image formation only a bit quicker and morevivid.

Imagination

To a man in the street there is perhaps hardly any difference between mental imagery and imagination. Perhaps one may confuse imagination with mere day dreaming which represents an element of wishful thinking in which not only adolescents but some time adult as well as children indulge. While there is often an element of fantasy in day dreaming, or in imagination, as defined by psychologists, there is also a creative thinking.

It is a process that leads to practical and constructive ends, though it may not always lead to tangible results.

Helmhotz studies his own creative thought process. He found that they were results of prolonged deliberate effort which often made him tired and distracted. Solution would come to him in the form of inspiration after some time.

Rosman found that creative ideas would come to an inventor only when he is somewhat in a relaxed mood. It would come when a person is asleep and sometime after he would wake up after a sound sleep. Rarely however, they appeared just before dropping off to sleep. As one can sleep only when he is free from distractions and worry, it follows that creative thoughts can never come to a worried and perplexed mind, but would appear only when mind has got over the state of perplexity, conflict or confusion.

Ribot and later Graham Walls studies the process more scientifically and through their investigations showed some difference in minor points, although in essential points they both agreed. They found four essential elements in imagination :

1. First of all there must be a desire to solve the problem. This Graham calls the preparation state.
2. For a long time this desire troubles the person without bringing out any solution. It is a long and painful period of racking one's brain. Graham calls this the period of incubation in which ideas often recur in the mind, but does not give any solution to the problem.
3. This is followed up by a period of illumination or inspiration in which the solution appears as a flash. Often the person is surprised as to how he overlooked this simple solution so long. He realises that the painful brain-racking process of the incubation period has really brought the solution in a subconscious form, and this has now suddenly risen up to the conscious level with a rapidity that surprises the person himself.
4. Lastly, comes the period of verification or revision, where the validity or correctness of the inspiration is tested by application.

Creative imagination may easily be confused with day dreaming, and one must not overlook that abstract thinking is the cause of both. The fact that some of the great inventors and discoverers had been mere dreamers in their childhood or adolescence would go to prove that one begets the other. We have already shown why an individual tired or distracted in the real world, covers up his inadequacies by building an unreal world of his own. This often happens during adolescence, when the causes of this frustration are perhaps greatest.

If left to itself this leads not only to a wastage of time but produces a ban and withdrawing habit providing a refuge which an individual would resort to whenever he feels frustrated in real life. Yet if properly directed, it may give the individual an opportunity to work out great things. Creative thinking is not the monopoly of a favoured or fortunate few. It is open to all who have a good stock of concrete images which are to blend and fuse together and to all who are ready to take sufficient pains.

Summary

Though commonly confused, rote or mechanical memory is not the same as meaningful learning or images. Because words are symbolised forms of experiences, there is a danger that the sense conveyed by the person communicating may not be understood by the person receiving information. If meaning is derived by the use of concrete objects, the chances of such misunderstandings are considerably reduced. Sometime, however, from the primary meaning an expression has many secondary or derived meanings, each of which becomes clear to a person who has had the experience of the thing, or situations in which such derived meanings have originated. From the derived meanings come the generalised or abstract meanings.

To enrich or clarify pupil's store of meanings, teachers should first of all make fullest use of the environment. Experiences are often classified into groups so that similar images may be formed.

Before abstraction, a careful survey of several concrete situations out of which such abstract situations have generated must be made. Whatever be the type of meanings, primary (concrete) or secondary, generalised or abstract, we must have a rich background of the concrete reality or specific cases and situations which make such meanings clear and remove chances for misunderstanding.

Meaning that is gained out of a concrete situation is stored inside the mind in the form of experiences. Images are, however, sometimes reconstructive. The impressions gained in a single situation are of course retained but very often few images blend together to form a new image which does not, of course, represent the reality, but becomes a new creation. But even this creation is the result of a background of concrete images.

While impressions take place in the presence of original objects and are results of perception, images occur in the absence of these objects, and are caused by a process of mental reconstruction of an experience undergone. When experiences are varied, there is a danger that before proper impression of an object is formed, a new impression is brought out, and both the impressions get blurred. It is not surprising, therefore, that for a person whose field of experience is limited, the images though few need to be well defined, while a scientist with stray experiences has wide area of floating ideas. This is really an unsatisfactory situation, and its remedy lies in enriching every image with experiences. All persons do not have the same type of impressions. Some seem to be more visual and they receive their impression mostly through the eye, while others may be auditory getting more impressions through the ears. There are persons who receive impression through other senses like the nose, touch or tongue or even through a sense of motion. Which of the senses of a pupil is predominating, can be found by the word or phrase list improvised by Kraplin or Smith. This will help the teacher to plan a course of instruction which may be more useful to a particular student. But this presupposes that instruction should be given either to individual or pupils divided into groups according to their imagery. It has also been seen that persons vary in their imagery. Some persons remember tunes as so many colours, while others remember colours as tunes. Besides these peculiarities, some persons have the remarkable capacity of quick perception. They can recall minute details after a short perception in which a normal person will hardly notice even half of those details.

10

PERSONALITY AND PERSONALITY DEVELOPMENT

What is Personality

Personality like intelligence is a term which is commonly used but its exact definition is yet to be arrived at. Personality is a global concept and it is marked by such characteristics by which a person can be distinguished from others. Generally we take notice of such persons who are able to attract our attention as somewhat different from others. Hypocrites first divided all human beings into four characteristic groups according to their temperament as follows:-

(a) Choleric or those who are easily excitable,

(b) Emotionally feeble and pessimistic or Melancholic,

(c) Emotionally insensitive or Phlegmatic, and

(d) Persevering and optimistic or Sanguine.

According to Hypocrites, these personality differences were caused by certain liver secretions, They affect our emotional life. Centuries after Hypocrites, Willim James in 1911 divided all human beings into two groups: One prone to accept the established ideals whom he called rationalist and the other ready to test and verify things whom he called empiricist. In 1923 Carl Jung had also a two fold division but on a different basis. He called the first group extrovert and held that their standard of judgement and reaction was related to the external world and the other was introvert whose standards were related to the internal or their own inner world.

Allport tried to find personality traits under five broad divisions namely: Intelligence, Motility, Temperature, Self-expression and Sociability. Each of these traits was subdivided into a number of factors. Allport's characteristics are twenty four as follows:—

Intelligence : (a) Capacity to remove obstacles, (b) Memory which is associated with learning, (c) Capacity to see interrelationships, (d) Creative imagination, and (e) Capacity to adjust to new situations.

Motility : (a) Capacity for work, (b) Methods of working, (c) Perseverance, and (d) General Ability.

Temperament : (a) Emotional strength, (b) Breadth or narrowness in the emotional field, (c) Capacity to control one's emotions, (d) Tendencies, and (e) Treatment towards other persons.

Self Expression : (a) Capacity to start work, (b) Insight, (c) Compensatory capacity and capacity to bear loss, (d) Extraversion or introversion, and (e) Aggressive or submissive attitude.

Sociability : (a) Social adjustment, (b) Capacity to share in social activities, (c) Self-centred or Self-evasive attitude, and (d) Character.

While Allport's subdivisions are comprehensive, even if they are somewhat overlapping, its critics hold that the absence of fixed standard for measurements will make allocations subjective and arbitrary.

Some Biological Considerations in determining Personality

Following Hypocrites, Earnest Kretschmer has classified all human beings into biological types, not according to bile secretions but according to their physical structure, and has allotted definite emotional roles associated with each physical make up. These are as follows:-

(a) Pyknics: Short and stout built persons among whom are found potential maniacs and aggressive persons in general.

(b) Asthenics: Tall and thin persons who are generally shy and withdrawing type and among which are found potential schizophrenic persons who suffer from split personality ordinarily talking to themselves.

(c) Athletes, or muscle-built

Researches have shown particularly the fact that there are more maniacs among pyknics and Schizophrenic among Asthenics. Persons tend to be stout and well-built and come under the pyknics category in an older age and in early youth they are more Asthenic. As prevalence of schizophrenia is mostly in the youth and maniacs are generally found at the age above forty, it is no wonder that he found more maniacs among pyknics and more schizophrenics among Asthenics.

In 1923, Gilbert attempted to divide personality in terms of alkaline secretions and held that aggressive tendencies are measured in terms of the quantity of alkaline secretion. Perman held that if the adrenal glands are over active one becomes more masculine, while if the rear lobes are over active one gets effeminate. An overactive thyroid is more active and persevering. Ross Stagner and Young, however, doubt about Berman's findings stating that our knowledge about the endocrine glands is yet incomplete.

Alfred Adler has, however, deduced certain sociological conclusions. Having found that most of the criminals and deliquents have some physical defects Adler traces the defect as the cause of their maladjustment not only at physical but sociological levels as well. If all persons had defects, then there would be according to him, no tensions. As the handicapped persons suffer from an inferiority complex their behaviour is adversely affected after the tension is thus caused.

Freud's view in Personality Determination

Freud has not denoted any definite personality type as such. He has traced Libido as the basic urge set up by the unconscious tendencies excited by Id. It is sexually inclined. Id which is controlled by Ego or the practical aspect of the self in a normal person. Ego is in its turn controlled by the Super Ego or the moral aspect of the self. Super Ego, according to Freud can not directly control the Id, but it does so always through Ego.

According to Freud, the personality structure is conditioned by the interaction of these forces from early infancy. The libido of a newly born infant is conditioned to its own body, later it gets fixed with its mother. If the fixation and later transference is not normal, it gives an abnormal fixation which Freud has called Oedipus complex. With girls, similar fixation with the father is possible. With the development of age and intellect, the libido is transferred to other persons, at first with persons of the same and later with the opposite sex. According to Freud, the urges of the libido are often running in opposite directions from the activities which are socially approved, and this creates conflicts which the Ego is not able to resolve and thus causes maladjusted personalities.

Freud's findings revolutionised the psychological approach to personalities although all persons do not agree with him. Terman had, for instance, found that instead of attachment to the parents of an opposite sex, boys get more emotionally attached to fathers and girls to mothers. It may further be said that in a joint family-structure in an eastern home, where there are other relatives superior to the parents in a social hierarchy, the findings of Freud would need considerable modification.

Social Influences on Personality Developments

Not only Adler, but a few other psychologists have doubted Freud's conclusions on personality development independent of social forces. Cooley first indicated the influence of the larger society, beyond the child's parents in the determination of personality. William Thomas studied some Polish families which have immigrated in U.S.A. and very soon displayed certain distinct behaviours from what they used to display at Poland. These were consequently the result of the impact of a new social environment. If the behaviours of the refugees from Hungary (after 1956) and of Eastern or Western Pakistan into different States of India, far away from their home-land, are studied we may obtain valuable information about change of personality traits due to social environment. The change is, however, due to three forces, the influence of the older environment, and the influence of the new circumstances.

Anthropologists have found out how certain stereotyped racial characteristics are found in every member of the race, conditioned by the expectations from each individual member of the society. Thus it has been found by Benedict that Zuni Indians of New Mexico, and by Margaret Mead that Tchambulis of New Guinea have more aggressive females and more timid males. The Tharu Indians of Jansar Bawar in U.P. show similar characteristics. All these are conditioned by the respective roles in those lands.

Cyril Burt in England and Eichhorn in Australia have found that most of the delinquents come from broken homes where one of the parents has been divorced or separated, or where the parents are found to be always quarrelling. As opposed to these findings, however, it has been found in U.P., that 80% criminals have come from well adjusted but rather poorer homes. It may be said that in a joint family-structure it is not parents alone that determine the personality development. There are, however, certain tribes in India which were called 'criminal' tribes. They were found to supply the potential criminals. Investigations have found that these have well settled moral codes within their own groups and their so called criminal tendencies are nothing but a sort of hostility to the larger group.

The environment of the school, in addition to home and immediate neighbourhood, no doubt, exerts a considerable influence on the development of the child. Education, no doubt influences the native tendencies of the child. It has been seen that students who have had some education tend to be broad-minded. Contact with one's own age group coming from different families and bringing different family traditions and traits does also help in developing the personality. Then we must not forget the tendency of hero-worship inherent in an adolescent, influencing the personality of the children. An ideal teacher can influence the growth of proper personality. This can easily be seen by comparing children from a good school with those from a bad school. And it is seen that a good family rearing as well as education in a good school are both conducive to a well-integrated personality.

Summary

Human society was concerned with what constitutes a personality. Since physical appearance attracts notice, it was studied first of all, but we find that from the time of Greek civilisation we have not been indifferent to emotional components of the personality as well. There is some definite similarity between what Hypocrites has said about bile secretions and what some of the psychologists say about the secretion of endocrine glands. But our knowledge, then and now, has been incomplete to establish a definite relation between these secretions and development of personality traits. Kretschmer has tried to connect personality traits with body built, but perhaps in this context the explanation given by Alder seems to be more convincing. It is the idea of a social superiority or otherwise that determines these traits. In other words, it is not the traits but their uniqueness in one's group that develops the traits.

Freud has studied the development of personality in terms of the fixation of libido and the adjustment of Id, Ego and Super Ego. His studies have been challenged by others, and may perhaps need some modifications in the light of the observations of eastern families where the upbringing of the child is some-what different.

That the social group from which the children have come had some influence on the personality has been confirmed not only by the study of delinquents coming from broken homes but also from different culture-contexts.

An objective study of the personality whether by Allport or by Benreuter's inventory, interviews or projective techniques give conflicting results, showing that personality being an all pervasive behaviour can not so easily be studied.

Personality and its Measurement

Differential psychology has become perhaps the most active branch of science. But it fails to explore all the dimensions of personality. It is extremely difficult to reach the new horizons of psychology as the personality is too complex to be analysed. Attempt has, however, been made to define personality from various angles. If we make a critical survey of the definitions already attempted, we can classify them under the following categories:-

(a) Omnibus definitions

(b) Configurational definitions

(c) Hierarchical definitions

(d) Definition in terms of adjustment

(e) Definition in terms of distinctiveness.

In spite of all the definitions of the term, it would be worth-while to arrive at a general definition representing a synthesis of contemporary psychology and its usage. The following definition may be accepted as a comprehensive one:-

"Personality is the dynamic organisation within the individual of those psycho-physical systems that determine his unique adjustments to his environment."

The definition represents a synthesis of the speculative thoughts in past ages and much of the scientific research in recent times. Mere definition of the term is not enough for our purposes as we are interested in identifying the elements which constitute personality. Psychology has embraced hopefully many possibilities, faculties, ideas, instincts, factors and dimensions.

Personality is rather an abstraction and character is often used synonymously with it. Some find it more convenient to use 'Temperament" instead of 'Personality'

It is, however, fortunate that almost all the psychologists have taken it as a psycho-physical disposition which develops from the interaction of human impulses. The concept implies certain organised system or structure which is gradually built up and which includes conscious sentiments and interests, complexes or mechanisms and the like.

There have been mainly two kinds of approaches for the assessment of personality for practical purposes.

(1) Typological approach, which can be roughly described as a synthetic approach is more or less concerned with a rough and ready estimate of a person as a whole. The oldest known classification was according to temperaments. It originated with a Greek medical school known as Hypocrite school and was based upon a theory about the varying proportion of four juices or 'humour" in bodies resulting in the following four temperaments.

(a) the Sanguine, (b) the Phlegmatic, (c) the Melancholic, and (d) the Choleric.

The Trait-Composite Approach

This is also an analytic approach and there have been many criticisms against this sort of atomistic study. That personality is a global unit which can by no means be analysed into several component parts, is maintained by few psychologists. But in spite of such vehement protest against the atomistic approach there have been considerable advances made by the factor analysts in this field. According to the former group, mere enumeration of person's traits and habits does not give a complete picture of the person, as the most important aspect of organised structure is ignored thereby. This has been emphatically put forward by Allport who is opposed to the monolithic or analytic approach. On the other hand, psychologists like Eysenck and Cattell have boldly faced the ideographic views but still insist on the necessity for trait-composite approach for practical purposes. It would be idle, according to them, to sit tight with the most vague and subjective approach.

Thus many traits have been discovered and assessments attempted. The term has been defined as a 'Collection of responses bound by some kind of unity which permits the responses to be gathered under a term.'

There have been various types of classifications of such traits as well:-

Unique traits — Common traits,

Surface traits — Source traits,

Constitutional traits — Environmental traits,

Dynamic traits, Ability traits — Temperamental traits, etc.

But among these the most important one is whether the trait is a unitary one or not.

Only recently psychometricians have favoured the conception of elements in terms of factors. The search for such elements has been carried out in many directions. A factor is rather an empirical generalisation. But there are difficulties with this conception of elements.

The first difficulty arises in the naming of factors. These factors very often seem remote from psychological fact and lead to confusion. The basic elements which are supposed to form the fundamental components of personality have unfortunately doubtful existence.

It is, however, assumed that the elements of personality are offered by the theory of pure or independent factors. On the other hand, the theory of focal and overlapping traits suggests the doctrine of functional autonomy. According to those who support functional autonomy, the dynamic substructures are unique and integrated, formed in the individual course of experience and heredity. The factorial approach assumed that they are uniform and they vary in weighages. But this assumption is perhaps mistaken. It is a fact that factorial techniques have some values for certain types of problems in psychology or sociology.

The doctrine of stimulus response elements however holds that personality is made up of a large number of independent characteristics or behaviour-tendencies.

The investigators have proceeded in different lines for exploring personality and discovering the structure of personality.

The problem of organisation and structure of personality is yet to be solved and the structure of personality depends on the consistency of an individual's conduct in an environmental situation.

The theory of partial identity often leads to an answer in the matter of generalisation and integration. It is a very serious question as to whether the inward cohesion in the structure of personality can be accounted for in this way.

The theory of traits is fairly established though they have been regarded as categories for the classification of habits. This is a biosocial approach and the biophysical approach considers a trait as a psychic force determining the active behaviour of an individual. Psychology has never been able to do without some conception of determining tendency and both attitude and trait are indispensable concepts.

The constancy of a trait is nearly an ideal and it is really difficult to discover these traits or assess them for an intimate knowledge of one's personality. To aid in the discovery of common traits a variety of devices is used.

The scientific evidence for the existence of traits comes from its constancy. Most significant of all the attributes of traits and their contribution to the problem of assessment is their interdependence, their uniqueness.

Cattell (1946, 1950, 1957) has made a comprehensive study of investigations into the structure of personality from many sources and different lines of approach. He has developed a theory of personality as a hierarchy of traits: that is collection of reactions or responses which are marked by some kind of unity and by a dynamic (teleological) direction towards a common goal. These traits can be verified and studied by means of correlation clusters and factor analysis. The former method reveals "surface traits", the latter "source traits". In the hierarchy, the basic, primary traits or "constitutional unities", called "urges" include needs and drives, directed towards some biological goal, as well as temperament and aptitude traits. The "environmental mould unities" are directed towards some intermediate goal acquired through the social or physical environment, and these include attitudes, sentiments and interests, which can be resolved into "urges". According to Cattell, attitudes are distinguished from interests through their definition in terms of direction or dynamic feeling (orectic) quality, which he conceives as a measure of the orientation of a vector. Thus, while most attitude tests measure only the orientation through a 180^0 plane-acceptance-rejection, Cattell thinks that many other planes could be used, such as curiosity-incuriosity, acquisitiveness—nonacquisitiveness. What is termed the 'strength' of an attitude is properly a measure of the amount of interest involved. Interest in Cattell's conception is regarded as 'libido-investment'. It will be seen that the distinction could be referred to in the terms of an earlier psychology as that between the affective and conative aspects of such traits.

It follows, therefore, that attitudes, interests and sentiments form a common group of study. In his later work (1957), Cattell affirms that, "Clinical, sociological and general experimental study of attitudes shows them to be linked by sub-goals, forming a lattice."

Four researches planned to test his hypotheses revealed seven well-defined factors having the qualities of drives, and three less clear. In descending order of clarity they were: sex, gregariousness, protectiveness, curiosity, escape, self-assertion, sex-appeal, rest-seeking, and construction. These are ergs. Five fairly well-defined sentiments and two less clear were: sentiment to profession, to sports and games, to religion, to mechanical or material interests, to the self, and possibly the super-ego and patriotic sentiments. He concludes that, on the whole, these represent new factors in a new dynamic modality.

Eysenck (1947, 1953), whose approach has been more from the study of pathological personalities, and who relies, made like Cattell, especially on factor analysis, constructs a hierarchy with four levels. At the 'type' level are three basic factors of neuroticism, introversion-extroversion, and general intelligence or 'g'. At the 'trait' level are such qualities as persistence, rigidity, shyness, etc., and these are related to elements of the third or 'habitual response' level, leading in turn to the 'specific response' level, which, is the lowest one.

In terms of factors, these levels would correspond to general factors, specific factors and error factors. Eysenck points out, however, that throughout the hierarchy, differences are in respect of degrees. The general factor is simply the group factor that is most widespread, while the specific factor is the group factor that is most limited in appeal.

Guilford's book, "personality" (1959), provides a comprehensive approach to the study of personality and an extensive survey of contributions by himself and others to its theory. It is impossible to summarise his conclusions in a few words, but in general it may be said that he accepts the hierarchical conception of personality structure with traits at different levels of generality. First there is the 'Type Level' represented by general social-adjustment types and also general emotional types; below this is the 'Primary-trait Level', the types of which are found by factor analysis, and are exemplified by such qualities as sociability and ascendancy. Next in order is the 'Hexis Level', the term used to describe 'consistent attitudes or dispositions of mind' and at the lowest level are types of specific actions.

Vernon in his recent book "Personality Assessment" has preferred objective study of personality to other approaches, including psycho-analytic one. He admits of the fact that personality is the area too complex and every approach has certain weakness. The propelling forces determining human behaviour are too many. It is, desired that a theory of personality and techniques should be constructed for getting at the right picture of the elements of personality.

We have assumed that personality is a complex whole and the judgement of it is extremely difficult. Still attempts have been made to explore the field from various angles by psychologists who are peripheralists and centralists.

The former group has objective approach, where as the centralists are more concerned with subjective facts of emotional components.

In view of this divergent trend it seems proper to employ a variety of methods for its assessment. There are difficulties that confront the investigator of personality. There are objective and subjective facts standing in the way. For example, the changing conditions of the physical and social environment, the changing physiological conditions within the subject, the motivational trends and patterns of the subject deserve special mention.

Similarly reports given by the subject of his perceptions, interpretations, feelings are subjective facts which influence the scientific study of personality.

In short, it may be said that variables of personality and the approaches made so far to study them are numerous. Very recently psycho-analysis has been tried for exploring this domain.

The unconscious level of personality organisation is now being attacked with the assumption that the psychic process involved has great resolving power when applied to the mysterious phenomena underlying personality structure. According to Murray, a need is a hypothetical process, the occurrence of which is imagined in order to account for certain objective and subjective facts.

Here, of course, emphasis has been laid not on the overt behaviour but on the inner conflicts, feelings, emotions, sentiments and beliefs.

Introspection and experiments demonstrate that an emotion basically determines the cognitive process underlying any behaviour pattern.

Thus need is a dynamic concept which has been formulated by Murray for explaining the mysteries of human behaviours. McDougall's instinct theory has thus been outdated by the theory of need.

The advantages of dealing with unitary traits, do not reduce the difficulties in their identification.

In spite of outstanding problems in the area of assessments, the 'factor analytic' technique has made a move in a definite direction. Few unitary traits have been established by cattell, Eysenck and others. The degree of success in a certain occupation or school subject partly depends upon intelligence and partly upon personality qualities. This is why the need for research on personality and its assessments is being felt more and more in recent times.

PERSONALITY MEASUREMENT

Personality is too complex to be analysed. There have been various attempts for measuring personality from different angles:-

(1) Subjective : method of impression.

(2) Objective : method of expression.

Of the subjective approaches, the following deserve mention: (a) ratings, (b) interview, (c) self-rating or questionnaire.

Of the objective approaches, situational tests deserve special mention. Besides, projective tests are being evolved for depth study of personality.

In spite of every attempt at the assessment of personality, much remains to be explored in this field. It appears that the various dimensions of personality have not yet been discovered as yet and the techniques so far evolved are not adequate.

Ratings

The objective of the rating method is to derive knowledge, about a person through others estimates and to turn them into numerical grades or scores. The subjectivity of judgements of personality is apparent. Ratings are therefore, regarded as grades obtained in specific areas on the reputation of the subject. They are however, inadequate as the sole criteria of a person's traits, or even as the entire source of date for the scientific study of personality.

There are various rating techniques, viz. ranking, paired comparisons, numerical ratings, verbal, graphic and other analytic scales.

Ranking and paired comparisons

This technique is advantageous when the number of cases is very limited. In the paired comparison method, the rater is given every possible pair of names and asked to say which of the two is higher.

Numerical Ratings

The outstanding defect of this type of scale is the variation in standard and distribution adopted by different raters.

But this is a very simple pattern. There is no really satisfactory way of comparing the ratings by different judges of different groups and this greatly limits the practical value of rating.

(a) Verbal and Graphic Scales

In the graphic scale each step is defined or described as concretely as possible, so that the rater no longer has to think quantitatively or bother about standards.

(b) Analytic Scales

This is the device of breaking up a general trait into a number of more specific components, which are separately rated and scores combined. In the marking of essays analytic schemes are often found to be no more reliable than impressionistic.

A number of steps have been taken to increase the reliability of ratings, i.e. agreement between different raters. It has been considered that there is the superiority of relative to absolute and of graphic to numerical ratings. There are definite advantages of breaking down traits into components. The following suggestions have been made by the psychologists:-

1. Choose only the unambiguous traits and find them correctly.

2. Rate all individuals on one trait at a time

3. Warn the raters of the personal bias and encourage them to be objective by obtaining independent judgements.

4. Ratings should be based on sample observations for a definite period.

Interview

Interview is the most comprehensive of all methods as it is based on observations of external appearance, gesture, other modes of expression and various behaviour patterns revealed during the interview. The reliability and validity of interview as a technique is not very satisfactory and it should therefore, be supplemented by other tests.

Interviews may vary in types. There may be individual interview, psychiatric interview and group interviews. Each has its value and limitations. So far as assessment of personality is concerned, the impressions, gathered in short interview, are hardly dependable. Interview may put an interviewees under considerable strains and yet the interviewers are liable to make wrong judgements.

Self-ratings

Ratings by the individuals of their own traits are known as self-ratings. This technique is popularly known as questionnaire. The questionnaires are easy to construct and use. In questionnaire, the responses of the subjects can be obtained in writing. This is why this technique has been widely used. So far as personality tests are concerned, the outstanding tests are those of Burnreuter, Cattell, Guildford and Eysenck. The main difficulty in using personality inventories or questionnaires is that the subject may either consciously or unconsciously fake his answers. Vernon concludes that despite the extreme weaknesses of questionnaires, they should not be entirely condemned. Well constructed questionnaires effectively administered in suitable motivating conditions can be of value both for experimental research or for clinical use.

Situational Tests

These tests are more objective in nature as the subject is unaware of the scoring system employed and consequently unable to guess the purpose of the test as well. The subjects are placed in miniature situations provided for obtaining their responses. But this may lead to considerable difficulty because of the subject's over awareness of the artificial situations. Although the validity of such personality tests varies widely the science of personality assessment is enriched by such objective tests of situational type.

The Projective Test

The projective technique holds its promise in playing an important part in personality assessment. This approach was adopted largely as a revolt against superficial testing of personality. Insight into the personality as a whole has been considered to be the primary objective of such a test. The advantage of a projective test is that the subject cannot guess the purpose of the test which brings out many unconscious urges and motives, traits and tendencies. The difficulty in applying such a test is that it demands skill and insight on the part of the experimenter. Rorschach's ink blocks and T.A.T. are the most outstanding tests in this field. Besides, other techniques of exploring the personality at the unconscious level have been evolved such as free word association, story telling test, object relation test, etc.

11

EXERCISE AND METHODS OF LEARNING

We all seem to know what constitutes learning. Yet a controversy may arise about its scientific definition, as all are not agreed as to what learning constitutes and the manner in which one may learn.

Associationist Conception

Associationists believe that when a new experience is brought about, our mind tries to locate its similarity with some thing familiar, something it has seen or known before and then to associate or connect the new fact with that old experience. This method, according to the associationists, produces certain economy. Instead of remembering so many isolated experiences one has to remember only few bundles of experiences whose connections are based on certain similarity or association. Disconnected items of knowledge may be too numerous to create confusion. But when grouped in a certain order they are like bundles of books arranged in a shelf and can be recalled when needed.

According to associationists, therefore, learning takes place when the mind is able to see the relationship between the new knowledge and the old. It is only when association of the new knowledge with the old one has taken place, learning is possible. Some associationists will go one step further. They would find in this mechanism not only better learning for the new items of information, but a better definition of the older one.

When a new boy enters the class, we try to recall the similarity he has with some person whom we have seen before. In doing so, we shall at the same time notice the points of dissimilarity. This improves our knowledge of the old and familiar things and also making them better defined. This is a process by which new things become known, and old things also get better known. This is known as the process of apperception.

Associations can be changed. They may be accidental, logical and systematic. Supposing I go to Delhi on a wet day when it is raining hard, my impressions of Delhi will always be associated with the rains, and perhaps my impression of Delhi will be that it is a wet place. As a matter of fact, this is merely accidental as Delhi has more dry days in the year than we think and the rainfall is not at all heavy. Yet because of the mere accident of my going there on a wet day, my association of Delhi will be with a wet place. My impressions will always be biased and wrong due to this accidental association. Many of our associations get biased because of the influence of chance factor.

But all our associations are fortunately not accidental. Often we reason out connections and find out relationship. According to associationists, therefore, learning is perfect if the associations are natural and meaningful.

Behaviourists' Conception

The psychologists who place more reliance on the behaviour that a living being displays when placed in a new situation are called behaviourists. Unlike the associationist who looks into the problem from the point of view of subject matter, behaviourist places more reliance on the responses, made by the learner himself. When a new situation confronts a living being, it is natural that he will try to react to it. So long as these reactions are disorganised and random lead no desired end, no learning takes places. Learning, according to the behaviourists, is the organised response that is conditioned or practised by the learner. They would further find out a reason why a learner practises. It is because the response helps in the adjustment of the learner to his environment. The behaviourists will draw some line of distinction between automatic responses like the reflex action of closing one's eyelid and responses that are chosen and organised. Automatic responses are not learnt and they show very little improvement, as they involve no organisation. Some psychologists would go one step further, and say that the slight extent to which some of the automatic responses are improved by practice shows the slight degree of organisation that is involved in them.

The behaviourists have brought forward the famous conditioned response theory. We owe it to the classical experiment of Pavlov. This Russian Psychologist had trained his dog in a peculiar way. Every day exactly sixty seconds after the ringing of a bell he would serve the dog with a dish of meat. One day, after many days of repeated practice, he did not bring the meat and observed the reaction of the dog to the sound of the bell. He found that as soon as the bell was rung, the dog became somewhat alert, but his mouth did not begin watering then. It was just sixty seconds after the sound of the bell that the dog's mouth watered, as if it was expecting its food then. Thus he found that the dog has connected or conditioned its response to two stimuli with which the object of its interest, the food, was connected. It knew that the sound of the bell had something to do with it and therefore, learnt to be alert.

But it also knew the implication of the time interval of sixty seconds, as then and then only the appropriate response, the watering of the mouth was visible.

The followers of the Conditioned Response Theory hold that learning in its fundamental form is essentially a modification of all natural responses, and their transference to artificial stimuli. In this particular case of Pavlov Experiment, the natural response of the accumulation of saliva, was connected not with the arrival of food, but with the artificial stimuli, namely with the sound of the bell, and the time interval of sixty seconds.

Being a physiological theory, conditioned response at once commends itself to those who want an objective but at the same time a physiological basis of the process of learning. According to this theory, a natural response may be modified by bracketing it with an artificial response and they together form a certain action which, may be called a reflex action. The response is simultaneous, as in the case of watering of the mouth at the very name of the delicious food, but sometimes we may modify the situation as in the case of ringing of the bell sixty seconds before the serving of the food. Here because of the time interval which has been inevitably followed, we find the response is consequently delayed. It does not occur at the mere ringing of the bell. This is clearly the case of a delayed response.

Followers of this theory hold that conditioning often takes place in our childhood and although the natural causes are forgotten, the effects or the response patters still remain. Childhood fears are thus result of conditioned response, e.g., fears for certain harmless animal like spiders and cockroaches often shown by adults. We may remember them as the results of conditioning of certain childhood experiences which have perhaps been forgotten. Perhaps these 'meaningless' fears display a meaning of their own. What has thus been done by accident can be done deliberately by an educator. If the educator wants a desirable type of responses, all he must do is to condition or arrange appropriate situations. The child will then respond in the way we desire him to respond. By repeated practice this response will be so conditioned that the response becomes apparently automatic. Learning thus becomes the process of habit. It is the educator, the teacher, who has to do all planning and arranging of situations in order to get a type of response that he desires. His task again is to arrange for repeated practice so that the response becomes ingrained.

The theory, no doubt, gives a plausible account of conditions of specific learning, particularly, in those situations which involve a certain amount of emotional response. It, however, fails to explain the cases of complex thought processes.

Thorndike's Laws

Thorndike also bases this conception of learning on the stimulus response theory, but he would add two more factors of requisites to the mere practice effect that brings about learning. Thorndike would try to look into the reason why a certain living being becomes ready to receive the stimulus at all and why he would act.

The subject would be ready to receive the stimulus only when such response brings a certain amount of pleasure. Satisfaction is, therefore, the first and foremost condition of learning. Without it no individual will react to the stimulus at all. Happiness derived from the response forms the motive force.

Thus the stimulus and the response should be related to one another. It is only when there is a natural connection between the way of acting and the result aimed at, an individual is motivated to repeat or carry on the process and learn.

Besides these two fundamental facts, Thorndike would add another condition to the very practice. The more recent has been the practice, the greater would be the learning effect.

The first solution of an adjustment according to Thorndike takes place in simple trial and error process. A rat kept inside a box which has a hole in it, will jump at random to get out. It is by mere accident that he hits upon the particularly favourable place from where he may get out if he jumps again. If he is taken into the box again, he will perhaps need fewer attempts to hit at the right place. And finally as soon as he is put into the box, he comes to the right spot wherefrom he can make a successful attempt to escape.

Analysing the situation, we find that the rat's first attempt involves a process of mere trial and error. He tried several places and made few errors before he came to the right spot from where he could jump successfully. This gave him the freedom, which is a pleasurable sensation.

Next time when the rat is put into the box he was motivated to try the process. Gradually he eliminates his unnecessary and unsuccessful jumps because he finds a connection between the action namely jumps, and the attainment of his goal, viz., freedom. This connection naturally involves a selection of the site and both the practice and the pleasure sensation of freedom provides stimulation. Further, if time elapses it is likely that the rat would forget the thing he learnt, and would have to repeat the process with unnecessary jumps before he hits the right spot again.

Thus Thorndike mentions four conditions for learning and provides that the learning to be effective should depend on certain laws which are as follows:-

(a) **Law of Frequency :** The more frequent is the practice, the greater will be the learning effect. Here Thorndike does not differ from the followers of the Conditioned Reflex Theory who also believe that it is practice that makes one perfect.

(b) **The law of effect :** If the situation motivates the learner it would provide greater chance of learning. While Thorndike takes away from the educator the right of determining which situations and stimuli are to be selected, the followers of Conditioned Response Theory would, give the choice of action to the learner. This places a greater responsibility on the educator, for he has to select not only desirable but desired situations.

(c) **The law or Recency :** The more recent is the practice, the greater would be the chance of learning. In this Thorndike has stated a thing which the followers of the Conditioned Reflex Theory might have implied but have never expressed. Any way, there is no variation in two theories with reference to this.

(d) **Law of Belongingness :** In order to motivate practice further, both the stimulus and the response must be connected or should belong to one another. In this too, Thorndike merely completes what the followers of Conditioned Reflex Theory have left unsaid. Surely the response in order to be conditioned, must belong or must be connected with the stimulus. But the connection has not been clearly stated in so many words as a necessary requirement for learning.

Gestalt View of Learning

Gestalt psychologists like Kohler and Koffka held that mental phenomena have a certain structure or pattern. The standpoint of the associationists had been to assume that individual items stand apart from each other, but this is not the case. A Gestalt psychologist does not look in to isolated items; he looks in to the total pattern or configuration. When we are looking at a certain individual or individual object, we are not unmindful of the total perspective in which that individual or the object happens to exist for the time being. Perhaps we are for the moment paying a greater attention to the particular individual. Yet the background effect the total panorama produces should not be overlooked. Ideas do not come to us in isolation. They are really parts of a total pattern or context by virtue of which they acquire a certain meaning and significance. According to this theory, when we learn a poem, we do not learn the individual words or lines of the poem but try to read the poem as a whole (or at least a significant portion of it which we may call a unit). This forms a complete unit of thought. If we happen to forget a particular line or stanza, the prompter just supplies the catchword and at once the whole chain of subsequent thoughts flashes back into mind. Why is it that supply of a single word helps us to recall the entire stanza? The followers of Gestalt School of thought would say that it is because the whole chain of words that form the stanza is so intimately connected (and the learning of the particular catch word has been so well knit with this chain) that the supply of the catch word helps us to call back into the mind the entire situation. The word in which stands out the midst of the chain of words is in the stanza.

Gestalt school of psychologists objects to the formulation or the problem of learning as implied by the four laws of Thorndike. Thorndike's basic position has been to find the connection between the stimulus and the response. These laws assume that for independent stimuli there are independent units of behaviour. Followers of the Gestalt do not believe in such isolated units. When we look at a certain scene, we have already organised our response to the total situation. What we call perception or learning, according to the followers of the Gestalt is the discovery of the relationships that exists between the elements on which we focus or concentrate our attention. Learning is thus not a building up of a wall by piling up bricks. It is the excavation of a huge mound to trace the hidden treasure. Gestalt theory assumes that learning takes place in a total situation and not in piece meal. In order to learn a poem it is easier to take the entire piece than to take it line by line or stanza by stanza, provided it is of a reasonable length. In case of longer poems also it is desirable to take one complete and meaningful unit of thought which may serve as the focal reference point. Learning by part proves less effective than learning by whole.

Dewey's Conception of Learning

According to John Dewey and his followers, learning is possible only when the individual feels a need for it. All learning according to him is purposeful taking place in the direction in which the purpose is being fulfilled. Ordinarily we do not observe how many cracks a wall has got, unless we are interested in its repair or are afraid of the wall collapsing. In both these situations, however, we are likely to observe minutely and when we do so, learning takes place. Dewey further assumes that when learning is taking place, an individual is participating in the situation as a single undivided organism. When we are playing, we are certainly interested in winning the game. We have thus an interest which motivates our action. Our entire organism, the body and the mind, are engaged together in this activity. It is in this type of situation where direct participation is possible, maximum learning takes place. This Dewey would call primary learning.

Dewey, however, admits that there is a scope for a different type of learning in certain situations where direct participation of the individual is not possible. Facts of the remote past or of distant lands can not be given in any other way except through a certain amount of communication. But whenever such communication is taking place, the actual learning that takes place is not much unless some opportunity for participation is provided. There is yet a third type of learning which may be the result of drawing inferences or conclusions from a topic learnt.

But here the situation should be presented in the form of a problem and the individual must feel the need for solving the problem.

Thus like Thorndike, Dewey believes in the law of readiness in as much as he recognises the need for motivation in learning situations. Dewey, however, places more reliance on the cause of motivation rather than on the effect. The goal must be worthwhile but pleasure would lie in the pursuit rather than in the attainment. The urge for pursuit, he feels, would come only when there is a felt need. He would further agree with Thorndike to the idea of belongingness. The situation should be meaningful, and the pursuit should take place in the direction of attainment. Both the goal and the significance of the effort in the direction of reaching the goal must be clear in the mind of the learner.

Like Kohler an Koffka, Dewey feels that learning does not take place by mere blind repetition or by thoughtless trial and error. He would modify Thorndike's law of exercise to the extent that exercise and repetition at each instance must be purposeful. Each renewed effort must be caused in such situations where there is a fresh motivation created in fulfilling one's need. Each exercise must be both purposeful and meaningful. One can not moreover learn in piecemeal. It is possible that we may concentrate on one aspect of the total process, but the background of the total situation is to be kept in view. Experience can not be subdivided into narrow compartments. Real learning takes place through the reaction of the organism to the whole and not part situations. There are of course certain focal points, but these are taken by the learner as mere means to reach the goal.

Summary

Opinion seems to be divided regarding the process through which a living organism tries to learn and gain better control over its surroundings. What it learns becomes helpful as it ensures an economy in future encounters by reducing the random effort which are noticeable in early efforts. Association shows that there is a certain economy if the new things learnt can be properly connected with a thing learnt in the past. It is only when the old and new get connected or associated, our ideas about the old things become clearer. The followers of this theory held that such association, may be quite accidental or deliberately planned and organised. They would, however, place more reliance on deliberate associations.

One school of behaviourist would place more reliance on Conditioned Response or Condition-Reflex Theory. Learning, according to them, takes place by repetition of process, when the connections between stimulus and response become ingrained. The followers of this theory would place all the responsibility for arranging the suitable situation and evoking desired response on the teacher or educator. It is for him to organise such situations and repeat the process so that learning may take place.

Thorndike, while admitting that sometime learning takes place by blind repetition or mere trial and error, would at the same time emphasize value of satisfaction derived. In other words, the outcome of learning situation should give some degree of satisfaction or pleasure (as pointed out in his law of effect).

He takes a commonsense view that the practice must be recently done, otherwise things learnt in the remote periods may be lost. He holds that the goal and the effort must be clear before the learner.

Kohler, Koffka and other followers of the Gestalt school feel that learning does not take place from parts to whole but rather from the whole to the part. Learning is not a building up process like piling up of bricks of information. It is the development of insight that comes into the mind of the learner to discover the relationships that exist between the particular parts of the situation for which the total situation stands as background.

Dewey's view of learning takes some thing from Thorndike and some thing from the Gestalt School. He also feels the need for belongingness and pleasure sensation. But according to him, the source of pleasure is not the attainment of the goal but really the effort. The individual must feel that his pursuit is worthwhile. This is possible only when the individual is conscious of the need for learning or exertion. He also agrees with the Gestalt school in considering the total pattern or background to which the individual learner acts as a single undivided being. But while an individual is interested in the total situation, he may yet select certain focal points for attacks. This will, however, be done so long as the particular focal point is connected with the main objective. Dewey makes a distinction between three types of learning. The first is one in which direct participation is possible. This is called primary learning situations which provide opportunity for Gestalt learning. But he admits that when direct participation is not possible, there is room for communication as well as for drawing inferences and conclusions. These are secondary and Primary learning situations and the degree of possible success in such situations depends on how they can be organised.

It may be profitable at this stage to look into the learning process that Dashiell has prepared to study the different conditions of learning, so as to make our study objective :—

The subject must be motivated. We can take an example from a simple experiment of maze learning of a rat. If we keep the food inside a maze and lead a rat through it to secure the food, he will not go and seek the food unless he is hungry. A well-fed rat may fall asleep at the door of the maze. It is only the hungry rat that explores and eventually finds his way. Dashiell thus agrees with Dewey that learning takes place in meaningful situations.

There must be some obstruction or barrier of some sort without which no learning takes places. In the above instance, if the food is supplied at the very entrance of the maze, where is the opportunity of the rat for learning? We thus find that through easy situation there is hardly any learning. There must be some obstacle to be felt as the same provides a motive force.

In every learning situation, the first movements are random and varied. This is seen not only in animal experiments but also in a complex situation as when one is learning to drive a car. Trial and error being the most fundamental process are gradually organised into definite patterns of behaviour.

Successful responses come mostly by chance. In learning by trial and error. or by conditioning perhaps the subject can not predict the results. In one, he hits accidentally and in the other he is made to do certain action at the dictation of another person. Hence in both these situations, the benefit of gaining an insight through the chance situation is perhaps lost. When, however the subject is conscious and alert, perhaps he will find a new meaning to the chance occurrence and this is called insight.

It is the effect that determines how an individual would select or fix the right responses. When a certain activity leads to a desired goal, the attainment brings some satisfaction. The connection between the effort made for its attainment and the goal itself proves meaningful so that learning takes place. Better motivation is perhaps possible when each repetition of the process brings some added satisfaction.

Learning may come rapidly or it may take a long time. When insight occurs, there is a sudden improvement. With trial and error and with conditioning there is progress no doubt, but the progress is slow.

Since learning depends on sense perception, loss or defect of any sense affects improvement of knowledge in that direction.

The common assumption that the blind hears better or the deaf sees better is not borne by facts. True it is that there is some compensation, but in its totality, the loss is greater than the slight gain.

Any fatigue, whether muscular or mental retards learning. Over-exertion must, therefore, be prevented and the physical conditions of ventilation or illumination must be satisfactory to provide freedom from physical fatigue.

Frequent practice given at regular internal is better than one long and continuous practice. It is better to repeat the process for ten minutes a day than to have one practice of two hours once in six days. This is, however, conditioned by the fact that such practice should be in complete units to be learnt at a time.

Age and maturity must be taken into account as well. Two experiments on identical twins offer good instance of this. Two identical twins are made to climb a few steps. The practice for the first was begun in the forty-six week, but for other it was delayed till the child was fifty-two weeks old. When the second child began its practice, it was seen that the first had already acquired some practice. In the 53rd week the first child could climb first steps in twenty six seconds while the second took forty-five seconds to do so.

Seven weeks later both the children took the same time. Thus though the second child had only eight weeks practice, yet it was equal to the former's fourteen week practice simply because the former began when it was still immature.

A review of the Theories of Leaning

Learning is a continuous process leading to improvement of behaviour. Various theories of learning have emerged. All these theories are based on certain observations. Some of them have been developed from behaviouristic standpoint, while others are the result of certain principles. Thus the principle of association of ideas has given rise to the traditional theory of association in learning, whereas the learning has also been explained in a more mechanical manner, viz, in terms of (connectionism) stimulus response. The latter approach emphasises the mechanical process by which bonds are built, strengthened and organised into systems. When applied in the field of education, this theory encouraged the educators to think of ways and means for creating S.R. bonds. Thorndike's laws of learning were enunciated for the purpose. But they could not explain the complex process of human learning. Modern theories by Hull and Tolman were evolved. Hull's theory of reinforcement springs from the law of effect and the concept of conditioning combined together. Tolman's theory of sign learning emphasised the importance of meaning in learning. Trial and error methods of learning have a much better place in Hall's theory while motivation, rewards and punishment have been regarded as signs helping the learning process in Tolman's theory.

Thus Tolman's view is very rational and adequate in accounting for human learning. In short, Tolman's theory links up the mechanism of early learning with the complex learning process observed in classroom situation. Hull has contributed to the theory of learning by introducing learning as conditioning and emphasising the role of need reduction for reinforcement of the S.R. connection. But Hull's theory has a number of limitations which were rightly pointed out by Tolman. It was Tolman who has tried to make an advance in the theory of learning by giving credit for insightful learning for signs and meanings.

It appears, that behaviouristic school of psychology explains learning in the light of the experience of animal behaviour. The behaviourists has deliberately avoided the role of experience in learning and attached no importance to the mental function, like intention and willingness in learning.

Thus there are serious limitations in the theories of learning, emerging from the behaviouristic school of psychology. The various laws of effect, conditioning and reinforcement presuppose a mechanical set-up in the learner. Though the question of reinforcement cannot be fully explained without any reference to intent and experience, a part explanation has only been sought by a haphazard interpretation of trial and error in the light of need reduction. A concept of conditioning ignores the motivational aspect of learning and is thus subject to criticism. It is unfortunate that a tendency towards oversimplification of the complex learning process has led to the development of theories almost in a mechanical manner. But there are certain characteristics of complex human achievements calling for a more comprehensive theory of learning. The role of experience, intention and insight, of criticism and construction and of generalisation of learning is to be taken into account while building up a rational theoretical framework in this field.

Human experience in perception and cognition plays a very prominent part in learning. Gestalt psychology is concerned with the problem of perception, which has been almost ignored by the behaviouristic school. Human perceptual experience cannot be fully explained in terms of pure sensation. There is something more which remains to be discovered. In any learning or perception the quality of each component is determined with reference to the whole. In Wertheimer's words, the characteristics of any Gestalt are determined not only by its parts but also by internal arrangement.

So far as the formation of Gestalt is concerned, Wertheimer holds that there are various perceptual phenomena in the visual field. The laws underlying the formation of Gestalts or whole configurations and the factors which influence their formation deserve special mention.

According to Koffka, configurations tend to become as clear as the conditions permit. A good form implies units, harmony inclusiveness and consciousness. There are several factors contributing to the formation of a good gestalt such as similarity and proximity of elements. Besides this, closure and clarity facilitate gestalt formation. These help one to organise perceptual situations through experience and to promote the learning situation of the classroom by means of stimulating cognition. In the whole process of perception, cognition and learning, in relation to any learning situation, a very important factor known as 'insight' creeps in. As in the course of experience by repetition, analogy, analysis and practice, the parts become related to each other and insight becomes clearly structural. A constant organisation and reorganisation in the perceptual field goes on in order to find improved means for reaching a goal. This character of insightful behaviour is one of the most important features in effective learning.

Insight of course calls for the intellectual ability in the learning. Hillgard gives a list of characteristics of insightful learning.

In early learning by insight it is important that all aspects of the problem situation are accessible and the learning process can be used in new situations. In short, the underlying principle of Gestalt psychology is that each individual is active in his effort so as to organise and give good structure to his learning with the derived satisfaction. Judd in his experiments has shown the importance of generalisation and verbalisation in any learning. In his own opinion, verbalising insight can lead to enhanced structuring. Insight may be aided by modelling the abstract knowledge.

In conclusion, it may be said that learning as insight has been as a concept much indebted to the theory of Gestalt psychologists, like. Koffka and Kohler as the problem of insight is closely connected with perception.

12

TRANSFER OF TRAINING

Developments of the Faculty Theory

The field of learning is vast and if we want learning to be really useful, we shall certainly wish that whatever power or faculty has been developed through the learning situation in one field should be useful in many other fields. If the school teaches a boy to be honest, it certainly does not like to limit the exercise of that quality only inside the examination hall, for instance. The boy should be honest in every walk of life, whether he works as a cashier in a firm or as a judge in a court. If the training given in school situations is not applicable in life situations it should be considered as insufficient or ineffective.

Thus a certain amount of transfer is not only desirable but is necessary. The subject matter of a particular study and the specific power that the study develops are no doubt, connected. The study of certain subjects facilitates preparation for studying a few other subjects. A little grounding in mathematics is necessary to understand the principles of physical sciences or statistics.

The idea that the study of certain subjects confers on the learner certain specific powers is as old as Plato. It was Plato who said that arithmetic sharpens wit and geometry increases the power of apprehension or general understanding of a situation. In other words, a study of arithmetic not only makes a person better able to compute (calculate) quantitative proportions, but it has an additional use of making a person witty. Likewise, the study of geometry in addition to developing powers to distinguish shapes also enables a student to understand or grasp any similar situation. A person is thus advised to study logic when one is not able to differentiate.

John Locke formulated the theory in a logical manner and propounded what is known to day as the transfer theory. Locke supposed that the study of certain subjects can develop certain faculties like memory, reasoning, power of judgement. Study of mathematics, it was supposed, develops the reasoning power, while study of a classical subject is helpful to train our imaginative powers. Other curricular subjects in a like manner were considered by him helpful to develop certain other faculties.

It was felt that the development of the faculty was the primary concern while the knowledge of content of a particular study was considered to be less important. The process of learning thus gained more importance than the content. Training in a particular subject is considered as a mere means to an end. What was being taught was of little significance by itself. Whether the subject matter was of any practical value, whether it was connected with life or not became matters of little consideration. Pupil's interest was not the criterion for relation of the subject matter. The pupil's mind has to be properly disciplined. Thus the faculty theory developed the theory of Formal Discipline.

Many modern educators feel that this theory of Locke has set back the wider interest of education in many ways:-

1. It has helped the retention of some of the less useful subjects in the curriculum. After the development of the modern European languages as a result of Renaissance, subjects like Latin has lost their practical utility in every-day life and would have perhaps been studied by few research workers. It was Locke's Faculty theory that justified their retention in the curriculum. As subjects for study they were no longer useful, having lost the utility of international communication and their place was taken by the modern language like English and French.

2. Though of great practical utility, the study of scientific subjects was delayed for a long time, simply because the educators could not agree as to what particular faculty of mind would their study develop. Even when they were eventually introduced in the curriculum they were taught in a formal and logical manner. More attention was paid to the method of teaching than to the content taught.

3. No effort was made to make the curriculum useful or interesting. Because of the supposed disciplinary value, they were just imposed upon the pupils.

The present educators, therefore, do not follow this theory blindly.

Limited Transfer Theory

As the studies in social and natural sciences developed, it was clear that the study of these subjects were found to be vital to our every day life. They were considered to have certain intrinsic values of their own, apart from the values of training of certain faculties.

Psychology essentially ceased to be a speculative subject when it acquired an experimental character. Psychologists would then like to perform experiments and ascertain objectively whether any transfer has taken place at all or not. Between 1800 and 1928, as many as ninety-nine experiments have been performed in a recognised manner, on the problem of transfer of training to see whether training given in one situation could be effectively transferred into another situation. James performed experiments on memory. A group of subjects was asked to memorise a certain thing, while, another group containing pupils of equal ability were left free. After a time both the groups were asked to memorise another thing, say another poem. Now if the first group would show better efficiency, one may conclude that their earlier act of memorizing has been effective, otherwise, the power of remembering had not been transferred from the first to the second situation. Others performed similar experiments on other learning abilities. By means of an experimental group which was made to learn something and by a control group which did not get a chance of learning, their learning ability in a new situation was tested. It was found that in 32 cases there was an evidence of considerable transfer. In 49 cases the transfer was just partial. In eight cases the transfer was so insignificant that it could be neglected and in five cases there was positive proof that no transfer had taken place. In the remaining five cases it was difficult to predict whether any transfer had taken place at all or not.

In short, in two out of six cases there is a positive proof of appreciable transfer. In three cases the transfer is only partial, while in one case either there is no transfer, or it is quite insignificant. This simply points to the fact that transfer is, on the whole, possible only to a limited extent.

We may now analyse the conditions and find out which factors would decide whether a transfer would take place or not. When the situation is identical either in the procedure or in the attitude, we find that a transfer is possible. Thorndike, for instance, found that when a person was made to learn two poems one after another and these poems had same metre or they conveyed a similar thought, then the effect of learning the first was transferred into the second so that the second was learnt quickly. Judd found that practice in solving one kind of problems helps the learner to solve other kinds of problems so long as the basic situation of problem solving remains the same. When one is working on simultaneous equation in Algebra for instance, he will acquire some power over the problem solving of a different type of simultaneous equation. He will need additional practice for working with certain other features of problem solving. It is on account of this that we do find that even in a new type of problem, one who has solved problems of any kind has a certain advantage.

Insight into a configuration (shape) or general perception of patterns are possibly transferred. So are good habits of work, neatness and orderliness. But these are only partially transferred.

Criticism of the Partial Transfer Theory

Even this theory of limited transfer is not free from criticism. Many psychologists hold that Thorndike's identical element theory does not really show or prove that there has been a transfer. When the elements are identical, what has happened is merely repeated exercise. It is agreed on all sides that repeated exercise helps retention and that learning is re-inforced by practice. The so-called 'new situation' is merely a recapitulation of the old element. For example if a boy has learnt the English words. 'Revolve' and he next learns the Latin root 'Volva' i.e. to roll, he is not learning really a new word but transferring the power acquired from his knowledge in English. He is really practising the basic elements of English word for a second time and when this additional practice is given there is some gain.

They likewise find fault with Judd's experiments, and show that a student clear in solving algebric problems does not show the same competence in solving a problem in Economics. There is no general ability of problem solving.

They are merely specific fields, and in each field larger the number of problems solved, the greater is the practice and quicker gets the speed for solving future problems.

Kohler working with apes found that the more intelligent ones solved their problems of food procurements, by a sudden insight when confronted with certain obstruction. He concludes that the content of the total situation or configuration is subconsciously visualised by the ape. All the while he is trying to concentrate on a specific aspect of the situation that is presented to him in a problematic form. Apparently, the ape was idle, but really he was actively engaged in manipulating the total situation in general. He managed to succeed in his attempt at solving the specific aspect, as a matter of course. An experiment was performed with four hens, three apes and a child, each of whom had to procure the food from a box. In each case he kept the food inside a box which we may call 'B' and which appeared to be somewhat lightly compared to another box 'A' which did not contain any food. After a number of practices each of the subjects learnt how to procure food from the box 'A' and the experimenter by altering the position of the boxes made this recognition well established. Then he quietly changed the box A and replaced it by another 'C' which happened to be more brightly coloured than the box 'B'. It was found that all subjects invariably tried to find the food in box 'C' and not in the box B. This clearly shows that the subjects did not recognise the box B at all, what they did is to learn that the food was in the brighter one of the two boxes. So long as B remained the brighter of the two, there was no difficulty. This experiment thus shows that with a change in the situation, learning loses its value. Thus transfer from one field to another is doubtful. Learning and perception in relation to the whole field of experience and the entire field situation can hardly be repeated in toto.

Our present Theory

Today we seem to doubt the very theory of identical elements put forward by Thorndike, as two fields can not be entirely identical. Apparently the old law of exercise is being presented in another form. As a matter of fact, similarity of two situations gave the learner some advantage by affording him a chance of practice. Thus the theory of transfer is challenged in certain quarters.

If, however, the subject-matter be adopted to the intellectual level of the learner, a certain amount of insight helps in broadening and generalising the zone of perception. This is not really a case of transfer. As, a new situation is interpreted in the light of past experiences of a similar situation, the past experience gives a new meaning to the situation and facilitates successful encounter with the new situation.

It is, however, found that certain routine habits formed by mechanical practice may persist or may be recalled for use. It is thus a case of recall of identical elements or added opportunity for practice. In language study for instance, grammar and spelling form the routine habit which can be taken from one situation and be used in a similar situation. Certain desirable attitudes, dispositions, methods of attack, ideals of accuracy, neatness and social values like honesty may be inculcated generally, and are capable of wide applications in similar situations.

Summary

Need for wider application of desirable habits taught in school to life situations is generally felt. This at first gave birth to the faulty-faculty theory, started by Plato and followed by Locke. The limitation of this theory has been found as it leads to the retention of useless subjects in the curriculum, utter neglect of the content of the curriculum and indifference to children's natural urges. With the introduction of social and natural sciences it was found that contents of courses had a certain value. Researches in experimental psychology proved that we can not conclusively say that ability acquired in one situation is likely to be transferred in toto in another situation.

This gives rise to Thorndike's theory of limited transfer. This assumes that if situations are similar, some transfer of the traits acquired in one situation may take place. Experiments made by the Gestalt psychologists like Kohler, however, shows that the individual does not remember an isolated experience, but the whole field, and since the whole field can not be recalled, there is really no effective transfer possible. Other educators criticise Thorndike's theory of limited transfer as superfluous, for after all, if two situations are identical, what is happening is not transfer, but merely an added practice. It is the practice that offers facility in the solution of difficulty in the second situation. The question is on the significance of developing certain desirable school habits.

Provided a certain thing has been learnt in a wider context, something, be it transfer or repeated practice, remains to be used in another situation. Modern educators, therefore, try to develop the desirable attitudes and offer subjects for instruction and greatest opportunities for enrichment of experience and practice. The habit thus formed in the school environment will be useful in the social environment. In this case the school situation and the social situation become more or less identical. Thus the basic conflicts or problems of life are really brought inside the school-room for the child to solve. No matter whether by providing opportunities for transfer or by giving added practice it would at any rate give him the power to meet the basic conflicts of real life situation. Thus to connect the school with life seems to be the objective of our study of the problem of transfer of training. It is thus really not a transfer of training, but training for transfer that we look forward to.

Teacher as on evaluator

The teacher has multiple roles and functions in different situations in the context of education. He, not only teaches, he has also the function as an evaluator. The purpose of the evaluation is to measure the output of his teaching as well as the outcome of the learning by his pupils. Thus evaluation helps to review the methods of teaching in the class-room and revise in the light of the results of the review.

There are certain tools and techniques of measurement and evaluation, no doubt; yet a resourceful teacher has a scope to develop his own tests of different kinds for the purpose of assessing pupil's behaviour. He may start building up a battery of ad hoc tests for measuring the achievement of the pupils and he may supplement them by diagnostic tests. In short, testing programme should evolve out of the needs. It is only a part of the total evaluation which should be designed for probing into the various areas of the pupil's performance, learning, achievement, attitude and personality. The purpose of testing should be quite clear and the principles of evaluation should be followed in every situation. Recently attempt has been made to integrate testing with teaching as it is believed that teaching and testing should go together. It is observed that the pupils in the class-room differ not only in intelligence but also in interest, attitude and many other personality traits. It is also experienced that the pupil's achievement does not only depend upon intelligence: so many factors can be attributed to the success or failure in pupil's academic life.

Obviously, the teacher has the obligation to know the individual differences precisely for counselling and guidance. In order to know the individual differences, he has to take recourse to testing and observation within the class-room as well as in different school-situations. Sophisticated testing is not always feasible in the limited time available to the teacher. Yet he needs to have an objective assessment of the basic differences in terms of his pupil's potential. It becomes practical to combine the different techniques of assessment including rating and case-studies. I.Q. testing has become fashionable in certain quarters in spite of its limits and limitations. It is a common experience that pupil's work-habit, motivation and persistence contribute no less than intelligence to the pupil's achievement in the classroom. Moreover, statistics indicate that about two-third of the population has around average intelligence. Thus not much is achieved from practical point of view by using the time-consuming intelligence-tests. In stead it is profitable to know the pupil's functional general abilities through his class-room interaction and performance. What is more important is the qualitative analysis instead of the quantitative measurement of the cognitive aspects of the pupil's behaviour. Numerical marking is therefore being replaced by qualitative grading in many progressive countries as it serves a better and perhaps more practical purpose of evaluation.

As testing is but one form of evaluation, there are other methods including rating scales, check list, situational tests and observations. It is a fact that each method has its own limits and limitations and the teacher has the responsibility to make the best use of them. In many cases the subjectivity factor creeps in and undesirable bias of the teacher-evaluator vitiates the purpose of testing. Of course there are measures to increase objectivity of the tests and examination procedure through adequate care and caution. The teacher should be aware of the ways and means which would make evaluation meaningful.

13

GROWTH, DEVELOPMENT AND EDUCATION

Human growth is related to the inherent process of development at various stages in different areas. In spite of the mystery around the process certain consistent patterns are noticeable in the dynamic life of a growing individual. Development involves an orderly progression from lower to higher levels. Rates and forms of development, however, depend upon the environmental stimuli although true developmental sequences are universal. Theory of Cognitive development provides information about how students learn and perceive at different levels. It also offers clue as to how they may be taught most effectively. In fact, development takes place simultaneously at various levels and not in isolated areas. Thus the teacher has to consider the total developmental process including physical, emotional social and cognitive development. Piaget's four major stages mainly viz (i) sensory motor, (ii) pre-operational, (iii) concrete operational, and (iv) formal operational—appear to involve qualitative differences in learning orientations and capacities as well as in cognitive structures. We learn what we do and therefore, learning is abstraction from action. All learning is said to involve both assimilation and accommodation. The children assimilate stimulus features into existing schemes and accommodate the existing schemes into modified or new schemes. Thus Piagetians see people in continuous dynamic interaction with the environment. Assimilation of familiar aspects and accommodation of those to unfamiliar ones continues until a state of equilibrium is reached. The students at the pre-operational stages (early primary grades) learn facts. Creativity is another area belonging to cognitive domain which deserves special mention with reference to human development. It is obvious that the proposed stages of development vary from psychologist to psychologist. For example Freud, Erikson and others have proposed stage-theories of social and personal development while Piaget has stressed the cognitive development for explaining human growth. Similarly Berg's stages of the development of moral judgment refer to the cognitive but not the affective aspects of life.

There is often a confusion around the concepts of 'growth' and 'development'. Development is, no doubt, more comprehensive as a concept as it implies something more than growth. No doubt development occurs during growth but it may also occur when no growth is observable. No matter, whether growth and development are supplementary as concepts for explaining the dynamic process of maturation, education plays a vital role in the area of cognitive development. It facilitates the developmental process by creating suitable stimuli and environment. Environment is very significant as a contributory factor in the area of development. For example, developments in language depend upon the language spoken in the country in which one is born.

Basic to developmental psychology is the concept of stage involving sequence. It is a gradual process, no doubt, but it involves a series of qualitatively distinct stages. Thus, the learning theorists differ from the developmental psychologists in the basic approach to understand life. When applied to education the developmental model places heavy stress on the concepts of maturation and readiness.

It may be worthwhile to make certain observations on the implication of the various theories of learning and motivation. While cognitive theories stress perceptions and thinking, motivational theories attempt to explain the initiation, direction, persistence and intensity of goal-directed behaviour, Behaviourist theory, on the other hand, stresses reinforcement through reward and positive feedback. Teachers may, however, take advantage of all these theories by applying them in class-room situations appropriately, They can also take advantage of intellectual curiosity, achievement, needs and other motivations by using suitable materials, examples and stimulating questions. A basic motivational goal for teachers is to help students, look upon school-tasks as challenging and enjoyable.

Cognitive explanations of behaviour emphasise the role of person's thinking about what is happening to him or his perception of reality. This has been supported by a number of studies which illustrate that cognitive perceptions are real as they influence behaviour.

As mentioned earlier, the concept of need is related to the dynamics of behaviour as Murray defined it as a construct that stands for a force and organises perception.

Few psychologists today corroborate the view that Murray provides a way of looking at differential interest patterns that students bring to the class-room. Although interest is potentially a source of activity or behaviour, it goes without saying that they may differ widely. The teacher can identify and build upon these interests, he can also allow the students to grow from the past history of positive reinforcement. A systematic exposure to environmental stimulations will, no doubt, lead to the development of the dominant interests. The teachers should take note of the wide variety of the student's interests and to integrate them through curricular and co-curricular activities. It's a failure on the part of the teacher to ignore student's interests as a source of motivation and learning. Today, we find student's frustrations finding their expression through anti-social activities. At the root of this frustration of-course we may find the unfulfilled needs including love-needs and other emotional needs, Even the students need for esteem and appreciation has to be respected for the development of a balanced personality. The knowledge of the developmental principles helps the teacher to understand the pupils in a realistic perspective.

In the present context of education we find a dismal picture of the student - life full of confusion and insecurity. They are torn between extremes, between love and hate, courage and cowardice. Education, as such is hardly offering any solution to the crisis at home, in the class-room and community. Thus the consequences of educating children need to be well visualised and strategies built up accordingly. Piaget was one of the psychologists to recognise that human beings are born as active, exploratory and information processing organism. He looks upon people's adoptive activities as more fundamental and important than the external stimuli. His basic unit of cognition, speech and behaviour forms the scheme which he uses rather loosely. The two fundamental mechanisms in the formation and use of all schemes are accommodation and assimilation. In other words, human beings grow as a result of their new learning, adaptation and assimilation. It is important that the differences in rates of acquisition of schemes should be recognised as outcome of the following factors :—

(a) Maturation

(b) Individual experience

(c) Social transmission

(d) Internal Self-direction.

In short, the concepts used by Piaget are useful to a teacher for understanding the processes used by human beings to interact with and adopt to their environment.

14

THEORIES OF CHILD DEVELOPMENT

In summarizing Piaget's theory, we can see that the substance of his findings is very relevant to the educator along with the methods he employs. The method by which he collects data is frequently referred to as "clinical method," which means that the child actively searches for the solution of the problem. The examiner stimulates and challenges the child to reflect on his own answers and to use this discourse as a means to clarify his own thought. Piaget wholeheartedly believes in the child's autonomy and his active participation in his own cognitive growth.

Applying Piaget's findings about children's cognitive growth to teaching could have a revolutionary impact on the planning of the curriculum. The content itself would be influenced or the logical processes by which we think and by which we attempt to solve problems could become a major area of focus in any educational endeavor. Thus there would be a more systematic emphasis on systems of classification, on reversibility, on logical transformations, and on the process of logic in general.

In conclusion, Jean Piaget's theory demonstrates that there are regular patterns in cognitive development which are experienced by everyone. Such an understanding allows us to predict is an individual modes and range of comprehension all along his course of development.

The next theory to be discussed is that of Freud. Freud's theory of development holds that the young child goes through five definite phases in the first five or six years of life and only two more in the remaining fifteen childhood and adolescent years. One of Freud's basic assumptions is that the first five years of childhood are the most formative ones for personality development.

During the oral stage, the child gets pleasurable auto-erotic stimulation from such manipulations of the oral erogenous zone as sucking, drinking, and eating. In the second phase of this oral stage, the oral-sadistic stage, the child exhibits sadistic tendencies through biting during the cutting of teeth. At the end of the second year, the anal stage begins, changing the source of pleasure from the oral to the anal region. He "holds back" and "lets go" to get more pleasure and to exert power over his parents. The oral and anal stages are sometimes called pre-ego periods, since the id impulses are not yet restrained by the ego.

One basic Freudian concept concerns libidinal forces. "Libidinal" energy will have to be defined as the yet unknown force which directs human development. Terms such as "drive, desire, and urge" may be "libidinal energy." This force or energy, which in part is sexual, must be realized as an aspect of the human system.

Freud believed that these forces were attached to various experiences throughout the life of an individual. Therefore it would seem valuable to define these three levels. One is the conscious experience, all those life events which remain within the individual's perceptual and/or cognitive awareness. The second is preconscious experience, which are all those events beyond the individual's immediate recognition but within the realm of his conscious recall. And the third is unconscious experience, which is entirely beyond the individual's perceptive and rational awareness. I have mentioned the above levels of experience because the last two have become the center of most psychoanalytic investigations, and are seen as the most potent determinants of all human motivation.

These libidinal energies from three major analytic processes, are known as the Freudian triad of id, ego, and superego. The id comprises the sum of the "pressure of excessive wishes." This pressure originates in unconscious libidinal energy. The id possesses, further, the unfulfilled libidinal striving of an organism. In other words, the id is all the desires which we must overcome to be human, and not to be mere creatures. The ego is charged with controlling the conscious actions of an individual. It is a combination of all his past experiences which confront him and help him to take actions in the present. The superego is assumed to be made up of personal experiences which have been affected by the higher ideals and attitudes of significant adults and peers in the life of the individual.

The phallic phase—sometimes referred to as "little puberty" begins with interest in manipulation of the sex organs. Infantile masturbation and "impulses for knowledge and investigation" appear in this phase. His newly developed intellectual curiosity draws the child to the problem of sex. The discovery of the ego accompanies the beginning of narcissism. The development of the ego changes the child's total outlook toward the world.

At puberty, the sexual impulses break through to produce the subordination of all sexual component-instincts under the primacy of the genital zone. Whereas pleasure-seeking was the aim of all the infantile forms of sexuality, physiological pubertal changes create another sexual aim, that of reproduction. This phase of psychosexual development is called the genital stage. Pubescent sexuality manifests itself in three different ways : (a) through external stimulation of the erogenous zones: (b) through internal tension and a physiological need to release sexual products, a condition not present in the childhood sexuality; and (c) through psychological "Sexual excitation" which may be influenced by the former two.

Pubescent development not only awakens sexuality, but also enormously increases nervous excitement, anxiety, genital phobia, and personality disturbances "because of the outstanding power of the "lust dynamism". Biological changes bring about behavioural changes, since one's lust collides with one's security. During adolescence, therefore, a person is especially vulnerable to the development of psychopathology.

Increased sexual tension during adolescence revives many of the old incestuous objects of the phallic period. Freud speaks of a second oedipal situation during pubescence. Freud comments that during adolescence a boy's first serious love object is most likely to be a mature woman, and a young girl's an older man-that is, mother and father figures.

But these are not the greatest dangers an adolescent faces in his further development. There exists the danger that friendship ties that are too strong will bind boys and girls to their own sex, with the possibility of inversion of the sex object. Related to the oedipal situation is the adolescent's task of freeing himself from his dependency upon his parents. The boy's libidinal attachment to his mother has to be released and he must also free himself from the dominance of the father. Unsuccessful attempts to resolve either situation will result in neurosis, since they will interfere with the selection of a heterosexual love object. The main task of the adolescent as seen by psychoanalytic theory may be summarized as being the "attainment of genital primacy and the definitive completion of the process of non-incestuous object finding".

It is assumed that the stages of psychosexual development are predominantly biological in nature, since they occur in a predetermined sequence. The biological nature of Freud's theory is further emphasized by the frequent use of the instinct concept. In his earlier theory, the two biological instincts are self-preservation and reproduction. The self-preservation instinct includes such ego motives as hunger, fear, and self-assertion. The reproductive instinct is sexual and in closely related to the physical energy called libido.

In summarizing thus far, Freud assumes that the emotional (libidinal) aspects of life permeate all human functions. Freud is very much concerned with the emotional relationships between persons. Each individual's life—his manner of perceiving, thinking, doing, and feeling—depends largely upon the relative balance of the three major affective processes—the id, the ego, and the superego.

ERIK ERIKSON'S THEORY

Erik Erikson modifies the Freudian theory of psychosexual development in the light of findings by cultural anthropology. The core concept in his theory of ego development is the acquiring of ego identity. This a accomplished in different ways from culture to culture. However, there is one common element which is present in all cultures, namely the idea that the child must receive consistent, meaningful recognition of his achievements and accomplishments. In each of the eight developmental steps that Erikson describes a conflict with two possible outcomes arises. If the conflict is worked out in a satisfactory manner, the positive quality is built into the ego and further healthy development can take place. But if the conflict is resolved unsatisfactorily, the developing ego is damaged.

Here is a list of the eight basic stages in chronological order-comparing them to corresponding Freudian stages:—

(1)	Trust vs. mistrust	Oral sensory
(2)	Autonomy vs. shame and doubt	Muscular anal

(3)	Initiative vs. guilt	Locomotor genital
(4)	Industry vs. inferiority	Latency ,
(5)	Identity vs. role diffusion	Puberty and adolescence
(6)	Intimacy vs. isolation	Young adulthood
(7)	Generativity vs. stagnation	Adulthood
(8)	Ego integrity vs. disgust, despair	Maturity

Pubescence, according to Erikson is characterized by rapidity of body growth, genital maturity, and sexual awareness. Youth is confronted with a "physiological revolution" within himself that threatens his body image and his ego identity. He becomes preoccupied with what he "appears to be in the eyes of others" as compared with what he feels he is. Adolescence is the period during which a dominant positive ego identity is to be established. Erikson maintains that the study of identity has become as important as the study of sexuality was in Freud's time. Particularly as for the adolescent, identity (which is the establishment of sameness with one's previous experiences and a conscious attempt to make the future a part of one's personal life plan) becomes subordinated to sexuality. If ego identity is not satisfactorily established at this stage, there is the danger that role diffusion will endanger further ego development. Where this is based on a strong previous doubt as to one's sexual identity, delinquent and outright psychotic incidents are not uncommon.

Vocational identity is still a great concern for many adolescents. During the initial attempts to establish ego identity some role diffusion exists. Adolescents at this time frequently over-identify with movies heroes, group leaders, athletic champions, etc. At this point, youth rarely identifies with his parents. On the contrary, he rebels against their dominance, their value system, and their intrusion into his private life, since he has to separate his identity from that of his parents. However, there is a desperate need for social belonging. The peer group and gang help the individual in finding his own identity in a social context. Particularly during the time when the body image changes radically, when genital maturity stimulates imagination, and when intimacy with the opposite sex appears as a possibility, the adolescent relies on his peers for comfort by stereotyping himself, his ideals, and his adversaries.

Falling in love, which is a common and frequent occurrence at this age, is not of a sexual nature to the same degree as it will be at later ages. The "serious" love affairs through which the adolescent passes contribute to the development of the ego as one identification succeeds another, and the adolescent is aided in defining and revising his own definition of his ego. Ego identity to be established before marriage should be considered. A person must really know who he is and whom he wants, to become before he can decide who is a suitable mate for him. "Crushes," which occur frequently at the high school and college level, serve a genuine psychological purpose. This is why many would rather converse, and settle matters of mutual identification.

Maturity begins when identity has been established and an integrated, independent individual has emerged. He can now stand on his own feet, without emotional crutches from others.

Ego identity involves total integration of vocational ambitions and aspirations, along with all those qualities acquired through earlier identification, imitation of parents, falling in love, admiration of heroes, etc. Only the achievement of all these aspects of ego identity will permit intimacy of sexual, love and deep friendship.

Erikson's contribution of psychological thought is in his systematic reorganization of psychoanalytic theory in the light of anthropological findings. He has gone beyond the preoccupation of orthodox psychoanalysis. He has brought about a shift in emphasis to the social conditions and organizations in which the ego must be rooted for normal development.

Erikson's stages which are similar have been influenced by those of Freud. For example, feeding, and oral function, results in social trust when it is appropriately gratified. Autonomy should be established during the anal period. For the first time, the child will experience the autonomy of free choice in the power of "holding on and letting go when he wishes." Initiative is related to the phallic stage in the boy, which expresses itself in exuberance, a feeling of power, aggressive manipulation, and pleasure in attack. In girls, aggressive initiative may be present in the form of "catching"; it may be modified to making herself more attractive. Industry should develop during the latency period. Unable to marry his mother, the boy now must learn to become a potential provider and to gain recognition so that he may later leave his family and start his own. He must establish ego identity during puberty to incorporate genital maturity into his body image. In this way he establishes a sense of ego integrity, which is essential if he is to enter a genuine love relationship in which he abandons himself. We may conclude, therefore, that the stage concept, in general, is a vital and integral part of all psychoanalytic theories.

In conclusion, Erikson's modified form of psychoanalytic theory offers more helpful advice to the teacher. According to Erikson, it is not frustration per se that results in neurosis, but frustration that is not meaningful. Therefore, parents and teachers should only introduce culturally meaningful forms of frustration. Erikson assumes that, as part of the process of growing up, children must learn to encounter limits and restrictions which may be frustrating. But they will not produce neurosis so long as they are meaningful. Meaningful ways of frustrating children will challenge them, direct their activities, and bring about learning.

According to Freud, the first stage is the oral level (sucking and swallowing). The over indulged child at the first oral level is characterized as carefree, generous, optimistic, and unwilling to assume responsibilities. The child who is frustrated in his oral needs is said to become pessimistic, demanding of help from others, and dependent. The second oral stage is the oral sadistic (biting, devouring) level. Lack of satisfaction at this level results in an adult characterized by ambivalent attitudes toward others. Friendliness alternates with hostility, aggression with submissiveness, love with hate.

The anal stage follows the oral period. Here the libido becomes concentrated upon the process of the expulsion of feces and the clashes with the parent's needs to train the child. The child who fixated at the anal level of development is dominated by retaining characteristics as an adult. Frustration at this level results either in "regression" back to the oral stage or in personal characteristics of worries about fine details, cleanliness, parsimony, obstinacy, or, in extremity, sadism, or masochism.

The anal period is replaced by the phallic stage (touching, exploring, fantasizing about the genitalia) and the development of the Oedipus complexie, love for the parent of the opposite sex. In normal children the Oedipus complex is resolved as the child abandons the parent as a love object and identifies with the parent of the same sex. It is through this process that the superego (conscience) is formed and strengthened.

The latency period of middle childhood is a time of libidinal quiescence, during which repression and other psychological "defense mechanisms" appear, and social feelings develop. Puberty brings on the late genital period, a revival of the Oedipus conflict, the development of adult modes of libidinal satisfaction, the pre-dominance of homosexual choice, and finally the normal heterosexual choice of the love object.

The cognitive growth process is very complicated. Every child has some experiences and the environment has impact on us and therefore we attend to it. Yet, some children are curious and seek further information while others are withdrawn. Children do differ in respect of responsiveness and receptivity. Through interaction children absorb, assimilate, classify, organize and reinforce.

Educational Application of Development Principles

The objectives of teaching and learning are obviously related to the stages of development of the pupils and their capacity or potential. It is therefore, likely that the teacher has to be aware of various types of development viz.

(a) Physical Development,
(b) Cognitive Development,
(c) Language Development,
(d) Social Development, and
(e) Emotional and personality Development.

It is important that the child grows in all directions simultaneously as a human being. As his body grows, his mental function also starts at various levels. The most fundamental implication of development at psychology for education is that Educational experiences must be matched with cognitive and other developments of the learners. This can be done in a general way because most individuals of the same age range will be roughly at the same developmental level. Education involves optimizing instruction to meet the unique needs of each student. However, it is essential to recognise that cognitive development takes place rather slowly. Pupils acquire knowledge and skill as they grow.

According to Piaget, development in inherent, dynamic and continuous. The teacher should have definite ideas of the characteristic at each stage of child development. Otherwise his understanding of the pupils will remain incomplete. The developmental considerations thus help a teacher in meeting the individual needs of each child.

15

GROUP BEHAVIOUR

Men live in groups and are guided at times by group life and its norms. Their individual reaction is modified and their behaviour is adjusted and controlled by the social environment.

No doubt, the basic instincts and needs prompt our activities for their satisfaction. Yet they undergo certain modifications under group pressure. This is because man is basically a social creature. Group life generates new needs and expectations. Values and attitudes thus shape group behaviour. Satisfaction plays a prominent part in group behaviour. Individuals while interacting with one another tend to gain from their individual course of action. A group mindedness prevails when individuals sacrifice their strong individuality and come to a compromise for better adjustment. Individuals need company and co-operation for effective functioning. Man can not live alone in isolation. He is particularly a social animal. It is impossible for man to live in an environment cut off from other members of the community. His innate urge to co-operate and coordinate is strong.

Group life offers the child a social environment. The individual child needs love, encouragement and sense of security within the family and group. Without the group life the child hardly grows. Group interaction helps the child to grow socially and emotionally. Thus when a child comes to school he learns together and shares his experience.

He gets the opportunity to express his feeling of self-assertion, communion and combat and grows up emotionally, socially and physically. As mentioned earlier, the child grows through experience. He needs sympathy and suggestion for self expansion. At time a child feels dependent and looks forward to suggestions and sympathy from his groups. Sympathy provides sense of security and builds up the ego strength of the child.

At times a child is confused or defused and badly needs suggestion. The role of parents, teachers and even of friends is very significant.

Sympathy is the fellow feeling or feeling with others. This involves emotions when shared among members within a group. Emotion is aroused in case there is any accident or a sudden situation demanding common participation.

It facilitates social solidarity and brings harmony of actions even around an occasion or event.

Sympathy also plays a significant role in animal behaviour. It prompts them to share and profit from each others experience and knowledge of a group life. Sympathy may be expressed both in active and passive forms.

In a class room situation the teachers can take advantage of their interaction by arousing emotions for the right and good cause among the pupils. He can inspire them toward noble causes and creative activities.

Like sympathy, imitation is found to influence group behaviour, to love others instinctively as this tendency is ingrained in nature since childhood. A child learns to speak gradually. He copies from nearest adults other's behaviours even unconsciously. Imitation is very common when the relationship between the members is close and cordial. We imitate what we admire in others.

The children learn most by imitating their parents and teachers. Most of the habits and modes of behaviour are copied by children through imitation. Imitation is great social bond, a means of uniting a large number of individuals into one group.

Group behaviour is dominant when there is cohesion and communality. Group behaviour is something more than a collective behaviour.

Motivation and interest can be generated by applying group dynamics. Not only in the field of education, group dynamics are applied at present even in the field of industry for better production.

Cooperation, competition and conflict are the various modes of group behaviour which can be employed for producing the behaviour as end result.

In the present society we find competition and conflict more than cooperation. There is a struggle for survival of the fittest. It is the law of the present society. We can hardly ignore this stark reality. Yet there are certain occasions and causes which demand cooperation, and co-ordination for our greater interest. Any national enterprise demands co-operation in spite of conflicts and competitions within group.

Group Behaviour and Education

With the growing size of the class room and increasing load of curriculum there is hardly any time to pay individual attention in the class room. It is also not feasible to treat pupils individually. The present situation thus demands application of group dynamics, where a class is divided into groups for participation in assigned educational activities. This interactional approach very often proves economic and effective as well.

In group approach an individual finds it possible to contribute his best to the group performance and develops a sense of identity with the group. The spirit of social awareness is thus stimulated through this group activity.

16

CONFLICT—THE ROLE OF THE UNCONSCIOUS

Mind refers to the human thought, feelings emotions and desires, memories and motives. The contents of our mind may be analysed or observed by instrospection while some of our behaviours can not be explained by analysing our conscious mind. The conscious process can not always explain our certain behaviours.

There are certain disconnected thoughts and actions which have no connection with conscious process. There are hidden dimensions of our cognitive behaviour which we call unconsciousness.

In fact, conscious life consists of a small part of our mental life.

Group behaviour which is often the outcome of social pressure is guided mostly by the social desirability.

There are certain social instincts which are stimulated by the presence of other human beings. For example, there are instincts of self preservation, self assertion, gregariousness which are quite in keeping with the social awareness and sense of dignity.

Some writers like Hobbes considers rivalry as an innate disposition and a spirit of competition behind conflict.

Others consider 'herd' instinct playing significant role behind co-operation and conflict at times. In short, so many innate dispositions work behind the group behaviour.

As mentioned earlier, some general tendencies play their part in shaping our group behaviour. Not all of them can be traced at the conscious level. Most of our conflict have their root at the subconscious and unconscious levels. Imitation, sympathy and suggestions are the tendencies of the individual to take from other's modes of behaviour.

General tendencies are not the same as specific instincts which are aroused in specific situations. Conflict arises when our basic needs or desires are obstructed. This creates conflict or confusion.

When we are not able to decide and act when more than one idea or impulse tries to lead us to opposite courses of action, we face conflict. Conflict and hesitation are painful, no doubt. The mind becomes divided and it fails to meet any difficult situation with confidence or competence. Struggles go on and the state of conflict at the unconscious level become quite uncomfortable. At times one has to face situation leading to conflict of values and brings a scope of repression of socially unacceptable desires.

Some of the repressed wishes seek expression through dreams. Our unfulfilled desires sometime find their outlet through dreams. Psychoanalysts often use dream for explaining human behaviour at the unconscious or subconscious levels.

Repression is often taken recourse to by children to adjust to complex environment. It is also frequent in adult life.

It is hardly accessible to reasoning as it lies at the unconscious level. It is often claimed that repression is at the root of many mental disorders. They express themselves in dreams when some of the wished get an opportunity for free expression when self control and social checks are at the lowest.

Freud, Jung and others support interpretation of dreams for explaining our unfulfilled desires. In school situation, we find conflicts at various levels. There is conflict among children, among teachers, among students, teachers and parents. They are around various issues and roles. At present with the emergence of democracy in our education and schools we try to resolve the conflicts after proper diagnosis. When we have adopted the principle of democracy we have to accept the method of government of the people, for the people, and by the people. This approach reduces the scope for conflict for obvious reasons.

Besides co-operation, sympathy and suggestion very often play important roles for resolving the conflict.

Suggestion is an effective means of avoiding conflict and confrontation. A policy of give and take helps to come to understanding before the conflict states. It is often seen that suggestion comes from above for acceptance at the lower level. But it is not always so.

It goes without saving that repression at times is a necessity for the development of a complex. The formation of complex helps conflict resolution as complex is an idea or a group of ideas strongly mixed with emotion that is repressed. The moral standard or customs do not permit the display of many crude complexes which acknowledges failure to cope with the demands of a challenging situation of life. Complexes are, therefore not always desirable as they may adversely effect personality. There are certain hobbies and obsessions which may become complexes. Yet they may contribute to socialization and community life. Exchanging visits and small gifts to sick friends are helpful to develop a social outlook.

Repression is quite common both in the life of children and adults. There are wishes which are not allowed to be expressed in social life and they find their place in the unconscious. They also seek their outlet in the dreams. There are certain symptoms of mental conflict like scratching the head, movement of legs during conversation, struggling shoulders, frequent winking and stammering. Frequent ships and omissions may be caused by conflicts as well.

Lying among school children may be due to repression.

Abnormal forgetting usually takes place as we tend to forget the unpleasant experiences and things.

The teacher and parents should realize the evil effect of repression on child mind. The child's personality may be thwarted and turned into neurotic as a result of too much pressure.

Mental conflicts and mental hygiene

Mental health is an important asset in every life. Life calls for adjustment to any change in environment, physical and social. It is through adjustment one maintains a balance between his needs and circumstances. A person can hardly find satisfaction unless he can make effective adjustment.

BIBLIOGRAPHY

ADMAS JEMES T., A Study of Adult Education and Frontier of American Cen.

ALEXANDER SAMUEL, Space Time and Deity, MacMillan 1920.

ALLPORT G. W., Personality Harper, N.V. 1947.

BURN MICHAEL, Scientific and Education, H. Hamilton 1956.

BRUBACHER JOHNS, Modern Philosophies of Education.

CAMPBELL C. A., Selfhood and Godhood, Allen and Unwin 1957.

COOK CALDWELL,Playway in Education, Hutchinson 1961.

CURTIS S. J., An Introduction to the Philosophy of Education.

EWING A. C., Second Thoughts on Moral Philosophy Routledge.

FOSTER MICHAEL, In Mystery and Philosophy S.C.M. Press, London 1957.

FLEW AG. N. (ED.), Essays in Conceptual Analysis, MacMillan 1956

HUME, A Treatise of Human Nature Part—4.

HENRY NELSON, Education in Rural Communities, Chicago Univ. Press.

KANT IMMANUEL, Fundamental Principles of the Metaphysics and Ethics, Longmans 1911

LINTO RALPH, The Cultural Background of Personality, Applenton Century Co.

LANDIS PAUL H., Man In Environment, N.Y.

MACMURRAY JOHN, The Form of the Personal—The Self as an agent, Faber London 1957.

MILTON G., Genius and Creativity, Harper N.Y 1965.

PERCY NUNN, Education--Its data and First Principles.

PEEPER JOSEPH, Leisure of Bans of Culture, Faber.

PROGRAMMING FOR WORLD AFFAIRS, Adult Leadership (July-August 1933).

ODHUM HOWARD W., Understanding Society, MacMillan Co. N.Y. 1947.

REID A.L., Ways of Knowledge and Experience, Allen and Unwin.

PERSCOTT DANIEL, Emotion and the executive Process, American Council of Education, Washington D.C.

SERGENT S. and SMITH, Culture and Personality.

SMITH B. O. et al., Foundations of Curriculum Improvement World Book Co. 1953.

WELLING M. H. et al, School and our Democratic Society, Harper and Brother N. Y.

SOCIOLOGICAL FOUNDATION

CHAPLIN F.S., Cultural Change.

COOK L. A., A Sociological Approach to Education Book Co. 1950.

DAVIS ALLISON, Social Class Influences upon learning, Harvard University Press 1945.

DAVIS KINGSLEY, Human Society, MacMillan Co. 1949.

FOSTER R. G., Marriage and Family Relations, MacMillan Co., N.Y. 1930

HENRY NELSON B., Education in Rural Communities — Chicago University Press 1982

H. FRANCIS I, Man and Society, Appleton Century N.Y.

JONES MARSHALL E., Basic Sociological Principles.

LINTON RALPH, The Cultural Background of Personality Appleton Century Co.,

MEAD MARGARET, Growth and Culture Pitman's Sons, N.Y.

MURRAY RAYMOND W., Sociology for a Democratic Society, Appleton Century N.Y. 1950.

SERGENT. S. S. and SMITH M., Culture and Personality.

SILVERMAN LEO, Analysis of Society, William Hodge and Co., London 1951.

PSYCHOLOGICAL FOUNDATION

ANDERSON JOHN E., The Psychology of Development and Personal Adjustment, Henny Holt & Co. N.Y. 1951.

DAVIS ALLISON, Social Class Influences upon learning, Harvard University Press.

GUILFORD J.P. Editor, Fields of Psychology Basic and applical, D: Vasc Nostrand N.Y.

MUNN NORMAN L., Psychology The Fundamentals of Human Adjustment, Houghton Heffin Co. Boston 1943.

MURPHY GARDNER, Psychology An Introduction to Psychology, Harper and Brothers N.Y. 1951

MUNRUE WALTER S., Teaching Learning-Theory and Teacher Education, University of Illinois Press 1952.

ROSE, Groundwork of Educational Psychology (Har etc.)

SKINNER B.F., Educational Psychology Prentice Hall.

STAGNER ROSS, Psychology of Personality, Mc Graw Hill N.Y. 1948

THORNDIKE, Educational Psychology.

VERNON P. E., The Structure of Human Abilities

VERNON P.E., Personality Tests and Assessments, Methum & Co. Ltd. 1953

VULKART EDMAND H., Social Behaviour and Personality, Social Science Research Council.

WOODWORTH R., Psychology, Methum.

YOUNG, Motivation of Behaviour Waley.